# Implementing the Learning Organisation

## The 17-Day Learning Programme

PATRICK J. THURBIN

**FINANCIAL TIMES**
PITMAN PUBLISHING

To Dad who encouraged me to begin and Daisy whose belief enabled me to finish.

PITMAN PUBLISHING
128 Long Acre, London WC2E 9AN

A Division of Longman Group UK Limited

First published in Great Britain 1994

© Longman Group UK Limited, 1994

**British Library Cataloguing in Publication Data**
A CIP catalogue record for this book can be obtained from the British Library.

ISBN 0 273 60385 X

All rights reserved; no part of this publication may be reproduced, stored in a retrieval system, or transmitted in any form or by any means, electronic, mechanical, photocopying, recording, or otherwise without either the prior written permission of the Publishers or a licence permitting restricted copying in the United Kingdom issued by the Copyright Licensing Agency Ltd, 90 Tottenham Court Road, London W1P 9HE. This book may not be lent, resold, hired out or otherwise disposed of by way of trade in any form of binding or cover other than that in which it is published, without the prior consent of the Publishers.

Phototypeset in Linotron Times Roman
by Northern Phototypesetting Co. Ltd., Bolton
Printed and bound in Great Britain
by Biddles Ltd., Guildford and King's Lynn

*The Publishers' policy is to use paper manufactured from sustainable forests.*

# CONTENTS

*Foreword* — v

*Preface* — vii

*Introduction* — 1

1  THE LEARNING ORGANISATION – MYTH OR REALITY — 6

2  USING THE 17-DAY PROGRAMME — 30

3  CLARIFYING THE PURPOSE AND REVIEWING THE ORGANISATION — 36

4  CREATING THE VISION OF THE LEARNING ORGANISATION — 78

5  IDENTIFYING THE CULTURE AND THE OPPORTUNITIES FOR CHANGE — 104

6  ASSESSING THE BENEFITS — 135

7  IMPLEMENTATION — 156

8  LESSONS FROM PRACTICE — 203

*Index* — 246

# FOREWORD

I welcome this opportunity to contribute a foreword for a book whose subject matter has claimed so much of my business thinking and practice over the past decade.

During the mid 1980's a number of us, particularly in manufacturing businesses, somewhat belatedly became aware that our international competitiveness was being negatively impacted by the static knowledge and skills of our people at all levels. It was a small but critical step to translate this understanding into programmes to lift knowledge and skills on a continuing basis.

For me the use of the word 'Learning' came from Rob Meakin, Rover's personnel director in the late 80's and early 90's. Also, it was Rob who persuaded me that what became named 'The Rover Learning Business' should be separate from the personnel function.

The Rover Learning Business story is recounted as one of several practical examples in Patrick Thurbin's excellent book. The fact that there are such stories, and from such diverse organisational backgrounds, is testimony to the power of an idea whose time, if anything, is overdue.

Rover's need to establish what we now term a 'Learning Organisation' came from the imperative to secure the company's survival. Now it contributes to Rover's increasing competitiveness and value as a business.

Prior to the mid 80's Rover was not unique in holding that investment meant hardware, not people. Also industrial Britain the early 1980's, I felt, viewed continuous 'Learning' for all employees as vaguely socialist and fundamentally unnecessary. I am happy to say that I consider such views to be exceptional today.

Now the trend is the other way. Employee learning on a continuous basis is understood, by and large, to be essential to a business's competitiveness. Indeed fast learning, aggregated across a business, may be that business's only competitive advantage.

Much has been said and written about the 'Learning Organisation', most of it interesting but largely unhelpful. Patrick Thurbin's book is different. It is both interesting and very helpful – a practical 'How to' solidly based on experience. I wish that 'Implementing the Learning Organisation' had been written much earlier. When, of necessity, I experimented, this book would have saved me much grief and would have compressed the time and dramatically reduced the cost.

For those who have yet to embark upon the 'Learning' odyssey, you have available now a valuable book which will start you off and see you through. I am grateful to Patrick Thurbin and I know you will be too.

Sir Graham Day
Hantsport, Nova Scotia
Canada

# PREFACE

The contemporary notion of the learning organisation has been developed from work by leading academics Chris Argyris & Donald Schon in 1978. It has since proved a focus and rallying ground for academics, managers and those seeking to understand and improve the performance of their organisation. Studies attempting to explain organisational learning in terms of developing a corporate culture and introducing strategies for change abound.

Attempts to differentiate between learning with the notion of profitability as a motive, and the social aspects of the wider learning organisation, encompassing the hospitals for example, have in many ways confused the manager attempting to gain from the literature. Learning organisations, like religions, have many beliefs and practices.

To put it simply – people create and work in organisations and attempt to achieve some overall output or service. In return they are enabled to continue in that form and develop new forms. Learning seems an obvious descriptor for how people achieve that outcome. Learning for both people and organisations leads to a change in behaviour. There are obviously hundreds of learning organisations but are some better at it than others and how can one accelerate and influence what is learned? How to initiate learning that is good for both the individual and organisation in terms of acceptable rewards?

It is natural that exemplars of an effective learning organisation have been identified. Organisations such as Grand Metropolitan Hotels, Rank Xerox and the Rover Group openly claim to be learning organisations. Others include Canon Inc., Japan; TSB Group, Komatsu, Japan, Digital Equipment, British Airways, Guardian Royal Exchange, Lucas, IBM, GKN, Massey Ferguson, Gatwick Airport, American Express in the UK and USA, Shell, Cadbury Schweppes and a variety of Health Authorities. There are, of course, many others.

Looking at the above list of organisations it becomes patently obvious that not all learning companies get it right first time.

Some common themes have emerged from studies of learning organisations:

**The Trigger** There has to be a recognised need or trigger that stimulates the setting up of processes to focus on learning in the organisation.

**The Belief** People in learning organisations believe that transformation of the form of the organisation, its services and products in order to meet new challenges is a strategy. They welcome the risks associated with learning.

**The Action** Learning is by trial and error with existing strategies for business development, management development and training all incorporated.

**The Benefits** Organisations attract and retain calibre staff and perform well on recognised performance criteria.

This book will help the reader understand the ideas behind the learning organisation, the benefits that can be gained and how to set about implementing learning to achieve those benefits in both the short and longer term. In short a foothold and then a plan of how to get there.

Many people have contributed to the learning that is being conveyed in this book and above all thanks should go to Derek Taylor, Ian Hinton, my friends and mentors over many years, and Olga Reeve for her support and good humour during the writing of this book.

# INTRODUCTION

Books linking learning and managing in organisations abound. The area became significant for managers and businessmen in the early 1980s with Reg Reavans promoting action learning as a way of regenerating an enthusiasm among middle managers for handling change. Since then the focus has moved between books promoting individual learning as the way forward and those concentrating on broader organisational learning. The lead has always come from the academics who provide the steady backdrop against which professional managers try to view their world. Challenges to the academics have been provided by business gurus such as Harvey Jones who appeals to the manager who wants to learn from seeing an expert at work.

In the UK academics such as Tom Boydell and Mike Pedler gained much fame and following by focusing on the power of self-development, an area that has been developed by a host of writers. This appeal to the individual in the form of self-analysis approaches and the move towards personal mastery in order to build the foundation for a learning company is still very popular.

The trainers meanwhile emphasised theories of learning styles as a way of matching training approaches to the individual. This gained support from those managers who were trying to harness the learning capabilities of members of their teams through team-building approaches.

In the late 1980s the focus moved to the learning organisation; the orthodox ways of describing organisations based on theories of Taylor, Fayol and Weber were increasingly being challenged. Books such as: *Creative Organisation Theory*, Gareth Morgan (1989) and *The Fifth Discipline – The Art and Practice of the Learning Organisation*, Peter Senge (1990) became market and fashion leaders.

This thrust towards the learning organisation emphasised the role of the individual. Slogans such as 'empowering the people', were taken to heart as the way forward. The area was further supported by the availability of information technology and the growing idea that information was a resource that transcended conventional organisational structures. Hence flat organisational structures and creativity and innovation at all levels was now seen as a reality.

An alternative to this academic, and at times philosophical debate, emerged. The emphasis was much more on achievement with books written in every day language providing examples of best practice that stemmed from observing successful companies, for example: *In Search of Excellence – Lessons from America's best run companies*, Tom Peters and Robert Waterman (1982). This type of book appealed to managers who were seeking a lead to achieving business success through organisational learning and strategic management.

As national economies slumped so individual expertise and the way individuals could learn to create successful businesses became very popular, epitomised by *Trouble Shooter*, Harvey Jones and the emergence of the video-supported learning packages from the *Financial Times*. Concepts of Quality were used to promote Quality Circles and then TQM as an approach to harnessing learning in organisations with the obvious influence from Japanese companies.

The learning organisation as a notion is complicated in that both learning and organisation are terms that most managers would find relatively easy to talk about and describe. They are both commonplace and at the same time complex notions. When used together as the learning organisation we have a notion that becomes useful only when some enormous assumptions are declared. Some of these assumptions are that:

**(a)** Learning organisations support the formal cognitive processes associated with training and educational events. The informal learning process is often underestimated.

**(b)** The organisation is an entity to which learning can be attributed and that observable changes in behaviour and outcomes follow. This is difficult to prove and many would argue that chance and happenstance play a big part in organisational outcomes.

**(c)** To compete in an ever-changing environment an organisation needs to learn to adapt in order to survive and grow. There is, of course, lots of evidence to indicate that organisations both large and small are not very good at survival let alone growth. The big question is what are the key things to learn and to what extent does learning lead to managers developing mindsets or perceptions that are counter-productive to running a successful organisation.

**(d)** The amount of change required of both the organisation and individuals is achieveable and will be welcomed. This sense of optimism underpins notions of the learning organisation whereas the reality, for many managers, might reflect cynicism and survivalist, or at least protectionist, activities aimed at maintaining the status quo. To these realities, learning can provide a major threat.

There are two major camps or belief groups who provide the arguments supporting distinct approaches to creating the learning organisation. Firstly, those favouring a mechanistic or purposeful approach where learning is seen as an organisational tool that underpins the policy-making and strategic activities aimed at initiating and managing change for organisational success. Secondly, those favouring the more philosophical or open approach, valuing learning in terms of leading to personal growth of the individual and the contribution of the organisation to a wider society. This view leads to action that sets out to empower individuals in organisations that are seen as victims of rigid mindsets of the managers and dominant power groups. Individuals are encouraged to adopt more risk-taking activities and emphasise informal aspects of organisational processes.

Attempts have been made by some writers to bridge the gaps between these two groups or camps. This book does bridge the gap and also provides the reader with some tools and guidance on how to turn theory and philosophy into practice that will bring both short-term and long-term rewards.

The book is structured as a learning process; essentially in two parts. First, a 17-day learning programme that, dependent on the pressures of work and need, would be spread over, say, four to six months. This involves completing a series of practical reviews of the organisation and some focused reading. By using this approach the reader will gradually build up an awareness of all the aspects of the learning organisation and have done this in their own organisational setting. The second part provides detailed guidance and advice on how to set about creating a learning organisation. It is envisaged that most organisations need at least two to three years before the notion is fully integrated into the total enterprise.

The final section provides some examples from which the reader is unashamedly expected to borrow ideas.

This book is based on a wealth of experience and integrates many of the accepted best practice approaches with the latest academic research. The reader is therefore introduced to:

### 1. The Learning Organisation – Myth or Reality.
Where to start and how to fit the notion of the Learning Organisation into conventional organisational development and well-tried management concepts.

### 2. Using the 17-Day Programme.
How to use the book to conduct a feasibility study in your own organisation that will determine how and where implementation can begin. An essential precursor of any action.

### 3. Clarifying the Purpose and Reviewing the Organisation.
The first review will set your organisation in context and identify opportuni-

## 4  Implementing the Learning Organisation

ties for applying the notion of learning. The impact of your own personality and style on the approach to implementation is explored and emphasised.

### 4. Creating the Vision of the Learning Organisation.

This review will provide a clear picture of how the vision and mission for your organisation can be used as a trigger for formulating your design for the learning organisation. Attention is also drawn to the influence that your leadership style will have on approaches to implementation.

### 5. Identifying the Culture and the Opportunities for Change.

A review of the organisational culture and identification of blocks to learning enables the learning organisation to be viewed as a long-term change programme. Previous change programmes, their successes and failures are reviewed.

### 6. Assessing the Benefits.

This final review looks at the key stakeholders and how their requirements for performance from the organisation are measured. Opportunities for the learning organisation to support the stakeholders are explored and the ways of presenting the cost and benefits argument are presented.

### 7. Implementation.

Here the outcomes from the reviews are used to determine the best way of implementing the learning organisation. A three-stage programme of exploration, development and consolidation is described with total integration of the notion of the learning organisation into the enterprise envisaged as taking place over two to three years.

### 8. Lessons from Practice.

Experiences of both large and small organisations who are introducing the notion of the learning organisation are provided as stimulus for thought. Organisations such as Shell International, Motorola, Rover, International Computers, Royal Mail, Lucas, W. S. Atkins, Digital, British Aerospace, Rank Xerox and the Health Education Authority provide experiences from the multinational, the world of consultancy and the smaller enterprises.

Learning is fundamental to the success of all organisations. By following the stages outlined in this book and treating the experience as one of personal learning, the reader will be fully equipped to bring the benefits to bear for everyone involved in the wider organisational enterprise. The advice is practical and can be tailored to suit the particular context in which implementation is being considered.

Establishing a learning organisation does provide an exciting opportunity for the ambitious and professional manager. The reader who is determined to succeed will wrestle with the concepts presented in this book and adopt the practical advice that is set out. The results will show that implementing the learning organisation will provide the breakthrough that has long been prophesied by academics, practitioners and business managers.

## *References*

Morgan, G. *Creative Organisation Theory*, (California, Sage, 1989).
Senge, P.M. *The Fifth Discipline*, (Century Business 1990).
Peters, T., Waterman, R.H. Jnr *In Search of Excellence*, (Harper Row, New York, 1982).

# 1

# THE LEARNING ORGANISATION – MYTH OR REALITY

## INTRODUCTION

Any attempt to capture a complex notion in a few words is bound to lead to confusion. The two words 'learning organisation' can certainly claim fame to having created massive heart-searching amongst academics, writers and harassed managers worldwide. Story-tellers like to build up myths around their heroes or pet topics and there are many stories about what constitutes a fully-fledged learning organisation and about those that are not even at the starting point. This chapter will help separate the myth from the reality. The challenge for you is to establish your own reality as to what the learning organisation might be.

Various suggestions are given as to the start point for your quest and the reasons why the learning organisation might be able to help. The conventional wisdom from the academics is then presented to help explore the boundaries of the notion of the learning organisation. In a field such as this it is also important to see how the recognised counsultancies approach the subject and this is backed up with some examples of practice from two leading companies.

The notion of the learning organisation has to sit alongside a host of well-tried and accepted approaches to managing and developing organisations. This chapter therefore provides an overview of how management development and the whole field of Human Resource Development fits in with the notion of the learning organisation.

Many would also argue that the enormous experience and techniques of those using an Organisational Development (OD) approach to managing change are in effect demonstrating all the elements of the learning organisation. A summary of what constitutes OD. is therefore presented in order to help you set this important area into context.

Finally the notions surrounding Total Quality Management (TQM) are introduced. Increasingly organisations are travelling down the Quality road and there is no doubt that for many this provides the bedrock from which the learning organisation will spring.

The chapter is aimed at helping you build up an initial set of arguments and views as to what the learning organisation might be and how it fits into your own organisational setting. The following definition may provide an initial trigger to help you to begin challenging some of the myths surrounding this important notion.

> *A learning organisation is one which improves its knowledge and understanding of itself and its environment over time, by facilitating and making use of the learning of its individual members.*

By the end of this chapter some of the myths will have been challenged and a sense of reality will have begun to emerge.

## DETERMINING YOUR START POINT – A TRIGGER

We have all heard the story about the stranger who asked a local for directions: 'Well it depends,' was the reply, 'but if I were you I wouldn't start from here'. Let us look at some possible start points.

The Chairman or Managing Director of a large or medium-sized company will probably be attempting to find out whether:

- the approaches being taken in directing and guiding the organisation can be improved
- the learning organisation can be used to overcome some major problem that the organisation will have to tackle or is currently facing
- the learning organisation can fit into plans for changing the direction of the organisation
- the learning organisation will help develop top teams and key managers
- the investments made in developing the organisation are the right ones
- implementing the learning organisation requires the use of external consultants
- the learning organisation should become part of the strategic management activity.

For the Divisional or Unit Manager in a large or medium-sized organisation concerns could include:

- is the learning organisation able to help grow and develop the organisation in order to meet performance targets?

## 8  Implementing the Learning Organisation

- can the learning organisation help to build the key managers as a team?
- can the learning organisation help to improve the organisation's ability to be innovative in developing new products or services?
- does the learning organisation provide an opportunity to create a working environment that will raise morale and lead to improvements in productivity of the operations?
- where does the learning organisation fit into the whole field of TQM, Management Development and other Training initiatives?

For the manager or entrepreneur running a small business your concerns could include:

- can the learning organisation be used to help identify the best way to develop the business?
- what will be the advantages or benefits of introducing a learning organisation approach?
- will the learning organisation provide a way of tackling problems of growth?

For the Human Resources Director concerns could include:

- how does the learning organisation approach fit into the other human resource strategies such as management development, training, Total Quality Management?
- what is the link between the learning organisation and the strategic development of the business or organisation?
- how can the learning organisation be described or sold to other senior managers?
- how can the learning organisation be used to change the culture of the organisation?
- is it necessary to engage consultants in order to introduce the learning organisation and what is the best approach to take?
- where does the learning organisation fit with self-appraisal and development activities?
- what benefits could follow from introducing the learning organisation approach?
- is it practical to introduce the learning organisation approach into the organisation?
- can the learning organisation form the basis for setting up a new Division or Unit within the organisation?
- how long does it take for the learning organisation to show a return on investment?

Some of the above ideas may have provided an inspirational trigger or at least struck a chord as to how the learning organisation can be of use to your organisation.

## THE ACADEMICS – CONVENTIONAL WISDOM

One of the key roles of the academic is to attempt to explain how organisations and people within them operate and the concepts and ground rules that define this operation. The use of metaphors that depict organisations as organisms (surviving by learning and adapting – having a life of their own, etc.) or as mechanisms (input, output, process, systems, feedback and control) are those that are most likely to be used. By using these metaphors academics can quickly communicate and persuade their audiences to think in particular ways. Quite often the outcome is mostly persuasive in terms of appreciation but less capable of translation into practice. In addition the academics will be deriving their persuasive argument from an academic background or discipline. This will be primarily sociology, psychology, systems theory or cybernetics. In some cases the attempt will be to mix these all together and operate from a very broad base. Why not, you may ask. Each theorist can provide an important insight into the way to think about and begin to explore possible approaches to implementing the learning organisation.

Perhaps the most well-known academic writers in the United Kingdom are Mike Pedler, John Burgoyne and Tom Boydell, with Peter Senge holding the ring in the United States of America. Learning organisations are described by these and other academics in terms such as:

- transformation
- change
- participation
- innovation
- altering the way people work
- adapting
- management style
- delegation
- fostering employee involvement

The inference being that a learning organisation is one that adopts some or all of these characteristics.

### Mike Pedler, John Burgoyne and Tom Boydell

These authors come from a background of management development and psychology. They started working together in 1976 and became well known for their interest and ideas in individual or self-development. This focus in many ways created problems for individuals who were attempting to pursue development in organisational settings. The idea was thus extended to embrace organisational learning. Their philosophy is underpinned by the following two statements:

*The Learning Company is a vision of what might be possible. It is not brought about simply by training individuals; it can only happen as a result of learning at the whole organisation level.*

*A Learning Company is an organisation that facilitates the learning of all its members and continuously transforms itself.*

Two key notions underpin their work. Firstly, the suggestion that there are eleven dimensions or features of a Learning Company and secondly that there are levels or degrees of learning in an organisation.

These two notions were described by Professor John Burgoyne in an article published in the *Royal Society of Arts Journal* (April 1992) entitled 'Creating a Learning Organisation'. The three levels of what he described as 'degrees of learningfullness' in organisations are: first where the organisation learns and uses processes and procedures; this is seen as being essentially a bureaucracy. The second level is where the organisation learns to adapt and survive and the third is where they begin to develop in such a way as to support the wider enterprise which includes all stakeholders and interested parties. Within a learning organisation Burgoyne sees four fundamental processes taking place: Policy, Operations, Thinking and Doing. Individual learning is viewed as flowing from visioning through Thinking to realisation associated with action and Doing, whereas collective or organisational level learning is represented through Policy and Operations as collective action. The model suggested by these four processes interacting does raise the notion of the learning organisation above one that is focused purely on training and management development, but for many practising managers does not provide an easy route to implementation.

The article does provide perhaps a more practical focus by describing the eleven characteristics or features of the learning organisation. These characteristics cover the complex range of the organisation's activities. The inference is made that developing these characteristics could lead to creating learning organisations.

At a Corporate level the strategy formation and policy-making processes are seen as benefiting from a greater focus on collective learning and evaluation of outcomes. More people being involved in the policy-making process. A greater use of information technology or at least a more open approach to the creation and use of information is recommended as a basis around which people can become increasingly empowered. This would also include a more open approach towards the design and use of accounting systems. Other characteristics would include: departments acting more as customers and suppliers, alternative reward systems being created, flexible organisational structures and collecting data from all organisational members. Two final characteristics highlighted by Burgoyne touch directly on the notion of a learning focus. Firstly, where the organisation forms links with suppliers and customers on joint learning activities and secondly where a climate for learning that encourages experimentation and risk taking is created. The suggestion given in the article is that there may be one or more of these eleven characteristics that are vital in any particular organisational setting if the learning organisation is to be created.

## Peter Senge

Peter Senge, Director of the Systems Thinking and Organisational Learning Programme at the Sloane School of Management identifies five disciplines as the key characteristics which everyone must develop in order to create a learning organisation. The five characteristics can be broadly interpreted as:

### 1. Systems Thinking.
Everyone learning that one action or set of events has an impact on how others think and act.

### 2. Personal Mastery.
The discipline of continually clarifying and deepening personal vision – developing patience, seeing reality objectively.

### 3. Mental Models.
Unearthing mental pictures of the world and holding them to vigorous scrutiny.

### 4. Build a shared Vision.
Leadership being used to create organisations, creating structures and activities.

### 5. Team Learning.
Teams, not individuals being key to successful organisations of the future and the only way in which organisations can learn.

The emphasis is on the element of systems thinking. Senge sees the learning organisations as entities in which people can and do expand their capacities to create the results that they truly desire. New and expansive thinking is encouraged and individuals learn together. Various tools derived from the notions of creativity and innovation such as surfacing and challenging mental models, building a shared vision and the creation of processes where open and risk-free dialogue can take place are used within the learning organisations. Senge advocates the use of 'microworlds', simulations that compress time and space to enable teams to learn about possible ways of working together and tackling problems. These 'microworld teams' reflect on, expose and test mental models and mind sets that they use when tackling problems. In this way problems that organisational systems (e.g. purchasing, order-getting, scheduling) can cause, and the influence of the perceptions of the individuals can be explored and changed. In this way blocks to learning are identified.

## THE CONSULTANTS – CONVENTIONAL ADVICE

The management consultancies such as McKinsey, Coopers & Lybrand and a host of smaller agencies are a natural source of advice for those wishing to explore ways of implementing the learning organisation. The management consultant trades on:

- being seen as an expert
- bringing to bear the outside view
- having tools, techniques and methodologies
- being seen as operating from a position of integrity and accountability.

The consultant is well aware that the client is rarely starting with a clean sheet and there will be many constraints surrounding any suggestions made as to a way forward. The approach taken by the consultant is usually based on the following premises:

- get close to the client before suggesting a way forward
- get in where the opportunity arises
- the desire to give value for money and thus establish repeat business.

Most major assignments centre around programmes of change and intervention. It is unlikely that the consultant would be forthcoming in suggesting a learning organisation approach. The problem is that there is little shared meaning among consultants, academics and practitioners as to the notion of the learning organisation. The larger consultancies have a wide client base and being client centred will resist pushing a particular approach whereas the minor consultancies may have identified the learning organisation notion as a niche market opportunity.

Some of the beliefs about the learning organisation shared by the consultants might include:

- that individual development needs to be conducted within the context of organisational developments and the wider corporate strategies
- that management processes need to be identified and their functions integrated into the structure of the organisation
- that reward and incentive systems must be built into any change programmes.

In many ways it can be seen that the consultants do not need to have a clear approach to the learning organisation. Their portfolio of approaches already has Organisational Development, Total Quality Management and Human Resource Development, Leadership, Change Management and Team Building as labels that are recognised and accepted in their market place. The notion of the learning organisation is one that is of value primarily to those inside organisations who wish to make use of the concept of learning associated with action and reflection as a focus for change and growth.

An example from some work by Tom Peters and Robert Waterman when they were with McKinsey illustrates how a top consultancy approached the notion of the learning organisation.

Peters and Waterman developed and expounded what is known as the McKinsey 7-S framework and their eight attributes that characterise the distinctive or excellent companies. A learning organisation would on this premise need to learn and become effective in all of these areas. The McKinsey 7-S framework suggests that the following seven variables have to be taken into account when developing an organisation, all of which are complex and interrelated. Strategy and structure are described as the hardware, with skills, systems, style and staff being the software. Peters and Waterman emphasised to practising managers the belief that these software characteristics could not only be managed but that they could be bound within a set of shared values. This does create a clear picture as to some of the key elements of a learning organisation.

In addition the eight attributes that Peters and Waterman suggested would characterise an excellent company can be broadly described as:

### 1. A bias for action.
This suggests that flatter organisations are more likely to lead to action with small teams being given the authority to act.

### 2. Close to the customer.
A focus on satisfying the customer that now dominates all Total Quality Management thinking.

### 3. Autonomy and entrepreneurship.
Creating the environment where autonomy will work, encouraging risk taking and recognising success.

### 4. Productivity through people.
Ensuring that people are given the space to explore and create their own motivation. Respecting the individual.

### 5. Hands on, value driven.
Allowing people to see what the key values of the organisation are and demonstrating that management believe in these values.

### 6. Stick to the knitting.
Keep doing what works well. Aim always to improve the things that matter.

### 7. Simple organisational form, lean staff.
A small central staff group and a simple organisational structure.

### 8. Create loose tight properties.
Maintain tight control on some activities, say keeping close to customers but be loose in areas for example where innovation and team working are involved.

These attributes can easily be interpreted as a set of exhortations to be posted on the company noticeboard or printed in executive diaries but they are more than that. For the learning organisation they provide a set of beliefs which perhaps underpin management thinking and action but there is still the problem of the lack of an overall philosophy or guidance for executives and managers on how to proceed.

It is interesting to see how McKinsey set about introducing the notion of the learning organisation into their own internal way of working. The idea they used is that organisational learning is about the creation and management of knowledge. With this new focus the consultancy attempted to balance serving clients with creating knowledge. Practice Centres were broken down into thirteen that were industry focused and eighteen, known as centres of competence, that focused on functional specialities. This drive was to create an organisation where staff could easily tap into what people had learned. Personal networks were seen as key to a change of emphasis with staff formally contributing to institutional learning. A high level of contribution is seen as a requirement for promotion. The consultancy established a database called Firm Practice Information System (FPIS) which is used as a control in that, for example, client billings cannot be made until a summary of how the consultant intends to approach a project has been submitted. The FPIS also requests team leaders to input what has been learned from an assignment at regular intervals.

An additional development was the introduction of a Practice Development Network (PDN) which encouraged users to input what they saw as core documents from the practice. This database was then edited out at regular intervals. This approach suggests a very centralised form of the learning organisation.

These efforts by the academics and consultants raise the question as to how bespoke does an approach to implementing a learning organisation have to be and what general lessons and good practices are there to date. Two examples from the world of practice are given below to help address that question.

## THE PRACTITIONERS – CONVENTIONAL ACTIONS

Reports from the world of practice are based on interviews with Chief Executives, reports in magazines and journals or sometimes in books written by the person who initiated and implemented the change programme. The insight provided is always a simplified or cleaned up version of what probably transpired but they are useful in that they provide a backdrop for those considering implementing the learning organisation. Two examples are given in order to demonstrate the breadth of current practice.

### Xerox Corporation – Chief Executive – Organisational Architect

A reported interview with Paul Allaire, Chairman and CEO of the Xerox Corporation – reported by Robert Howard, Senior Editor, Harvard Business Review 1992.

> When most companies re-organise, they usually focus on the formal structure of the organisation – the boxes on the organisation chart. The change we are making now is more profound than anything we've done before. We have embarked on a process to change completely the way we manage the company. Changing the organisation structure is only one part of that. We are also changing the processes by which we manage, the reward systems and other mechanisms that shape those processes and the kind of people we place in key managerial positions. We are trying to change our informal culture – the way we do things, the behaviours that drive the business.

The interview then continues to spell out an approach where managers at various levels in the organisation worked in teams towards formulating targets and objectives in these areas and then other teams carried out the implementation. The picture is painted of the CEO needing to act as a modern-day architect with a flair for vision and design but also being able to

## 16  Implementing the Learning Organisation

structure and lead the implementation to produce economic benefits and growth for the organisation.

Xerox would, from this account, appear to have focused on learning as a means of changing the organisation. Appointed as CEO in 1990, Allaire spent two years systematically and methodically tackling the task of organisational redesign of the document processing business which accounted for some 80 per cent of the company's 1991 revenues of $17.8 billion.

Some of the key features of the programme are given to illustrate the trigger and response.

The trigger:

- the business was facing severe competition
- a quality programme had already been used to combat the threat from Japanese companies
- the need was identified as achieving a technological transformation
- the functions of the product were being incorporated in the technology and systems of the key competitors
- the need to re-address the customer was seen as paramount
- new skills had to be acquired.

The response comprised an eight-point plan:

1. The determination to create an organisation that can evolve as technology, skills, competitors and the business change.

2. Six young managers appointed to examine the structure and practices needed by the company to be successful. They were charged with learning about the latest thinking in strategy, management, organisational design and seeking new organisational models from outside the company.

3. A 15-month design process initiated involving 75 managers throughout the organisation. Principles of the change programme were internalised over that period.

4. Four possible scenarios for Xerox's future were developed in three months.

5. Seven months later the business division concept had been completed.

6. A new team was formed to work out the details of the new organisational model. Some 15 senior managers plus five support staff. They were charged with communicating the changes across the company. They met two days per week for four months.

7. Sub-groups involving 50 managers were set up to identify new skills required of the managers.

**8.** The new organisation was launched with the people involved in the programme in key leadership positions.

Xerox are by any measure a large corporation and the fact that the CEO promoted the change would seem to be a key feature of the support given by middle management. But the programme did harness creativity and stimulate learning in all parts of the organisation. Learning was addressed in areas such as:

- the formal processes of planning, control, reporting and reward
- the personality and character of managers required for the key posts
- the development of a more entrepreneurial approach from business divisions
- the informal networks and practices linking people together, the value systems and culture
- the need to create tension between autonomy of managers and integration
- the skills required for key managerial posts, how to define these and select the people to fill them
- the identification of a more sophisticated appraisal system
- the use of benchmarking against competitors
- developing pockets of innovation.

## British Telecommunications – Learning Organisations – BT UK sales (Reported in *Personnel Management* January 1993)

A report of BT's efforts to use the learning organisation approach in many ways challenges the growing belief that the behaviour of managers, through the demonstration of competences, is more important than the underlying shared mental models, shared vision of the future and collective team learning.

The trigger:

- BT UK Sales operation was faced with a major organisational change, introduction of new work patterns and the need to improve sales performance.
- Some 3000 sales and support staff plus 250 managers were involved in the change.
- Large business customers were being transferred to national accounts division leading to a reduced customer base but the same sales targets.
- Faced with the need to create new sales grades.
- Move from knowledge base as a sales strength towards an account management skills base.

The response:

**1.** A decision to focus on learning around areas such as teamworking and creativity in order to provide lasting solutions.

**2.** Trainers helped management identify the qualities for effectiveness needed by the new sales staff. Areas such as learning ability and an holistic approach to problem solving and personal flexibility were identified.

**3.** Two-day development workshop for 1000 sales staff. Senior managers trained in assessment centre techniques and the workshops focused on job-related exercises, aptitude tests, personality preference tests, feedback sessions for individuals. Emphasis was on helping individuals identify learning points that could be applied in their work. Also individuals were encouraged to consider their career direction for later discussion with their line managers.

**4.** Line managers trained in course management and job skills development in the workplace.

**5.** Training programmes around needs were set up.

**6.** Output from the workshops used to determine organisational decision making in the areas of manpower planning, succession planning and formulating training plans.

**7.** Regular reviews of team performance including the identification of learning points and planning the future application of learning.

Some initial hostility to the above programme was reported where managers saw the programme as an intrusion plus fears that the information at workshops would be used against the individuals. These fears were only partially allayed until the programme was under way and the potential benefits could be seen.

The programme is seen to involve three levels: learning, applying and developing.

*Level One*: participants attend a development centre to review performances and abilities – applying this learning at the workplace. Reviewing this with line managers.

*Level Two*: team managers review the learning and use coaching to help overcome blockages.

*Level Three*: organisational learning where top managers review their learning with inputs from Levels One and Two.

BT report that the programme has cost some £200,000 in training investment. Savings of some £60 million are reported.

In the many reports that are quoted as demonstrating that the learning organisation has been implemented, the common themes of linking individual development and learning with that of the organisation (usually the top management policy makers) and basing learning on the work and business come through. How these links are made and how these then translate through into bottom line performance are often left to the reader to surmise.

The following section illustrates how these links and translations to bottom line are made through conventional training and management development strategies.

## WHERE DOES TRAINING AND DEVELOPMENT FIT IN?

Training people for performance in their present jobs and development of their potential for future jobs is part and parcel of organisational life. Leadership training, team building workshops and enquiries into the practical and psychological aspects surrounding motivation form the backbone of the human resource development activities. It is important to understand where these approaches fit into the notion of the learning organisation.

### Human resource development

The Human Resource Development movement evolved from what was the training and personnel function. Human Resource Management is used as a wider description that includes all the historic personnel (pay, conditions, contracts) functions. So where does all this training and development fit?

The directorate or top management are charged with the overall direction of the enterprise. Traditionally this would involve the study of:

- the external environment in which the organisation operates
- the macro-economic context
- the industry structure
- the competitors
- key shareholders and interest groups
- the internal environment and culture of the organisation
- historic and current financial performance
- major strengths and weaknesses
- success or otherwise of key strategies
- performance and requirements for key senior personnel.

The corporate group is then expected to identify the future position that the organisation wishes to reach in terms of quantifiable objectives. The contribution of the Human Resource Management function in this process is to ascertain the human resource assets in the organisation in terms of numbers and skills levels. Also, to consider the changes to this skill base that will be required to support the wider corporate objectives and associated strategies. The Human Resource function would also become involved in helping to identify the organisational structure and form required to support the corporate planning process itself and the individuals at the top level. This mixing of the business planning and human resource planning creates a blurring and at times confusion as to where the drive for corporate development should begin.

Managers in the Human Resource functions have in many ways created for themselves a split role. Should they simply concentrate on supporting the business concerns of profitability, productivity, etc., by recruiting, training and developing the human resources to fit the specified need or do they have wider responsibilities to the employees and managers in terms of ensuring that the organisational climate and culture is harmonious for all concerned? Is it their function to ensure that processes are in place that will create an organisation capable of responding to the environment while at the same time developing the internal operational processes to improve management activity? Not an easy choice and in many organisations it leads to purposes and issues for the function being fudged.

The key point to be made is that whatever role the Human Resource function adopts the focus must be on both the formal and informal learning that takes place around the above issues. The opportunities for learning are enormous. Also, if the function is to take an active part in setting the foundations for organisational learning what should their role be in relation to those charged with the profitability and development of the organistion?

## Management Development

Management Development is usually, but not always, linked to an appraisal process. Targets for individuals are agreed and from this training and development programmes are set up. These programmes take many forms but share some common principles or ideas of best practice. Programmes need to be:

(a) work-based or linked to the business itself in order to gain more commitment from the delegates where learning is seen to be linked to 'pay-off' at the work place.

(b) designed to take account of the current perspectives of the delegates in

## The Learning Organisation – Myth or Reality 21

order for the learning to be seen as relevant and realistic.

(c) in tune with the climate and culture of the organisation in order to gain buy-in from the delegates.

Development programmes based on these lines tend to re-enforce the existing work practices and organisational culture. This ensures that identifiable pay-offs can be obtained both by the organisation and the delegates. Management Development programmes can also include an element of self-appraisal where individuals are encouraged to identify and follow programmes of self-development. In some organisations this has been formalised into the adoption of learning contracts where individuals form a contract in conjunction with their seniors to complete a learning programme to reach defined levels of competence. Obviously an organisation that promotes formal management development at the team and individual level can be seen as behaving as a learning organisation.

The following questions need to be posed in terms of whether or not the outcome of a Management Development process in itself constitutes a learning organisation. In particular:

- does the learning need to be formalised?
- at what level in the activities of the organisation should the learning be focussed?
- who decides the level at which learning priorities arise?
- how is the informal learning that takes place captured and utilised?
- how can new learning needs for both the organisation and individuals be identified and realised?
- to what extent does the learning involved in management development programmes link to outcomes for the organisation and the business?

Questions such as these have for many executives and managers created a view that subscribes to the idea that 'management development' is not only seen as an employee's right but that it must be a good thing, although not all would support this broad view.

## Organisational Development

Where an organisation wishes to change direction or the culture, possibly following a major re-organisation or takeover then more radical approaches to learning are introduced. The field of organisational development (OD) has grown over the years and organisations have become famous for their excursions with these change programmes.

The central concern of those driving OD programmes is that the effectiveness of the organisation relies on having an appropriate set of beliefs and cultures in place to support the corporate direction and strategies. Organisational development thus takes the form of a long-term programme of change in the way the organisation is structured and the way people behave. In this way an organisational capability is created that will seize the opportunity or survive the threats from the external environment.

Most OD programmes use external consultants as facilitators who begin by working with the Chief Executive or the top team to identify the changes that are required to the existing culture and the organisational structure. The new values and beliefs are then communicated to senior and middle managers through workshops, team events and discussion groups. The change is thus spread throughout the organisation.

The underlying notion behind OD is that it is possible to change the culture to a predetermined stance and that when this has been achieved the organisation will proceed steadfastly until the next major change is identified as being desirable. Examples of such programmes would be where the Chief Executive decided that the organisation needed to become more competitive, more marketing orientated, more customer responsive, more quality conscious, etc.

Organisational development consultants are not value free themselves and when studying an organisation prior to recommending a change programme would probably subscribe to the following beliefs:

- the programme has to be owned and driven by the Chief Executive and the top management team
- the changes must be organisation-wide
- a change agent or facilitator must be used to conduct the programme (preferably an external consultant)
- the programme should be presented in everyday management language
- the tasks created by the work itself should dictate how the organisation is structured
- the reward system should cover job performance, people development and developing management processes
- people should be open and able to handle conflict and confrontation
- people should conflict over the tasks and not interpersonal relations
- there should be a clear recognition of shared values and beliefs
- systems should exist where people can learn from experience.

This approach does move a bit closer to the notion of the learning organisation where the need to change is identified and the associated learning needs at an organisational level are crystallised; the change itself being linked very closely to business needs and hence tangible pay-offs.

Once again we need to pose some questions in relation to the learning organisation, in particular:

- What determines the start point for an organisational development programme and what consensus is needed that the programme is appropriate?
- To what extent do the intended outcomes of the programme have to be clear and quantifiable?
- What evidence is there that such programmes lead to real change in behaviour and performance of individuals and teams?
- Does management development fit within an organisational development programme?
- How far reaching does the programme need to be within the organisation in order to have impact?
- Over what timescale does an organisational development programme run?
- Do such programmes saturate individuals such that having introduced one then a period of respite has to follow?

There is no doubt that organisational development programmes are here to stay. They represent the way in which leaders and power groups in organisations act out their strategies for taking their organisations into new areas of performance. Many are successful, others less so. For the notion of the learning organisation they obviously form the conditioning upon which concepts of the learning organisation have been developed.

The criticism of OD programmes tends to be on two counts. Firstly, from those who reject the notion that the Chief Executive or top team can effectively define a culture that will fit the strategy and secondly, those who favour change arising from those more closely engaged in the work itself.

There is a growing concern that people who are subjected to a change programme will set up defensive routines. These stem from the line managers' innate belief that their power and authority are key to their success in achieving the task. That subordinates are most easily motivated by the work itself and the associated rewards. This is coupled to a view that judgements about a subordinate's performance should not be highlighted as this would threaten an already uneasy link in the power chain. Most managers will recognise these behaviours as being the norm rather than the exception at all levels. To be effective an OD programme would therefore need to tackle these more underlying beliefs about 'how to manage'.

Many see the way forward for OD programmes to be one that emphasises creating a climate in which people are given the space and resources to evolve a more effective way of working. Relying on groups to develop ways of working that rely on local knowledge that in many cases will be almost impossible to gauge or measure at a corporate level. The emphasis perhaps swinging much more towards a learning focus in order to achieve commitment and consensus rather than a change programme that sets out to obtain compliance to a previously identified set of behaviours.

## Teamwork, motivation and leadership

Most organisations would subscribe to the notions behind training that encourage effective teamwork, appropriate leadership and creating opportunities for individuals to maximise their potential for self-motivation. In spite of years of training, legions of books and articles, managers are still struggling to learn the mysteries behind these areas of management activity.

This section does not set out to expound all the theories that underpin these subjects. But some pointers from current practice would suggest that:

**Leadership** can be either a visionary and imaginative role or a controlling and directing role; the view being that most individuals would have difficulty fitting both roles.

**Motivation** that most managers just get in the way and restrict the motivation of subordinates. Others favour a psychological viewpoint where the personality characteristics of the individual need to be identified and these used as the basis for helping them reach a level of self-motivation.

**Teamwork** that individuals have preferences and styles that are based on personality characteristics, developed styles of tackling problems, and learned ways of behaving. To develop effective teams you need to encourage openness between individuals and have clear procedures for operation.

It is clear that managers are learning when testing their leadership, managing and working in teams and attempting to create a climate in which individuals can be motivated to give their best. But in order to link this learning to the notion of the learning organisation we need to pose the following questions:

- how is best practice in leadership and management communicated in the organisation?
- how can perspectives on leadership and the other management approaches in the organisation be identified and shared?
- is there any link between how leadership and teamwork are approached within the organisation and organisational performance?
- to what extent do these activities of management create or influence the climate and culture of the organisation?
- how vital are they to events requiring high levels of innovation and creativity?

These areas of management involve massive and deep-seated learning for individuals. There are formalised training programmes established for all these areas but within the organisation itself learning tends to be very dynamic and context based. In many ways the performance of an organisation is determined by these very basic and everyday management activities. Within the notion of the learning organisation the view would be that these management activities need to be reviewed and questioned almost continuously in relation to organisational performance. Once set in the organisational culture they become very difficult to change.

## Implications for the learning organisation

The activities of the Human Resource Developers can be seen to fit very neatly into the notion of a learning organisation. Areas such as management development, leadership and teamwork training are the underpinnings of the learning organisation. But the notion being considered here is more than the sum of all these parts. We must not cling to the myth that management development, extensive programmes attempting to change the culture of the organisation and the whole management training kitbag will produce effective managers let alone effective organisations. It needs something more – a unifying or collective vision and will to achieve great and exciting things within organisational settings. The opportunity is there but without the notion of the learning organisation the vision will not be created or realised.

The notion of the Learning Organisation must encompass all these human resource development activities such that they can be integrated with corporate strategy and ensure that learning at the organisational and individual level identifies with the right issues and that ways of overcoming blockages to learning are found.

# WHERE DOES QUALITY AND TQM FIT IN?

TQM is a management-led approach where the focus is on quality in all aspects and functions of the company operation. All employees are seen as satisfying customers in all they do with the focus being on the prevention of errors and faults rather than detection. In effect a cultural change in the company from inspection to prevention. A strong emphasis is on meeting customers' requirements and identifying internal customers. Most quality programmes also involve extensive teamwork activity to provide improvements in:

## 26 Implementing the Learning Organisation

- planning analysis
- problem solving
- communications
- motivation
- team responsibility.

The concept of organisations progressing through a series of development stages culminating in maximising benefits from a quality focus is suggested. The four stages are:

1. Producing output that meets customers' requirements. (This is now implemented through the introduction of BS5750/ISO 9000).

2. 'Doing it right first time and every time.' Companies set out to identify wasted effort, monitor processes and implement preventive efforts.

3. Introducing functional analysis to identify unnecessary activities. Discontinue time-wasting reporting activities and free-up time.

4. A focus on the twin objectives of improving product responsiveness and improving the efficiency of the product development process. Shortening the product development life cycle.

This fourth stage is seen as providing a range of business benefits such as customer loyalty, profitability etc.

Total Quality Management has links to the notion of a learning organisation. The TQM philosophy is to improve on product and service performance and delivery while at the same time focusing primarily on the customer. The approach is usually promoted as requiring a change in how the company operates and needs to have the commitment of top management and the involvement of all employees. This 'total involvement' approach is based on the view that the contribution that every employee can make needs to be harnessed, both skills and enthusiasm. This leads to programmes being introduced where individuals and teams are given the skills, tools and authority to investigate problems and introduce improvements. Teamwork is the key and management involvement is vital.

The following list of fundamental requirements of a Total Quality Culture have been suggested by Lesley and Malcolm Munro-Faure:

1. Know your customer.

2. Know your competitors.

3. Know your cost of non-conformance.

4. Measure your performance against key customer-driven parameters.

## The Learning Organisation – Myth or Reality 27

5. Make sure each employee understands and is committed to the Quality Objectives.
6. Management commitment to continuous improvement of Quality within the business.
7. Define the purpose of each department and activity in terms of satisfying external and internal customer requirements.
8. Enable employees to fulfil their commitment to Quality by influencing the programme of continuous improvement.
9. Replace inspection and correction techniques to control the Quality of output with preventative actions.
10. Never accept non-conforming output in the form of product or services for external or internal customers.
11. Plan effectively before undertaking actions.

The detail and prescriptiveness of the above requirements gives the flavour of TQM programmes.

Quality gurus such as Philip Crosby, Edwards Deming and Joseph Juran hold varying perspectives on how to approach quality but share some common tenets:

- without attention to quality business will fail in the long run
- full commitment from management is essential
- the approach is hard work
- extensive training is required
- active involvement of all employees is required.

Of all the gurus, perhaps, Edwards Deming provides the greatest link between TQM and the notion of the learning organisation being promoted in this book. Deming has spoken of the need for the total transformation of Western style management. He produced his 14 points for Management in order to help people understand and implement the necessary transformation. Deming said that the adoption of these points indicated that senior management intended to stay in business. His health warning was that these points needed careful discussion in the context of the organisation being considered. The points are given below to illustrate how some of them can be seen to link to the notion of a learning organisation.

1. Create constancy of purpose to improve product and service.
2. Adopt a new philosophy for new economic age by management learning responsibilities and taking leadership for change.

3. Cease dependence on inspection to achieve quality.
4. End awarding business on price.
5. Improve constantly and forever the system of production and service to improve quality and productivity and decrease costs.
6. Institute training on the job.
7. Institute leadership.
8. Drive out fear.
9. Break down barriers between departments.
10. Eliminate slogans, exhortations and numerical targets for the workforce.
11. Eliminate quotas, work standards and management by objectives – substitute leadership.
12. Remove barriers that rob people of their right to pride of workmanship.
13. Institute a vigorous education and self-improvement programme.
14. Put everyone in the company to work to accomplish the transformation.

The TQM approaches adopted by organisations have in many ways been examples of massive culture change and learning programmes. In some organisations notions of effective leadership have been coupled with those embodied in TQM. In this area effective leadership is seen as expressing the vision of the leader as to what the organisation has to become and what the leader believes in and wants to achieve; in this way defining what the organisation is all about. This leads to actions such as production of mission statements and a communication of beliefs and objectives to all employees. The linking ideas between effective leadership and Quality are then promoted as follows:

Effective Leadership:

- Develop clear beliefs and objectives
- Develop clear and effective strategies
- Identify critical processes
- Review management structure
- Encourage effective employee participation.

Quality:

- Satisfy customer needs
- Get close to customers

- Plan to do all jobs right first time
- Agree expected performance standards
- Implement company-wide quality improvements
- Measure performance
- Measure quality management and fire-fighting
- Demand continuous improvement
- Recognise achievements.

There are many areas in TQM that support the notion of the learning organisation and, where these approaches are adopted, there have been many success stories. The learning organisation notion provided in this book has a wider and perhaps more fundamental approach to instituting organisational learning and development than that offered by TQM. Where an organisation has introduced TQM or is in the process of doing so then this wider notion should be more easily assimilated. Alternatively, where an organisation has not adopted TQM, say beyond the BS5750 or ISO 9000 stage then the learning organisation notion provided will help that organisation move on in its thinking.

## References

Pedler, M., Burgoyne, J. and Boydell, T. *The Learning Company* (McGraw-Hill, 1991)

Senge, P.M. *The Fifth Discipline* (Century Business, 1990).

Peters, T. *Liberation Management*, (MacMillan, London, 1992).

Munro-Faure, L. & M. *Implementing Total Quality Management*, (Pitman Publishing, 1992).

Article – *Harvard Business Review* (1992). 'Xerox Corporation, The Organisational Architect.'

Article – *Journal of Personnel Management* (January 1993). 'British Telecommunications – Learning Organisations'.

Article – *Royal Society of Arts Journal* (April 1992). 'Creating a Learning Organisation.'

# 2
# USING THE 17-DAY PROGRAMME

**PREPARING FOR AND MANAGING THE STUDY**

Having set the scene and provided some of the background ideas behind the notion of the learning organisation it is time to introduce the learning programme itself.

As in all learning a degree of personal discipline is required. The first decision should be to tackle the learning programme in such a way that it can be completed within a period of time that maintains enthusiasm while not becoming a burden. Most managers are familiar with conducting feasibility studies in order to determine the possibilities and potential problems surrounding the introduction of a new product, service or approach. This is how the learning programme should be approached and thus completing the programme in a time period of 17 elapsed weeks (one day per week) is recommended. This will allow for the ideas to develop and be tested out with colleagues.

For most managers taking out one working day a week for this programme will present a major problem. The general belief is that managers fill up any space created in the week with new activities, hence always being in a state of busyness. The first step is therefore to conduct a short review of how your time is actually being spent. This analysis need only take a few hours of reflection and the determination to make more effective use of your time.

One way to tackle this is to consider the key purpose of your job; next to determine the six key areas that, if carried out well, will lead to satisfying the purpose of the job. These areas may include a mixture of man-management and functional activities. Then break down each of the six areas into, say, three sub-tasks. Based on a typical week, make some allocations of your time spent on each area. Decide from which areas you are going to wrestle that spare day. This is the point at which some major decisions have to be made as to how much discipline and reorganisation of your workload is going to be necessary if you are to complete your own learning programme.

As the learning programme unfolds, the amount of data and information that will be accumulated will grow. Ideas, problems, opportunities and suggestions need to be captured as they occur. Depending on your preference for data collection it would be advisable to set up some form of data base. This can be either a simple paper-based or PC-based system. What is important is that it is in a form that allows for simple recording and subsequent ease of recall.

It will also be necessary to decide whether or not other people will be involved in the study. This presents both an opportunity and a problem. Identifying, setting up and briefing task teams is a good way of increasing the coverage and cascading the learning but there is a time penalty and additional communication requirements. The final choice will depend upon personal style, organisational culture and the overall purpose of the feasibility study. It may be wise to make the decision after you have looked at the topic areas that are to be studied.

## TOPICS TO BE STUDIED

Four main topics are covered in the programme:

(a) Clarifying the purpose of the study and reviewing the organisation.

(b) Creating the vision of the learning organisation.

(c) Identifying the culture and the opportunities for change.

(d) Assessing the benefits.

These topics are covered fully in the following chapters but it is important that an overall understanding of what is involved is gained at this point.

### Clarifying the purpose of the study and reviewing the organisation

It is suggested that four days are allocated to this topic. The learning in this section will focus on clarifying the purpose and intentions behind the feasibility study. These will vary enormously from individual to individual as much due to personality and personal style as to the context in which the organisation is operating. An opportunity is provided to consider the influence of both personality and preferred style when tackling problems where creativity is required. This will help to make you aware of any biases that will be influencing your approach to implementation.

Classical views of the organisation operating in an external environment are used to help create a clear picture of the organisational context and opportunities for growth and development. Use will also be made of the notions of processes and the use of metaphors as ways of describing the internal environment of the organisation as seen by the major internal groups. An historical viewing of the organisation will be used to help build up a picture of the major events that have helped shape and create the existing organisational form and activity. Pressures for change will be explored and related to the need for the organisation and individuals within it to focus on learning as a way forward. A review will also be made of the organisational learning that has become ingrained and the mechanisms and processes that are reinforcing that learning.

## Creating the vision of the learning organisation

It is suggested that three days are allocated to this topic. This section provides an opportunity to consider your preferred leadership style and gauge the impact that this will have on your thinking and approach to implementation.

A first step is then taken to identifying your personal vision for the learning organisation and to test this out with colleagues. Help is then provided to establish the mission or sense of purpose that will be needed to support that vision. The notion of a separate identity for the learning organisation from that of the host enterprise is then presented along with suggestions as to how these eventually need to become integrated.

An opportunity to review how the organisation currently values and employs conventional management development and training to address learning needs at all levels is provided.

Finally a review of the main power groups and change leaders in the enterprise provides a first step in determining who will need to be aligned with the notion of the learning organisation.

## Identifying the culture and the opportunities for change

It is suggested that seven days are allocated to this topic. The organisational culture will be identified and used to consider areas where blockages to learning may be occurring. Ways of overcoming these blockages will be considered. The phasing of any envisaged changes that are considered essential to matching the purpose of the wider enterprise with the required learning will be identified. This linking between the overall purpose and learning is a key consideration at this stage in the feasibility study. It provides a focus for ways in which support from key players in the organisation can be attracted and begin to form some commitment to the ideas behind the learning organisation.

Initial plans will be developed as to the key activities and phasing required for the implementation of the learning organisation. How best to integrate existing learning processes is seen as crucial to this stage of the study.

### Assessing the benefits

It is suggested that three days are allocated to this topic. The focus will be on identifying the external and internal stakeholders in the organisation, and clarifying the range of outcomes and benefits that they would expect and value from the implementation of the learning organisation. Some creativity will be required here in order to determine ways of achieving the required level of satisfaction and hence support from the stakeholders.

Ways of measuring and evaluating the outcomes of the activities attributable to the learning organisation will be identified. This will include conventional cost-benefit and more evaluative models and approaches. Options for communicating and cascading the learning from the feasibility study will be considered.

The emphasis in this final section will be on how to ensure that the notion of the learning organisation is accepted by the organisation as a way forward.

## STEPS IN THE LEARNING MODEL

In order to conduct the learning programme a seven-step model will be used for each of the topics outlined above. The steps in the model are illustrated in Fig. 2.1. This will provide a sequence of learning that involves:

1. Thinking through the purposes behind the topic, clarifying objectives and deciding how to tackle the learning.
2. Taking action by collecting data and information about the organisation in order to provide a basis on which to clarify thoughts and perspectives.
3. Learning by undertaking some focused readings where views are presented, on the topic being studied, from the world of the practitioners and academics.
4. Forming perspectives and hypotheses by matching your views and findings with those from other practitioners and academics.
5. Learning by testing out your revised perspectives on others either inside or outside of the organisation. Hence confirming their reality and developing the arguments needed to persuade others.

34  Implementing the Learning Organisation

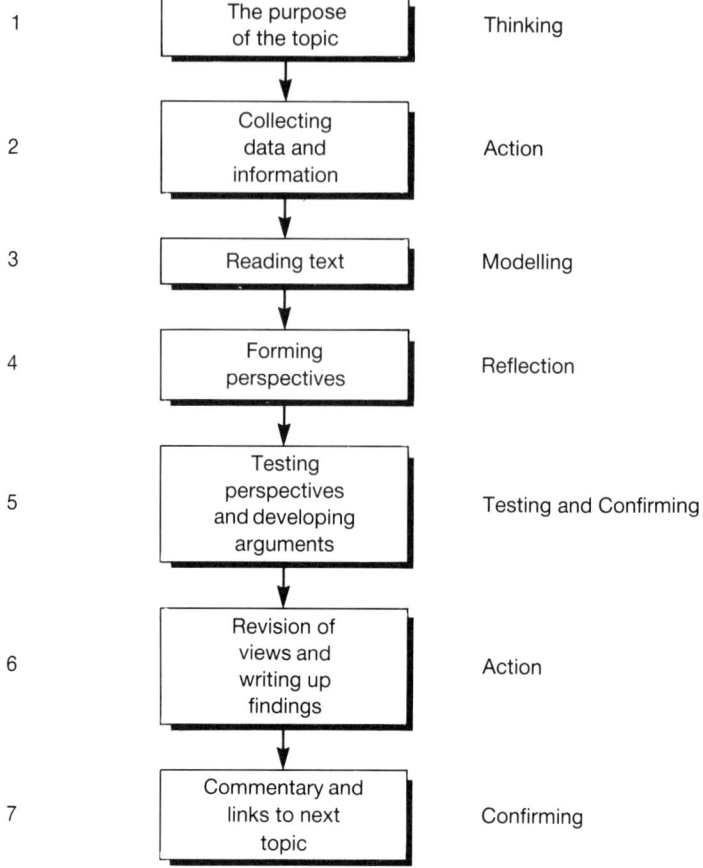

Fig. 2.1  *The seven-step learning model*

6. Reflection and revision of your views and committing these views to some formal documentation or database.

7. Confirming your views by testing them against the commentary provided and linking to the next study topic.

Some managers will find certain of the above steps more attractive than others. This is normal in that individuals have different preferences for learning. Some like the action and data collection steps while others prefer the more reflective and contemplative approach. It is important that an effort is made to learn from all the steps and that rationalisations for taking short-cuts are not introduced without an attempt at resistance.

The next four chapters all use the seven-step learning model as the approach to learning and when completed will provide the backdrop against which the final implementation design can be undertaken.

Before you tackle these four chapters it is recommended that you skim read Chapter 7 which covers a detailed guide to implementation.

Having read this you will then be much more purposeful in tackling the study itself. Study and implementation go hand-in-hand and practising this back and forth approach to learning is essential. In truth it is probably what you do already.

# 3

# CLARIFYING THE PURPOSE AND REVIEWING THE ORGANISATION

## INTRODUCTION

It is suggested that four days are allocated to this topic over an elapsed period of four weeks. An outline study plan is shown in Fig. 3.1.

The approach will be to provide guidance on how to conduct each of the steps in the learning model which involves consideration of the influence of your personality on the study approach, decisions on the purpose and conduct of the feasibility study followed by a review of the organisation. Checklists and proformas are provided to help focus the information from these reviews. A series of selected readings then help the reflection stage. Finally, an opportunity is provided to test out perspectives before moving on to the next study topic.

LEARNING MODEL – STEP I

### PERSONALITY AND CREATIVE STYLE – A SELF-ANALYSIS

The key ingredient in this feasibility study is perhaps not surprisingly yourself. Most senior managers have taken part in personality type tests either when being selected for posts or when involved in management training and study programmes. There are many variants of these tests and no doubt some managers see these as valid, others see them as unrealistic. Two of the more well-known tests are the Myers–Briggs Type Indicator (Myers–Briggs Type Indicator and MBTI are registered trade marks of Consultancy Psychologists Press, Inc.) and the Kirton–Adaptation–Innovation Inventory. The popularity of the MBTI can be seen in that around two million managers worldwide are reported to be taking this test each year. It is worth spending some time considering the influence that

| Step in the learning model | Activity | Sub topic studied | Study days |
|---|---|---|---|
| 1 | • Self-analysis/personality creative style<br>• Thinking through purposes and objectives of the feasibility study | – | 1/2 |
| 2 | Review of the organisation:<br>• External environment<br>• Internal environment<br>• Performance measures<br>• Historical perspective<br>• Pressures for change<br>• Opportunities for growth and development<br>• Opportunities for new learning | – | 2 |
| 3 | • Reading text and reflection | • Impact of personality and style on planning and problem solving<br>• Organisations, their form and development<br>• Managing and risk taking<br>• The use of creativity and innovation in developing organisations | 1 |
| 4/5/6 | • Reflection and testing of views<br>• Recording views, ideas perspectives and concerns | | 1/2 |
| 7 | • Reading text | • Commentary and links to next study topic | |

*Fig. 3.1 Study plan*

personality and the ability to be creative will have on the study outcomes. These two self-analyses are only intended to provide a broad insight into the use of these two well-proven psychological tests. The reader is advised to contact the British Psychological Society for a listing of qualified individuals who are able to administer and evaluate the tests in a professional manner. In this way the reader and other managers can obtain a more reliable and objective assessment on these two important psychological instruments. Contact addresses are provided at the end of this chapter for further information about taking these two tests and being trained in their administration.

| **Extrovert (E)** | **Introvert (I)** |
|---|---|
| • Favouring action<br>• Impatient<br>• Interested in others<br>• Impulsive<br>• Like being in a group<br>• Prefer talking<br>• Like collaborations | • Like quiet when working<br>• Forgetful of people<br>• Dig deep<br>• Work alone and like it<br>• Hate interruptions<br>• Learn by reading |
| **Sensing (S)** | **Intuitive (N)** |
| • Like routines<br>• Apply learning quickly<br>• Good at estimating job times<br>• Logical<br>• Good at precise tasks<br>• Accept the current reality<br>• Like getting the facts | • Always trying to improve things<br>• Work in fits and starts<br>• Like working to hunches<br>• Tend to over-complicate tasks<br>• Question the status quo |
| **Thinking (T)** | **Feeling (F)** |
| • Like establishing order<br>• Like to be treated fairly<br>• Clumsy with people's feelings<br>• Good at analysis | • Avoid conflict<br>• Like praise<br>• Like pleasing others<br>• Like people<br>• Sensitive to your impact on others |
| **Judging (J)** | **Perceiving (P)** |
| • Like to plan<br>• Like to complete<br>• Finish one job at a time<br>• Prepared to start work without all the facts<br>• Methodical | • Wait for the last minute<br>• Adapt to the situation<br>• Indecisive<br>• Avoid unpleasant jobs<br>• Work well under pressure<br>• Use checklists<br>• Inquisitive |

*Fig. 3.2 Personality traits*

## Personality

The Myers–Briggs inventory purports to measure personality types based on theories developed by Jung. The inventory is normally completed by the manager and subsequent analysis and feedback provided by trained psychologists. For the purposes of this learning activity you are asked to consider which of the categories of suggested personality traits match your self-perception. It is important to remember that there is no particular merit in any preferences or combinations of these traits. The value is that they will indicate where you will naturally focus when collecting and analysing information and where your focus will be weaker. These strengths and weaknesses also apply to how you approach problem-solving and decision-making. As this study progresses then the ability to be aware of your built-in biases will become increasingly important.

### Actions

(a) There are four pairs of preferences shown in Fig. 3.2. Consider which description comes closest to your self-perception, e.g. E or I, S or N, T or F, J or P based on work situations.

(b) Decide which of the combinations shown on Fig. 3.3 gives the best fit and check this through discussion with colleagues and friends.

(c) Note areas where your personality type preference may lead to a bias in your approach to this study.

It cannot be too strongly emphasised that this will only provide a very subjective guide to your personality traits. By taking time out to have these tests completed by a trained psychologist you will be able to obtain a more valid assessment.

In Step 3 we will look at how personality traits or cognitive preferences can affect the type of decisions and strategies that a manager adopts. Particularly when working under pressure. But first we will consider your preferred thinking style in respect of creativity, problem-solving and decision-making.

## Creative Style

The approach developed by Michael Kirton suggests that everyone can be seen to operate on a measured scale from highly adaptive in style preference to highly innovative. Adaptors being those who prefer to improve on existing practice and innovators are those who prefer to reframe problems in a way that often confronts accepted practice. Table 3.1 will help you to see to which side you naturally incline.

| The high ADAPTOR in response to problems | The high INNOVATOR in response to problems |
| --- | --- |
| Is characterised by precision, reliability, conformity, methodicalness, prudence. | Is seen as undisciplined, thinking tangentially, approaching tasks from unsuspected angles. |
| Seeks solutions to problems in tried and understood ways. | Often queries the problem's basic assumptions; manipulates problems. |
| Reduces problems by improvement and greater efficiency, maintaining continuity, stability and group cohesion. | Is catalyst to settled groups, irreverent of their consensual views; is seen as abrasive, creating dissonance. |
| Challenges rules rarely, cautiously, usually when supported | Often challenges rules, past customs, consensual views. |
| Produces a (manageable) few relevant sound safe ideas for prompt implementation. | Produces many ideas including those seen as irrelevant, unsound, risky. |

*Table 3.1 Adaptor and innovator responses*
Source: © Dr. M. J. Kirton, reproduced with permission

It is important to note that someone who is a high match with one style can exhibit the other style but that the stress required to maintain this increases with time and can have personal detrimental consequences.

To further develop awareness of your own style preference it will help to reflect on situations in your work where creativity – the ability to come up with a new way of tackling a problem or situation – was required. In this situation:

- how important was it to generate a completely fresh or new approach?
- did you approach this in an adaptive or innovative way?
- was this your preferred style?
- was it the most appropriate approach in the circumstances?
- how could you have led or initiated an alternative approach?

In Step 3 we will look at how these style preferences will have an impact on your conduct of the feasibility study. But bear in mind that both adaptors and innovators are required in an organisation and that both styles lead to creativity and support innovation.

It is again strongly recommended that you contact the Kirton Occupational Research Centre in order to obtain a professional assessment of your preferred style and the detailed implications.

| Extrovert (E) | Introvert (I) |
|---|---|
| They are motivated by what happens in their external world. <br> They need to talk with people in order to reach understanding and make sense of their reality. | The focus is more on their inner world. Their own mind is their source of inspiration. <br> They like working quietly without interruption before checking out ideas and views with others. |
| **Sensing – thinking type (ST)** <br> Like systematic decision-making using hard data, valuing order, control and certainty. <br> Averse to risk-taking and use procedures to solve problems. Cause and effect is their normal approach to problem analysis. <br> They focus on today's problems. Have difficulty looking ahead. | |
| **Intuition – thinking type (NT)** <br> Tend to ignore detail and look for patterns. <br> They are prepared to take risks in their thinking. <br> They reduce complex problems to simple ones. <br> There is a tendency to appear impersonal. | |
| **Sensing – feeling type (SF)** <br> Emphasise people's opinions in decision-making. <br> Focus on short-term problems and the implications for other people. <br> They like being in harmony. | |
| **Intuition – feeling type (NF)** <br> They project their personal views as facts. <br> They like to get the feel for a situation and do not use rules in decision-making. <br> They include people when structuring problems. <br> They ignore specifics and look for themes. <br> They like breakthroughs and new ideas. | |
| **Judging (J)** <br> Prefer to work in a planned way. Their emphasis is on controlling work, through organisation and structure. They want to decide, finish and move on. | **Perceiving (P)** <br> Prefer to be flexible and spontaneous. They want to understand rather than control. They are confident in their ability to adjust to the context in which they find themselves. |

*Fig. 3.3 Personality – the combination of traits*

## Purposes and objectives of the feasibility study

In Chapter 1 various triggers or start points for the study were suggested. These included:

- seeking new ways to direct and guide the organisation
- the need to overcome a major problem facing the organisation
- the need to improve organisational performance.

As in any study it is important to be clear as to the overall purpose and set some realistic objectives in terms of outcomes. Some guidance is provided to help in this clarification of purpose.

The triggers given above suggest that most people see themselves working within a system over which they have limited influence, and trying to cope with outside forces and constrained by boundaries associated with their position. For this study the purpose should perhaps be to question the boundaries of the perceived system and some of the constraints. Exploring the potential for designing and implementing learning processes that will enable individuals and teams to help the organisation develop towards a more exciting future.

The purpose of your study could therefore be:

> *To determine the need for, and clarify how to set about, implementing an approach to directing and managing the organisation, with a major focus on learning in its widest form.*

The particular objectives that follow from this broad purpose will depend on two factors: the organisational level at which the study is being aimed and whether the focus is to be strategic or operational. Fig. 3.4 illustrates these options for focus and level and suggests that your study should embrace all of these areas. The decision obviously is in your hands but whatever approach is taken the study programme that follows will provide the support required. By following the study programme the following broad objectives should be achieveable:

1. To be able to describe the current organisation in terms of:

    (a) the external and internal environment

    (b) key organisational measures of performance

    (c) the key factors and events that have formed the organisation

    (d) strategic and operational pressures for change

    (e) opportunities for growth and development

    (f) current learning processes.

## Clarifying the Purpose and Reviewing the Organisation

|  | Corporate level (Cross-Divisional) | Divisional or Unit Level |
|---|---|---|
| Strategic | 1. Uses an organisational development *or* major change programme approach | 2. Uses a marketing/service development approach |
| Operational | 3. Uses a TQM approach | 4. Uses a performance/efficiency focus with management development and team building approaches |

Note that the learning organisation focus should encompass all four areas.

*Fig. 3.4  Clarifying the purpose of the study*

2. To formulate a vision for the learning organisation and identify areas where opportunities for a focus on learning will arise.

3. To identify ways in which the change to a learning focus can be approached.

4. To describe the ways in which the major stakeholders in the organisation can benefit from this focus on learning and how the activities can be evaluated.

The purpose and objectives set out above may be a sufficient start point for the study to begin. As the stages unfold it is important that you revisit these objectives (or those you have formulated) to confirm that the learning that is taking place is of value and in line with the overall purpose. This also applies if you have decided to tackle the study as part of a management team or if you have enlisted the help of a series of task teams. This reviewing activity is a key part of the learning process. Remember that what we are trying to do is to create a realistic vision of the learning organisation that is specific enough to lead to implementation.

LEARNING MODEL – STEP 2

## REVIEW OF THE ORGANISATION – TAKING STOCK

In this step a series of reviews are used to create a baseline for thinking about the current organisation and the potential for development and change. Some organisations will have already conducted reviews in all or most of the areas listed. Where this information is available then it should be used for your review. But in some areas it will be difficult to obtain information in the form requested and the recommendation is to substitute best guesses or use intuition when this occurs. Remember that it is your review. The seven areas to be reviewed include:

(a) External organisational environment.

(b) Internal organisational environment.

(c) Measures used to gauge organisational performance.

(d) Events and people that have formed the organisation.

(e) Pressures for change at strategic and operational levels.

(f) Opportunities for growth and development.

(g) Opportunities for new learning.

Each of these areas should be tackled quickly and to a depth that reflects the time available and the study purpose. A series of proformas and checklists are provided to help complete this review in the short amount of time that has been alloted. It is important to remember that much of this information will be based on hearsay and impressions and will reflect both the present organisational culture and the mind-sets or perspectives of yourself and others involved in the study. This should present no problems other than in managing the breadth of perspectives. Most managers find it relatively easy to open up viewpoints and expand on their ideas; your problem will be to focus down on these viewpoints and opinions without losing the rich insight that they provide.

Your broad personality traits and style preferences identified earlier in this section will have alerted you to some of the biases that will be operating as you tackle the steps in the study, remembering that your colleagues and other managers will also be using their own built-in biases when expressing their perspective and viewpoints.

### The external environment

Here we are attempting to build a picture of the factors external to the organisation that can have a potential impact on performance. This involves an attempt to forecast or predict the future. This is a key belief in the strategic planning and management of organisations where the attempt is made to match the strategies being pursued by the organisation to these forecasts of external opportunities or threats in the environment. Having made these environmental forecasts then management actions are determined in order to avoid situations arising where the organisation is constantly reacting to events.

The external factors usually include:

- markets or settings in which the organisation operates. These are often described in terms of clients or customers
- technologies that the organisation depends on or uses
- resources in terms of sources of capital funding, assets, people skills
- competition in terms of those organisations that are attempting to or operate in the same markets, use the same technologies and similar people skills, etc.
- industry or sector financing and investment structures and processes
- international and global trends and changes that are significant to the organisation
- economic trends
- social and demographic trends
- political, regulatory and legal trends.

From this list it is obvious that an organisation needs to learn more about these trends, their significance, time impact and the opportunities and threats that they pose for the organisation. Fig. 3.5 illustrates a method for capturing the relative impact and hence need for organisational level learning about these external factors.

## The internal environment

This review focuses on the key functions and the formal and informal management processes that operate within the organisation.

All organisations can be analysed in terms of their primary functions. These are usually described in terms of departments such as marketing, operations, services, support, etc. Some of these departments interface to the external environment (customer, supplier, etc.) whereas others are almost totally inward facing with other departments being their customers or suppliers. Overlaying these functions there are numerous management processes in operation, some of which will be formal, and set down in procedures, others will be informal and depend largely for their

| Factor | Opportunity | Threat | Potential impact on organisation | | | Priority for organisational learning | | |
|---|---|---|---|---|---|---|---|---|
| | | | H | M | L | H | M | L |
| Markets | | | | | | | | |
| Technologies | | | | | | | | |
| Resources | | | | | | | | |
| Competition | | | | | | | | |
| Industry/sector financing | | | | | | | | |
| International and global trends | | | | | | | | |
| Economic trends | | | | | | | | |
| Social and demographic trends | | | | | | | | |
| Political/ regulatory and legal trends | | | | | | | | |

*Fig. 3.5 The external environment*

continuation upon the individual styles of the managers and the organisational culture.

In order to identify areas where learning is taking place and where a greater focus on learning would seem necessary it is important to identify the:

- key organisational functions
- key formal management processes, their ownership and operation
- key informal management processes, their membership and operation
- potential for organisational level learning in order that the functions can perform their primary purpose more effectively.

It is worth noting that opportunities for stimulating creativity, innovation, growth and development of the organisation can all be found within these

| Function | Primary focus of the function | | No. of staff | Potential for organisational learning to achieve purpose of function | | |
|---|---|---|---|---|---|---|
| | External | Internal | | H | M | L |
| Marketing | | | | | | |
| Sales | | | | | | |
| Operations | | | | | | |
| Finance and investment | | | | | | |
| Accounts | | | | | | |
| Research | | | | | | |
| Development | | | | | | |
| Procurement and supply | | | | | | |
| Personnel | | | | | | |
| Customer relations | | | | | | |
| Central Admin. | | | | | | |

*Fig. 3.6 Key organisational functions*

functions and processes. Hence a clear analysis needs to be made in order to gain an insight into what is being learned and the opportunities for new learning.

## Functional analysis

Fig. 3.6 illustrates a method for assessing the potential for a focus on learning as a way of helping these key functions achieve their purpose. This is shown at the total organisational level and for some organisations it may be more revealing to then repeat the analysis at Divisional and unit levels. Where the analysis indicates that the potential for learning at the organisational level is high then these opportunities should be described, e.g. for

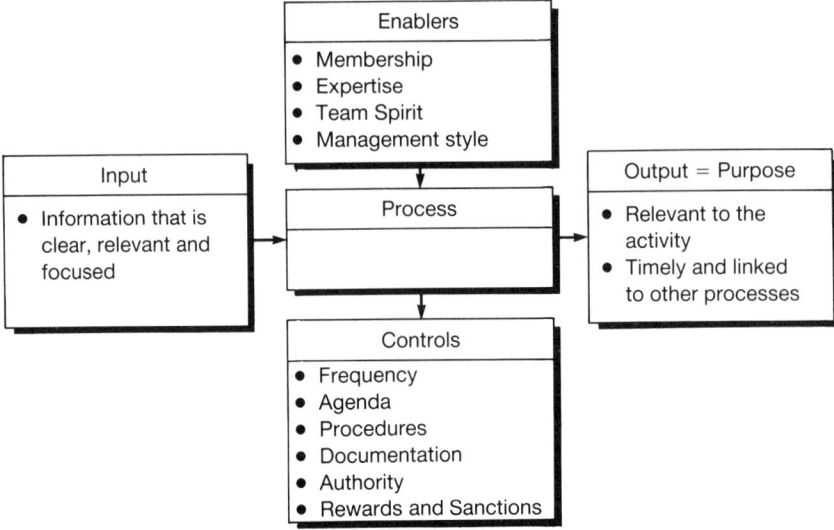

*Fig. 3.7 Organisational process model*

Marketing the learning could be around how to identify new product opportunities such that 50 per cent of future annual turnover can be derived from products that have been introduced in the previous 12 months. The focus on learning should always be aimed at improving the performance of the function.

## Process analysis

Analysing an organisation in terms of key management processes is less common but in many ways more telling than the functional analysis. The best way to understand this approach is to consider the model shown in Fig. 3.7. This suggests that for a typical management activity (process) such as operational planning or human resource planning there should exist:

(a) A clear statement of purpose and terms of reference. These are usually defined in output terms such as information-giving, problem-solving, decision-making, taking action on key issues, etc.

(b) Clear inputs in terms of information

(c) A defined membership that has the appropriate expertise and commitment

(d) A leader or champion responsible for the process operation

## Clarifying the Purpose and Reviewing the Organisation

(e) Controls that enable the process to achieve the purpose

(f) A management style used in the process that matches the purpose

(g) Clear links to other processes where appropriate.

The questions to be asked in analysing a particular process are as follows:

### 1. Process
What is the process primarily concerned with:

    (a) information giving and exchange?
    (b) problem-solving?
    (c) decision-making?

### 2. Output/Purpose
    (a) What are the outputs/purposes of the process?
    (b) Is everyone clear and agreed on these purposes?
    (c) Is the output relevant to the current activity?
    (d) What priorities would you place on this process and the particular outputs?

### 3. Inputs
    (a) What sort of information is required?
    (c) Who creates the input information?

### 4. Enablers
    (a) Who is involved in creating, running and developing the process?
    (b) Is there sufficient expertise and commitment among those involved?
    (c) Is there a good team spirit and effective team working?
    (d) Is the 'management style' used in conducting this process appropriate? i.e. authoritarian, democratic, etc.

### 5. Controls
    (a) Do people know when and where the process is conducted?
    (b) Are there procedures, rules, agendas, etc.?
    (c) Is there adequate documentation produced as part of the process?
    (d) Who has the authority to make things happen?
    (e) Are there any rewards or sanctions linked to the process?

Key management processes might include:

- Business Planning
- Operations Planning
- Human Resource Planning
- Investment Planning
- Project Planning and Management

## 50 Implementing the Learning Organisation

- External and Internal Communications
- Quality and Standard Setting
- Decision-making and Problem-solving
- Control, Reporting and Reviewing
- Organisational Development
- Budgetary Control
- Strategic Planning
- New Ideas Creation
- Departmental Performance Reviews
- Environmental Scanning

For any organisation the number and variety of management processes is potentially enormous. The identification of those that are key to the organisation and an analysis of their operation will form a vital step in focusing on the need for learning. This will involve all levels of management and be at the heart of the organisation. In conducting your analysis Fig. 3.8 will enable

| Process | Is the process | | Is the purpose of the process | | Is the focus of the process | | Scope for organisational learning | | |
|---|---|---|---|---|---|---|---|---|---|
| | Clear and established | Unclear | Clear | Effective | Long term | Short term | H | M | L |
| | | | | | | | | | |
| | | | | | | | | | |
| | | | | | | | | | |
| | | | | | | | | | |
| | | | | | | | | | |
| | | | | | | | | | |
| | | | | | | | | | |
| | | | | | | | | | |
| | | | | | | | | | |
| | | | | | | | | | |

*Fig. 3.8 Management processes and organisational learning*

opportunities for organisational learning to be identified and prioritised. Once again it is important to define the opportunity for learning in such a way that it leads to either clarification of the process, its conduct or the quality and relevance of the outputs.

## Informal processes and networking

Many organisations will have evolved a number of processes that are not formalised but easily recognisable by those working in the organisation as, '. . . the way it is around here . . .'

Where people are engaged in these informal processes they tend to form what might be called 'loose networks'. The predominant activity is the exchange of ideas and values as opposed to information and hard data. There are five obvious reasons why these informal networks and relationships evolve:

(a) The organisational activity is often so complex that informality becomes a survival tactic.

(b) The punishments associated with failure are such that managers prefer to try things out informally and thus avoid exposure if things should go wrong.

(c) Formal processes tend to become bureaucratic in their operation and have lives that extend well beyond their 'sell by' date. Managers eventually only pay lip service to these processes.

(d) Informal processes are quicker and perceived to be easier to conduct amongst the complexity of daily life.

(e) The formal processes and functions have been designed with stability in mind whereas most organisations are in a constant state of transition and hence instability.

The existence and operation of these informal processes can be identified by considering the following questions:

Informal Process and Network Checklist.
1. Are informal groupings within the organisation based on:
   (a) Social requirements?
   (b) Expertise/discipline groups?
   (c) Task groups?

2. Can any major organisational outcomes be attributable to these groups?

3. Identify two examples where an informal process has been used to

manage or where the formal process appear to have failed or been by-passed?

4. Is networking an obvious organisational phenomena?
5. If there is a need to find out quickly what action is being taken on key issues facing the organisation who are the people to contact?
6. Would the organisation be described as in a stable state, in transition, in a state of controlled chaos or uncontrolled chaos?
7. Who are the organisational politicians?
8. Who are the key influence groups?
9. Who holds the real power?
10. How are key decisions affecting the organisation really made?
11. What does the organisation do well?
12. What does the organisation do badly?
13. What is the best way to get some action in the organisation?
14. What are the four major things that need to be put right in the organisation?

This analysis of the informal processes and networking will have identified areas where more complex learning is taking place. Complex learning is where the problems and issues tend to be open-ended and require a confrontation and management of a range of alternative perspectives and deeply-held values. The proforma in Fig. 3.9 will help to capture this analysis and identify potential areas for a greater focus on the learning that is taking place.

## Performance measures

Classical management control approaches rely on being able to identify key objectives and describe them in quantifiable terms, e.g. financial ratios, service levels, etc. These become standards against which the performance of the organisation, teams and individuals are measured. Some objectives are not easily quantifiable, particularly with not-for-profit organisations, where qualitative measures are more common. These objectives become prime drivers for an organisation and hence dominate and direct decision-making and action-taking at all levels.

As this process of objective setting and performance measurement is the predominant approach to the management of an organisation it is obviously

## Clarifying the Purpose and Reviewing the Organisation 53

| Description of process | Purpose | Influence on corporate level action | | | Influence on operational level action | | | Should it be formalised | | Opportunity for learning | |
|---|---|---|---|---|---|---|---|---|---|---|---|
| | | H | M | L | H | M | L | Y | N | H | L |
| | | | | | | | | | | | |
| | | | | | | | | | | | |
| | | | | | | | | | | | |
| | | | | | | | | | | | |

| Description of network | Purpose | Influence on corporate level action | | | Influence on operational level action | | | Should it be formalised | | Opportunity for learning | |
|---|---|---|---|---|---|---|---|---|---|---|---|
| | | H | M | L | H | M | L | Y | N | H | L |
| | | | | | | | | | | | |
| | | | | | | | | | | | |
| | | | | | | | | | | | |
| | | | | | | | | | | | |

*Fig. 3.9 Informal processes and networks*

a key area of learning. An analysis of the existing formalised organisational performance measures will highlight areas where learning is taking place, i.e. learning how to get more contracts, develop new products, reduce stock holdings, improve customer service levels, etc.

In addition, an analysis of the informal objectives that groups work to and the associated performance measures will indicate where other types of learning may be taking place. Informal objectives that do not fit readily into conventional management control systems, might include:

- increasing design capability
- improving the internal image of the Division or Unit
- reducing the stress associated with high workloads
- increasing the ability to respond to tenders for new work

| Areas in which objectives are set | Specific performance measures | Opportunities for organisational learning are: | |
|---|---|---|---|
| | | Built into the management processes | Unstructured/ informal |
| Financial | | | |
| Budgetary | | | |
| Use of assets | | | |
| Operational | | | |
| Markets | | | |
| Services | | | |
| Products | | | |
| Human resources | | | |

*Fig. 3.10 Formal performance measures*

- recruiting people who fit into the existing culture.

Performance measures for these are usually ill-defined if defined at all.

Figs. 3.10 and 3.11 illustrate how to conduct this analysis of the use of both formal and informal performance measures.

For the formal measures you should identify where opportunities for learning can be either built into the management processes or best introduced in a more informal and unstructured way. Brief descriptions of what this learning should achieve need to be produced as this will help focus on initial areas for the implementation phase.

When analysing the informal performance measures the challenge is to identify whether the learning that takes place is made explicit or left at the tacit or implied level. Where organisational level learning or even team learning is being sought then there is a need to turn tacit or implied learning into something more explicit. By identifying the areas and the informal

| Areas in which tacit/implied objectives exist | Tacit performance measures | The learning that takes place is captured and shared, i.e. the tacit is made explicit ||
|---|---|---|---|
| | | Yes | No |
| Financial | | | |
| Budgetary | | | |
| Use of assets | | | |
| Operational | | | |
| Markets | | | |
| Services | | | |
| Products | | | |
| Human resources | | | |

*Fig. 3.11 Informal performance measures*

performance measures used then key learning processes can be set up so that organisational learning is captured and shared.

## Historical perspectives

Identifying the main events in the evolution of an organisation is a recognised way of highlighting what has been learned and what has been internalised. For example, an organisation that has previously withdrawn from a particular market, technology or channel of distribution is unlikely to favour a return. Conversely an organisation that has enjoyed growth and profitability by seeking new ideas and encouraging innovation is likely to continue to operate in this way. The learning has been internalised.

The following questions will help to identify the events and characters that have produced this form of organisational learning.

- Who were the key founders and major influencers at the formation of the enterprise?
- What particular beliefs and styles of developing and managing the organisation did they adopt?
- At what point in time was the enterprise seen to be successful and what created this success?
- During the past five years what were the two major successes and the two major failures that have influenced the present position of the enterprise? What were the main factors behind these events and what was learned?
- Has the structure of the organisation been changed primarily to react to events or to create new opportunities for growth and development?
- What major changes in ownership have taken place in the past five years and what was the effect on the organisation?
- What metaphors (e.g. tight as a drum, rats in a sack, swift as a cobra) would you use to describe the organisation, say, five years ago? What metaphors would you use today?

| Major historical event | Key learning that resulted | Actions taken by organisation as result of learning | Learning institutionalised * | |
| --- | --- | --- | --- | --- |
| | | | Yes | No |
| | | | | |
| | | | | |
| | | | | |
| | | | | |
| | | | | |
| | | | | |
| | | | | |
| * Institutionalised learning is that which has been either incorporated formally into the management processes or embedded in the culture. | | | | |

*Fig. 3.12 Historical perspectives*

### Clarifying the Purpose and Reviewing the Organisation 57

From this analysis it is possible to identify the events and aspects of the past that have created organisational learning and what has been institutionalised. It is important to attempt to capture the findings of this analysis at this stage using the proforma in Fig. 3.12.

## Pressures for change

A dominant belief among managers is that organisations occupy a strategic position in relation to others within a wider environment. Efforts are then made by senior management to either maintain that position or move to a more acceptable one. This is described as strategic management.

There are two predominant schools of thought around strategic management, the first being based on the belief that managers can predict and describe a desirable future and then move there in a rational and planned way. The second favours exploring the way forward based on living with uncertainty and establishing what is known as a situation of bounded chaos. The actions that flow from the strategic management process will obviously depend on which school of thought is being used. Both will also be

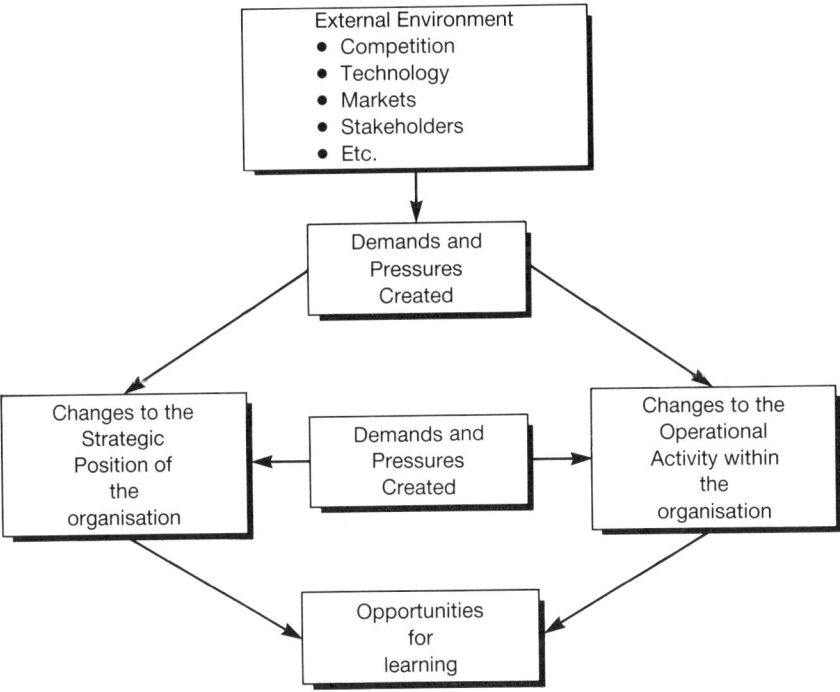

*Fig. 3.13 Pressures for change and opportunities for learning*

## 58  Implementing the Learning Organisation

**1. Current and Planned Changes to Strategic Position**

| Key Areas Affected | Description of Activities | Opportunity for Learning | | |
|---|---|---|---|---|
| | | H | M | L |
| Markets | | | | |
| Services | | | | |
| Products | | | | |
| Delivery channels | | | | |
| Funding/resourcing | | | | |
| External image | | | | |
| Collaboration/joint ventures | | | | |
| Corporate structure/ organisation | | | | |

**2. Current and Planned Changes to Operational Activity**

| Key Areas Affected | Description of Activity | Opportunity for Learning | | |
|---|---|---|---|---|
| | | H | M | L |
| Products | | | | |
| Services | | | | |
| Structure/organisation | | | | |
| Technology | | | | |
| Investment | | | | |
| Location | | | | |
| Processes | | | | |
| Controls | | | | |

*Fig. 3.14  Pressures for strategic and operational change*

## Clarifying the Purpose and Reviewing the Organisation 59

influenced by perceptions of the pressures that are giving rise to the need for change. The pressures will be the same in both cases but the responding action and end points envisaged will vary enormously dependent on these two fundamental beliefs about how to conduct strategic management.

Two sources of pressure for change can be identified; firstly that arising from the external environment and secondly from the operational activity from within the organisation, e.g. new technologies. These demands or pressures for change are illustrated in Fig. 3.13 and illustrate how this can be seen to create opportunities for learning in the organisation. Fig. 3.14 provides a method of analysing the organisation in order to describe the sources of pressure for change and the opportunities for learning that will be created.

## Opportunities for growth and development

The conventional approach used by organisations seeking growth and development is to assess the match, or otherwise, between organisational capabilities and opportunities in the environment. The approach is to use a SWOT analysis where the organisation's strengths and weaknesses are explored. The identified strengths are then matched with opportunities in the environment and ways of warding off threats identified. Attempts are then made to overcome any weaknesses identified in the organisation that could become victim to the external threat. The proforma for conducting this analysis is illustrated as in Fig. 3.15.

The analysis will show how the process of determining growth and development can provide a way of identifying the needs and opportunities for a range of organisational learning. Where the opportunity for learning is seen to be high then this needs to be described in terms of what outcomes will result. Learning processes can then be set up around these areas and the learning communicated across and through the organisation.

## Opportunities for new learning

The above reviews have tackled areas in the organisation where learning takes place around what might be described as conventional management activities. It is likely that by focusing on these areas a number of opportunities for organisational learning have been identified. Some of the areas covered so far have involved learning surrounding:

- personality and style preference associated with creativity
- factors in the external environment and their impact on the organisation
- existing functions and how they contribute to the organisational purpose

| Organisational strengths | Environmental opportunities | Opportunities for learning | | |
|---|---|---|---|---|
| | | H | M | L |
| | | | | |
| | | | | |
| | | | | |
| | | | | |
| | | | | |

| Organisational weaknesses | Environmental threats | Opportunities for learning | | |
|---|---|---|---|---|
| | | H | M | L |
| | | | | |
| | | | | |
| | | | | |
| | | | | |
| | | | | |

*Fig. 3.15 Opportunities for growth and development*

- existing formal management processes and the scope for setting up new processes
- informal processes, groups and networks that operate within the organisation
- the use of organisational objectives and resulting performance measures
- the existence of informal or tacit objectives and performance measures
- historical perspective of the organisation and the learning that has been institutionalised
- the pressures for change arising from strategic positioning and operational activity
- how opportunities for growth and development can be matched to the strengths and weaknesses of the organisation.

It would be tempting to see all the above in terms of just learning by experience. Unfortunately, although many managers are involved in these activities, the results of their involvement and hence learning are only realised over a longer time horizon. For example where a strategic decision

Clarifying the Purpose and Reviewing the Organisation 61

| Organisational review area | Relative importance as a learning opportunity | | |
|---|---|---|---|
| | H | M | L |
| Personality/creative style | | | |
| External environment/impact | | | |
| Links between functions and purposes | | | |
| Formal management Processes | | | |
| Informal management processes/networks | | | |
| Organisational objectives/ performance measures | | | |
| Tacit objectives/performance measures | | | |
| Historical perspectives | | | |
| Strategic/operational activity | | | |
| Opportunity for growth and development | | | |

*Fig. 3.16 Summary of key learning opportunities*

is made to invest in a new information technology system or a management team decides to focus on a new market area, then the outcomes and hence learning are either never reviewed seriously or the time lapse makes analysis impossible. Seeing the consequences of our own actions is rare in modern organisations, and negative outcomes are easily rationalised in terms of events outside our control.

What is needed therefore is to consider ways in which the intended outcomes of decisions and processes can be specified and measurements made over time to help managers learn from their decisions. The following questions may help identify areas in the organisation where such a reviewing process could be set up.

(a) In which of the key functions would evaluation of the outcomes of decisions lead to a major learning pay-off?

**(b)** Which of the management processes has the greatest multiplier effect on organisational action and expenditure of effort? How could this process and the effects of its decisions be evaluated and hence become a key area of organisational learning?

**(c)** How are the existing control and review activities in the organisation used as opportunities for learning? How could these learning opportunities be improved?

The ideas and thoughts that arise from considering these questions should be recorded at this stage of the study. They will help build up opportunities for learning that will be needed at the implementation stage.

It is suggested that the key opportunities for learning at the organisational level, identified from the reviews are captured using the proforma in Fig. 3.16 and their relative significance assessed. This will be used when considering possible approaches to implementation of the learning organisation, in Chapter 7.

LEARNING MODEL – STEP 3

## READING TEXT AND REFLECTION

In this section four sub-topics are introduced to help promote reflection on the findings resulting from the above reviews. The important point about these readings is that they will help develop your thinking and understanding about the behaviour of managers in organisations. Some of the notions that are presented may conflict violently with your own views and perspectives. When this occurs it is worth checking out your understanding of the notion being presented and your contentions with a colleague. In this way you may finish up changing your perspective. If not, at least you will have developed the argument that will be needed when considering your approach to implementing the learning organisation.

The areas covered by these sub-topics are:

- the impact of personality and style in organisations
- a view of how organisations develop
- how managers view risk taking
- using creativity in organisations.

## Impact of personality and style on planning and problem-solving

### Personality traits

In the Step 2 above you were invited to consider your personality traits and the style that you would adopt when tackling more open-ended or complex problems. This may have presented no surprises in that most managers are at times only too well aware of the impact that their personality and problem-solving approaches have on others and on the task at hand. Being aware is perhaps the first step but deciding whether and how to make changes to improve either the stress you feel, your impact on others or your job performance is quite a different matter. This represents a key area of personal learning and it is useful to consider how these personal characteristics come into play. Unfortunately, the whole area is bedevilled with techniques and philosophies that have by now become part of the folklore of management training and development. Some are applicable to the world of work, others less so. Typical applications of behaviour awareness techniques are transactional analysis, Jahari Window, team building (indoor and on mountain sides), sensitivity training, role playing, etc. Most of these have been experienced by managers.

Assuming that you subscribe to the notion of people having personality traits or characteristics then it is important to recognise how these traits can influence the way managers approach activities such as problem-solving and planning, etc. A widely held view is that different personality types develop dominant decision-making styles and have distinctive approaches when tackling management activities such as collecting data, generating and evaluating options. These personality types will thus have inherent biases to tackling activities that involve planning and decision-making. For example, Sensation (S) dominant managers seek precise data, convinced that they are realists and concerned with immediacy, whereas Intuition (N) dominant managers seek the wider picture and are happy to use more general data. Also that Thinking (T) dominant managers use logic, formal reasoning and prefer to generalise. The Feeling (F) dominant managers use value laden approaches and emphasise the more personal aspects when making decisions. These traits can be combined into four personality types:

STs – Systematic decision making with hard data. Focus is on the problems of today.
NTs – Stress is on analysis but take leaps into the unknown. Their interest is in simplifying complex problems. Tend to be impersonal.
SFs – Emphasise people's opinions, seek harmony. Focus on short-term problems.

NFs – Stress their judgement and experience. Emphasis is on broad themes.

When involved in problem-solving or decision-making managers have their own preferred or learned approaches. These approaches will obviously have an impact on where opportunities for learning occur and how to approach implementation of learning in the organisation. For some organisational processes, such as strategic planning, an awareness of how these personal biases are shaping the approaches used and outcomes is a key area of organisational learning.

Much of the work in this area of linking personalities and cognitions has been developed by Haley and Stumpf at the Leonard Stern School of Business, New York University and Fig. 3.17 represents the author's attempt to capture some of their ideas and theories.

This analysis suggests that managers may be at risk using their basic and learned approaches. The notion being promoted here is that managers may respond to their personality traits when under pressure and that learned ways may have built-in dangers for some decision-making situations. Being aware of the bias is perhaps the first step. Taking action to match the behaviour to the situation faced is the second. The importance of undertaking a professional assessment of your own personality traits cannot be over stressed and the sources given in the references should be contacted and the tests undertaken.

## *Creative style*

In Step 2 above you were invited to consider your style preference when faced with an open or complex problem. The style preference suggesting that when the emphasis was on creativity managers would either adopt an approach that favoured adaptation of the current situation, or one that emphasised innovation. The innovative approach often seeking to question and challenge the conventional approach, wanting to re-construct the problem.

In areas where creativity is important, e.g. new product development, new approaches to customer service, approaches to improve productivity, etc. both styles are effective and can be complementary. For example, one innovator with a team of adaptors might experience a level of rejection and become frustrated with what appears to be a painstaking approach. For the adaptors the innovator will appear unrealistic, emotional and unable to communicate clearly. Recognition of these differences does not mean harmony but will help to maximise the strengths of both styles.

Innovators can often be seen as abrasive in that they appear to be

## Clarifying the Purpose and Reviewing the Organisation 65

| Personality type | Potential weakness in approach | Bias which may limit performance | | |
|---|---|---|---|---|
| | | Data gathering stage | Decision making and response | Testing outcome against intentions |
| ST | •Reliance on standard approaches<br><br>•Rejecting novel approaches | • Highly analytical<br><br>• Ignores ambiguous data | • Conservative and short term<br><br>• Risk aversion | • Locked into initial preference<br><br>• Over simplification<br><br>• Reject evidence that does not fit |
| NT | •Adheres to previous beliefs | • Seeks patterns<br><br>• Over complicates<br><br>• Ignores contradictory data | • Long term<br><br>• Preference for innovation | • Seeks to confirm own preferences |
| SF | •Favours consultation<br><br>•Focus on discussion at expense of ideas | • Seeks emotional data | • Emphasis on people<br><br>• Preference for short term<br><br>• Solutions that are acceptable to people | • Seeks social approval |
| NF | •Uses imagery and vivid data<br><br>•Rejects standard problem-solving approaches | • Uses personal judgements and values<br><br>• Reduces uncertainty<br><br>• Relies on analogies | • Innovative<br><br>• Offers many solutions to obtain best fit | • Testing beliefs and views using imagery |

*Fig. 3.17 Personality types and problem solving bias*

attacking the consensus views and approaches favoured by the adaptors as well as other innovators. The initiating innovators may appear oblivious to the disruptions caused. The adaptors on the other hand find it easy to combine with others in the organisation in that they are prepared to work from the point which others have established. The predominant culture in an organisation and the nature of the work that managers find themselves engaged in can require that a natural innovator has to behave in an adaptive way or vice versa. It has been known for people to cope in this way for long periods of time with little diminution in the effect on their work but a slow destruction in their personal health and well-being. Managers tend therefore to gravitate to organisational environments that suit their styles. The more innovative incline towards turbulent or less stable situations and the more adaptive to those that are more predictable and certain. This has some key messages when considering implementation of the learning organisation. For example, learning can be initially threatening for individuals and groups where the status quo or dominant beliefs are being questioned or potentially changed. It is conceivable that the adaptors would be more able to cope with incremental and steady change based on a clear view of the future state of the organisation and the way of reaching that state. Whereas, the innovator would be more able to see ways and suggest approaches of how to explore original futures and the possible ways forward, being able to accept a much higher degree of uncertainty.

Evidence from research suggests that the degree of emphasis on adaptation and innovation when tackling problems varies between organisations, functions and departments. For example, in departments where problem-solving emanates from their own work (e.g. production) then adaptation predominates. In departments that interface to the outside world (e.g. sales) then the focus is likely to be on innovation.

Understanding and harnessing this preference for adaptation or innovation is one of the keys to managing the changes that implementing the learning organisation will involve. Where implementation is envisaged as involving radical change then both the adaptors and innovators have a role to play. Those with a preference for adaptation will be able to construct a clear view of the present position of the organisation and the features that are contributing to both the successes and failures, helping to suggest ways in which the organisation can adapt to the new position. Those with a preference for innovation will help to challenge the 'status quo' and to provide new and at times controversial ways of overcoming the perceived blocks and barriers to change.

It is important that the group that sets out to implement the learning organisation recognises the contribution that both the adaptive and innovative approaches can make to the change process. This will in itself become a learning process and managers need to be helped to move away from any casual stereotyping or tendency to make value judgements about preferred styles. Both styles demonstrate creativity and style preference should be seen as a strength to be harnessed rather than a characteristic to be 'dealt with'.

The obvious approach to achieving this climate where creativity can be harnessed is to free up and change the ethos of the organisation to one that rewards learning in all its forms.

By contacting the sources shown in the references you will be able to obtain a professional review of your preferred style and the associated implications.

## Organisations, their form and development

There are two popular views around the notion of an organisation. Firstly, that it is to do with structures and specifications of functions and formal processes. The second is where the organisation is thought of as being more to do with the perceptions, perspectives and mental models that people in the organisation use to conduct their affairs.

With this second view the organisation is seen as much more dynamic and made up of individuals and groups who hold sets of beliefs that have been learned or inculcated about what the organisation is and represents. Some of these beliefs would include the notions that:

- Individuals are engaged in both formal and informal processes.
- Allegiances and groupings have a strong influence on both operations and outcomes.
- Pressures for change are created by both external and internal influences.
- Individuals develop and maintain their performance in relation to interpretations of their task objectives and the control mechanisms.
- There are rules or approaches to managing organisations that if learned and followed lead to a greater probability of achieving success.
- Organisations are in a constant state of adjusting to their environment; sometimes stable, at other times under great tension and in turmoil.

The organisational reviews carried out in Step 2 above will have thrown some light on how the above notions operate in your organisations. They will also have shown where learning is taking place and where opportunities for enhanced and new learning exist. We need to look at the two major ways of viewing organisational development and management.

One of the more conventional and widely held views on what constitutes a successful organisation is where dynamic equilibrium is maintained with its environment. If the environment changes dramatically then the organisation responds. But in situations where the environment is constantly changing, in order to stay adapted the organisation needs to take rapid but incremental steps. Organisations, like a sailing ship on a breezy day, are therefore seen to stay close to a state of equilibrium, dramatic changes or swings away from this equilibrium are seen as undesirable; violent swings suggesting that a rational and logical plan is not being followed. Taking our sailing analogy one step further, we should consider what happens when we have more than one helmsman and more than one captain. Someone has to take charge according to conventional wisdom. This view leads neatly into a learned wisdom among managers that those implementing organisational strategies should adopt the following steps:

- establish a hierarchy of reporting
- set up information and control systems
- set up and run a reward system
- influence individuals to perform extraordinary activities for non-monetary rewards
- create a culture and set of management behaviours that will support the implementation of the organisational strategy.

This suggests that someone is in control, someone chooses the strategy, someone influences the behaviour of individuals and groups. Following from the above the approaches underlying Corporate Planning, Strategic Planning, Budgetary Control are quickly learned.

There is an alternative view to managing organisational development and this suggests that because the future is unpredictable that vision building and trial and error should be the hallmark of an effective organisation. Does this mean that most organisations are getting it wrong? One answer could be that managers may seem to be approaching planning and action in a rational and goal orientated way but in reality are probably relying on intuition, gut feel, the ability to respond and local knowledge and information. These two dominant views of the rational or the trial and error approach have major implications on how the learning organisation will evolve. This becomes evident when tackling questions such as:

- what does the organisation need to learn?
- what are the underlying rules for designing the organisation and its processes?
- what will lead to organisational success?

These are all answered according to beliefs that have already been learned and internalised by managers. Any attempts to answer these questions can therefore only be made when the basic beliefs of the particular groups of managers have been explored and understood.

### Clarifying the Purpose and Reviewing the Organisation 69

As this is so fundamental to setting up the learning organisation it is worthwhile having a closer look at some of the ways in which the rational, the visionary and what might be called the dynamic approach to organisational management are carried out.

## Rational corporate approach

This view tends to be top down and involves the following beliefs:

**(a)** The various parts of the organisational hierarchy are seen as having distinct roles, e.g. Corporate Direction, Operational Planning, etc. The Corporate group is concerned with long-term goals and direction in order to satisfy the stakeholders.

**(b)** Plans are generated that match the organisation's internal resources to the external threats and opportunities. Monitoring and control predominates.

**(c)** Organisational culture and style are designed to be appropriate to the needs of the external environment and conducive to motivation and control of the managers and staff.

**(d)** Organisational structures are set up to mirror the espoused strategy.

**(e)** By using the ability to predict changes the organisation responds and adapts itself before the external change creates a problem.

This approach is seen, by most managers, as both sensible and reasonable, leading to the encouragement of simple or single loop learning activities. That is where the consequences of action are used to inform the next action. The fundamental rational corporate models or beliefs are not called into question or challenged. As this form of simple learning is encouraged then the organisation becomes increasingly tuned to and able to deal with issues that are seen as essentially certain and predictable.

Organisations following this approach are identified by their adherence to Corporate Planning processes and teams focusing on strategy, budgetary cycles and controls; the overall aim is to achieve stability and maintain equilibrium in the environment.

## Visionary leader approach

This approach is similar to the rational approach but places much more emphasis on the informal groupings. Discovery and experimentation are encouraged. These are reinforced by empowering individuals and groups, encouraging creativity and risk-taking with an emphasis on emotional leadership.

These groupings are harnessed in such a way that their behaviour is eventually harmonious and conflict is eliminated in order to support the strategy.

## *Dynamic approach*

This approach to thinking about organisations and their management makes some major assumptions, namely that:

**(a)** Futures are unpredictable and thus long-term planning to achieve that future impracticable.

**(b)** Individuals in organisations receive a wide range of signals from their immediate and distant environments which they interpret according to their own (often subconscious) beliefs.

**(c)** Short-term planning is possible and lends itself to rational and logical planning.

**(d)** Outcomes of organisational activity emerge and strategies can only be seen through an historical perspective.

**(e)** The organisational norm is one of tension and conflict.

**(f)** Managers need to accept this apparent chaos and erect negotiated boundaries in order to take short-term actions.

**(g)** Managers need only accept satisfactory rather than ideal outcomes.

**(h)** Organisational learning is created when existing patterns of belief are challenged.

The underlying view is that successful organisations are those that create as well as adapt to their environment. In these organisations managers are encouraged to contradict the conventional wisdom and embrace the resulting tension and conflict. There is one central plan or vision but managers share an overall belief in short-term action and look for the strategies that emerge from the patterns of their work. The outcomes are intended and purposeful as in the rational approach but the method of how to get there is discovered rather than planned.

This type of organisation would be characterised by its ability to be creative and influence the environment in which it operates. Informal groups would operate in loose networks and alliances, forming and breaking up as the needs arose. Obtaining a position of stability in the environment would be seen by the management as both unrealistic and probably undesirable.

## Managing and taking risk

The review of organisational performance measures and how they influence learning was covered in Step 2. In this section a more detailed look at how performance measures link to learning is provided.

Most managers subscribe to a rational and logical approach to measuring and meeting a performance standard. They specify the required performance, collect and analyse information then select and take the required corrective actions.

This may sound like stating the obvious but the reality is that this approach is used even when the available information and objectives are unclear or uncertain. Faced with uncertainty, managers will often use a rational approach in order to reduce the risk to themselves and the organisation. Their response will be to:

- avoid taking action
- search for a low-risk response
- make an apparently logical decision then rationalise as to why the objective was not achieved
- try to shift the responsibility for action to another area.

By taking action that appears to be rational the managers are in effect covering up the uncertainty that they perceive and missing out on major opportunities for learning at the individual and organisational levels.

This uncertainty can be attributable to either a lack of agreement over the objectives or a lack of clarity over the cause and effect relationship surrounding the issue. The model in Fig. 3.18 suggests various ways in which managers could be encouraged to adapt their approaches to decision-making under these conditions of uncertainty.

|  | **Unclear objectives** | **Clear objectives** |
| --- | --- | --- |
| Unclear cause and effect links | Adopt an experimental approach where learning from outcomes is a priority | Take incremental action on the basis of intuition and gut-feel |
| Clear cause and effect links | Seek opinions and attempt to reach a compromise on desirable outcomes | Use a rational and logical approach |

*Fig. 3.18 Decision making in conditions of uncertainty*

Situations where the objectives plus cause and effect relationships are unclear is probably the norm rather than the exception for the daily lives of most managers. Encouraging managers to expose their defensive routines and adopt approaches that help them to cope and live with the unknown must be a key to organisational learning. Taking chances, allowing strategies to emerge, providing challenges, living with ambiguity and rewarding risk-taking moves the organisation rapidly towards a learning approach. One way to achieve this change of approach is to encourage managers to debate issues in informal groups. This leads to what has become known as forming communities of practice. Here managers engage in what they perceive as low-risk debates where beliefs can be challenged and informal learning achieved. A large element of political and social interaction is made possible by forming these practice groups.

## The use of creativity and innovation in developing organisations

In thinking about implementing the learning organisation the main concern will be about how to develop the overall capability of the organisation; then how to harness this capability to the purpose of the organisation.

The reviews carried out in Step 2 on the historic perspective, pressures for change and opportunities for growth and development are all based on the notion of a strategic management process in action. It is conventional to consider this strategic management activity to be the task of senior management and the approach taken as dependent on the age and size of the organisation. The strategy-making approach is usually considered as being either:

**(a)** entrepreneurial where the organisation is new and/or small and a key figure drives the strategy based on vision and intuition.

**(b)** adaptive where the organisation is becoming more diverse and complex such that the entrepreneur can no longer maintain the dominant ideas position. The organisation is then adjusting to external and internal pressures.

**(c)** planned where the organisation is large and has developed bureaucratic processes and expectations. Business and organisational analysts dominate.

When organisations reach the planned stage the usual response is to attempt to break the size down to smaller units that are then encouraged to grow in their own right.

If we take the conventional model of strategy formulation used to develop organisations the following six steps are usually prescribed:

- Vision building
- Strategic thinking
- Strategic formulation
- Business analysis and forecasts
- Strategy implementation
- Reviews of strategies and performance

The first four steps can be seen as predominantly thinking and the last two involve action. This conventional approach relies on logic, data collection and analysis and uses perspectives developed by the managers resulting from their experiences and beliefs. In essence it relies on what has been learned and on the knowledge and experience available within the enterprise; the idea being that this knowledge is explicit, i.e. clearly defined, and is available. The review process will have shown that this is rarely the case. Most organisational knowledge exists in a tacit or unstated form.

The strategic management activity then becomes an intellectual, or thinking process of ascertaining what an enterprise might do in terms of linking environmental opportunities and organisational capability. This conventional approach is criticised by researchers and practitioners on three main accounts:

(a) It has not proved an effective approach in helping organisations satisfy their stakeholders. Many reasons being given to explain why this happens.

(b) It does not relate to the way in which managers think and act when faced with everyday organisational events.

(c) It inhibits the creation of new or original ideas and restricts the process by which new ideas are converted into commercial products or services.

The difficulty is that most managers rely on logic and rational approaches as the cornerstone for establishing order and control in their work.

Senior management have therefore to deal with the conflicting requirements of order on the one hand and apparent disorder on the other. The paradox to be managed becomes:

- to promote order in daily operations in line with the stated strategic direction and policy constraints.
- to encourage questioning and contention that borders on chaos in order to promote creativity that will lead to innovation.

Many organisations are now embracing this paradox (rather than seeing it as a threat) and moving towards a more creative approach to strategic management. This is achieved by emphasising the need for imagination and use of intuition at the early stages of the strategic process. Creating tensions in the organisation between what is currently viewed as acceptable performance and a future enhanced performance. Then encouraging informal groups to question, critique and take limited action that will enable the appropriate strategies to emerge as opposed to being planned or forecasted. In this way organisations encourage managers to be creative and turn knowledge from the tacit to the explicit. Moving ideas through to innovation, gaining new insights, tapping into hunches and intuition. This is illustrated in Fig. 3.19.

|  | Coping with predictable Issues | Coping with ambiguous issues |
| --- | --- | --- |
| Using formal structures | Simple learning based on re-enforcing existing beliefs and past experiences | • Simple learning tends to submerge the ambiguity<br><br>• Rationalisation post event predominates |
| Using informal groups | Can tend to over-complicate issues and restricts concerted action taking | • Encourages creativity and promotes innovation around ideas<br><br>• Can be seen as threatening the status quo<br><br>• Needs visionary leaders |

*Fig. 3.19 Organisational learning – the need for formal and informal structures*

Not all organisations will be at the stage of development where there is a great need for complex learning and informal groups and networks. Being aware of the need and place for these approaches is imperative but the skill comes in knowing how and to what extent they apply in the context of the organisation, the managers and workforce that represent its current capability.

LEARNING MODEL – STEPS 4, 5, 6

## FORMING AND TESTING PERSPECTIVES

Becoming a reflective practitioner is the hallmark of an effective learner. Having completed the reviews and studied the above text you are now in a

## Clarifying the Purpose and Reviewing the Organisation 75

good position to indulge in some purposeful reflection. It may help to go back to the start point of the chapter where the purpose and objectives were spelt out.

This chapter represents the first steps in exploring the potential for designing and implementing learning processes that will help the organisation develop towards a more exciting future. Based on the reviews and readings it should be possible to articulate your perspectives on:

- the position of the organisation in the environment; the key factors in that environment that will create a need for organisational learning
- the key organisational functions and the priorities for organisational learning
- the way in which management processes operate and how they can be used to promote organisational learning
- the extent to which the organisation makes use of informal processes and networks and how these contribute to organisational learning
- what the organisation needs to do in order to be successful and who in the organisation defines success
- how performance measures are used to direct and motivate managers and what opportunities this creates for organisational learning
- what key events have shaped the organisation and what has been learned and internalised.
- what are the key pressures for change, how the organisation is currently learning about these pressures and how to respond
- what opportunities for growth the organisation perceives and how these are discovered and actioned
- which areas or activities within the organisation offer key targets and hence opportunities for organisational learning
- how organisational learning would add to achieving the existing purpose of the organisation
- to what extent creativity (new ideas or adaptation of existing ones) is important in the organisation and whether it is given sufficient opportunity to flourish?
- is the strategic management of the organisation focused on the rational-logical, the visionary leader or dynamic approach?
- is risk taking encouraged?
- is the organisation at the entrepreneurial, adaptive or planned stage and is organisational learning of potential help in moving between these stages?
- to what extent is the organisation able to cope with ambiguity and can organisational learning help?

Some of these perspectives may be important and appear more powerful than others. It will depend very much on your viewpoint and obviously on the results obtained from the reviews. It is highly likely that the demands of the reviews proved far greater than you anticipated and a lot of corners had to be cut. This may say something about the organisation and should begin to indicate the possibilities for wider studies. It is important to recognise that organisations rarely tackle reviews with such vigour or depth as most of the time is spent on operational responses with little encouragement for managers to review and reflect. Perhaps this is a pointer towards the need to create learning processes and management approaches that make organisational learning part of the daily work. For many people work does represent a massive learning opportunity. For example, a company might articulate the need to get more contracts or improve customer service but this really means that the need to learn how to do these things has been identified. This focus on the learning needed to solve a problem is key to approaching the implementation of learning in organisations.

It is also important that your key perspectives are tested out and revised in the light of feedback from colleagues, peers and subordinates. Many organisations now encourage managers to present their perspectives to subordinates for comment and criticism; the deal being that the manager in return commits to taking action to show a change in personal perspective. This is suggesting a very open style of management which some managers will either find threatening or be unable to handle well.

As a final point it is suggested that you make summary notes on your key perspectives and opportunities for organisational learning. These will accumulate as subsequent chapters are tackled.

LEARNING MODEL – STEP 7

## COMMENTARY AND LINKS TO CHAPTER 4

This chapter is probably the most difficult but still an essential step in setting the scene for your own learning organisation. Managers always find the internal and external reviews expose a great lack of hard or even semi-hard data. Most so-called organisational knowledge is made up of perspectives and firmly held beliefs in the minds of the managers. Some organisations may well have developed a culture where information and knowledge once gained is kept close to the chest and used as insurance against redundancy. Many organisational development and change programmes set out to change that type of culture but few are successful. The change needs to come from within the managers themselves and a focus on organisational learning will provide opportunities for managers to determine where they want to change perspectives and test out the benefits to themselves and to the organisation.

In Chapter 4 the emphasis moves towards ways of creating a vision for the type of learning organisation that will find some congruence or match with the overall purpose of the enterprise. Noting that the learning organisation will also help shape up and generate new and developing purposes for the enterprise. The place of the leaders and power groups in such a learning organisation will be explored.

## *References*

MBTI Tests can be obtained from Oxford Psychologist Press, Lambourne House, 311–321 Banbury Road, Oxford, OX2 7JH.

Information on the Kirton Adaptation Innovation Inventory can be obtained from Occupational Research Centre, Highlands, Gravel Path, Berkhampstead, Herts, HP4 2PQ.

Haley, U.C.V. and Stumpf, S.A. 'Cognitive Trails in Strategic Decision Making – linking personalities and cognitions.' *Journal of Management Studies*, Vol. 26, No. 5, September 1989, Basil Blackwell.

Jung C.G. *Psychological Types* (Routledge and Kegan Paul, London 1923).

Kirton, M.J. *Adaptor and Innovator. Styles of Creativity and Problem Solving*, (Routledge, London, 1989).

Myers, I.B. & McCaulley, M.H. Manual: 'A guide to the Development and Use of the Myers–Briggs Type Indicator' (Consulting Psychologist Press, USA, 1985).

# 4

# CREATING THE VISION OF THE LEARNING ORGANISATION

## INTRODUCTION

It is suggested that three days are allocated to this topic over an elapsed period of three weeks. An outline study plan is shown in Fig.4.1.

The approach will be to provide guidance on how to conduct each step in the learning model which consists of a review of your preferred leadership style and building a vision for the learning organisation. This is followed by a review of the organisation in terms of planning scenarios, power groups and current approaches to management development and training. Checklists and proformas are provided to help focus your thinking and capture the learning. A series of selected readings then help the reflection stage. These cover vision building and sharing of mental models, new roles for the leader and links between strategic planning and human resource development. Finally an opportunity is provided to test out perspectives before moving on to the next study topic.

LEARNING MODEL – STEP 1

### LEADERSHIP STYLE – A SELF-ANALYSIS

Most managers are at times totally focused on concerns about the way they are perceived by their seniors, colleagues and subordinates. Concerns range from whether they are liked, to how they come across and how effective they are as a leader. Views of past heroes, role models, favourite previous bosses, self-perception, image and experience all contribute to managers adopting a style of leadership with which they feel most comfortable. Those that attempt to maintain a posture that does not fit easily usually finish up found out or worn out.

### Creating the Vision of the Learning Organisation 79

| Step in the learning model | Activity | Sub-topic studied | Study days |
|---|---|---|---|
| 1 | • Self analysis/leadership style preference<br><br>• Creating a vision for the learning organisation | – | 1/2 |
| 2 | Review of the organisation's:<br>• Strategic direction and planning scenarios<br><br>• Management development and training approaches<br><br>• Power groups and existing change leaders | | 1 |
| 3 | • Reading text and reflection | • Vision building and shared mental models<br><br>• New roles for the leader<br><br>• Strategic planning and human resource development | 1 |
| 4/5/6 | • Reflection and testing of views<br><br>• Recording views, ideas, perspectives and concerns | – | 1/2 |
| 7 | • Reading text | • Commentary and links to next study topic | |

*Fig. 4.1 Study plan*

It is likely that your leadership style will by now be deeply ingrained and although it is possible at times to demonstrate some flexibility the common view is that dramatic changes in style are not sustainable. The importance here is to recognise the strengths that your preferred leadership style brings to your thinking about the learning organisation and the resulting biases.

Most organisations do not undertake real changes in direction until they approach a crisis or survival is threatened. The task of helping such organisations to recognise, let alone change to a more learning focused approach obviously places great demands on the leadership style of the person who has decided to implement the learning organisation. Alternatively, many organisations who perceive a crisis looming will be satisfied with making short or medium-term responses. Learning for these organisations will not be a priority. Both of these types of organisational contexts do not lend themselves to easy adoption of the more long-term learning organisation approach.

There are five key factors to consider when thinking about leadership style and the learning organisation. These are that:

(a) an individual's leadership style does not have a great deal of flexibility

(b) mature organisations will have a developed culture that creates a leadership style requirement

(c) organisations will not seek a change of leadership style unless faced with crisis or survival problems

(d) an organisation that is growing will attract and reward leadership styles that take them from the entrepreneurial to the adaptive and bureaucratic stages of development

(e) the person considering implementation of the learning organisation will bring to bear personal leadership style preferences and hence design biases.

The approach that will be used to help you review your preferred leadership style is based on research findings that have differentiated styles among managers, according to the emphasis given to interpersonal relationships or to the structure of the task in hand. Fig. 4.2. provides some broad statements that should be used to check which one most closely represents you firstly in normal working situations and secondly when under stress, e.g. under normal conditions you may be Style 'B' but under stress move rapidly to Style 'A'. You may, of course, decide that you stay within one style band even when under extreme stress.

These categories are only broad indicators of styles and any manager knows from experience that they are dependent on and influenced by:

- your basic personality
- your subordinates' needs
- the task in hand
- the constraints and boundaries created by the organisation
- the cultural values and expectations within the organisation
- the personal, positional and expertise power of the manager
- the response of your subordinates to the particular leadership style.

### Creating the Vision of the Learning Organisation 81

**Style A**
- Operates in the present, emphasises the immediacy of matters
- Seen as an organisation man
- Seen as in charge
- Demands performance from subordinates
- Subordinates feel information is withheld at times
- Seen as argumentative
- Tends to undervalue some subordinates

**Style B**
- Uses groups to share ideas
- Identifies well with subordinates
- Likes working with teams
- Seeks to understand the cause of any conflict
- Subordinates sometimes feel that their individuality has been lost
- Seeks to please everyone
- Does not seek to demonstrate or attract power

**Style C**
- Accepts others without criticism and is non-judgemental
- Seen as very supportive by subordinates
- Likes being in groups
- Rarely highlights subordinates' mistakes
- Seen as emotional and sensitive to the moods of others
- Subordinates feel that sufficient direction is not provided
- Not an open supporter of the organisation and its culture
- Seen to be often praising subordinates
- Avoids confrontation and conflict

**Style D**
- Seen as imposing management controls
- Supports the organisation's rules and procedures
- Likes routine activity
- Seen to resist tackling open-ended issues
- Does not promote the formation of groups
- Seen as unemotional
- Appears to prefer to work alone

*Fig. 4.2 Leadership style preferences*

Bearing this in mind the categories can be described as representing styles as follows:

## Style A

Where the task in hand tends to dominate the behaviour of the manager. The fear of failure at the task and loss of power and influence to achieve an outcome are the driving motivational forces. In normal circumstances this predominantly directive style can be seen as kindly and fair but under stress is likely to revert to a more autocratic style. By engaging in argument to avoid direct conflict opportunities for compromise and forming coalitions is often missed. This style is often associated with a high pressure, tight deadline task where subordinates recognise the manager as a technical expert and identify with the outcomes. In most organisations this style is not only highly valued but essential for achieving targets.

## Style B

Here the manager is concerned to link the task to the team. The manager is seeking self-fulfilment and is determined that subordinates will be satisfied with their situation. In normal circumstances the manager would be seen as an effective director of the workforce where ideas and objectives are fully explained and work is completed to schedule. Under pressure the fear that people might become dissatisfied tends to result in compromises being made regarding the task.

## Style C

This style values the relationship with subordinates perhaps more than the task in hand. The desire for approval from the team and the fear of rejection are the driving emotional forces. The lack of direction felt by subordinates and the tendency to reward personal loyalty to the manager can encourage the team to become isolated from the rest of the organisation. In normal circumstances the manager would be seen as an excellent developer of subordinates but under pressure would become an idealist at the expense of the task.

## Style D

This manager likes to impose management controls and relies heavily on the use of rational and logical methods. Procedures and rules are used extensively to manage and control both the subordinates and the task. The dominant motivation is to survive in what appears to the manager as a series of uncertain circumstances. By not becoming involved with subordinates this manager seeks to avoid dependency and any influences on action.

### Creating the Vision of the Learning Organisation

This review probably presented no surprises as to your preferred style and how an emphasis on task or on relationships with subordinates can be interpreted as a change in style. Fig.4.3. provides an illustration of the styles and can be used to recognise how you react under pressure. For most managers style represents years of personal investment and has become internalised at an emotional level. Style for many represents a learned defence mechanism, a way of dealing with organisational life that is rarely brought to the open and questioned. There are some key learning opportunities in this area of leadership style, particularly for the manager who operates with Style D and is not committed to either the task or to the team.

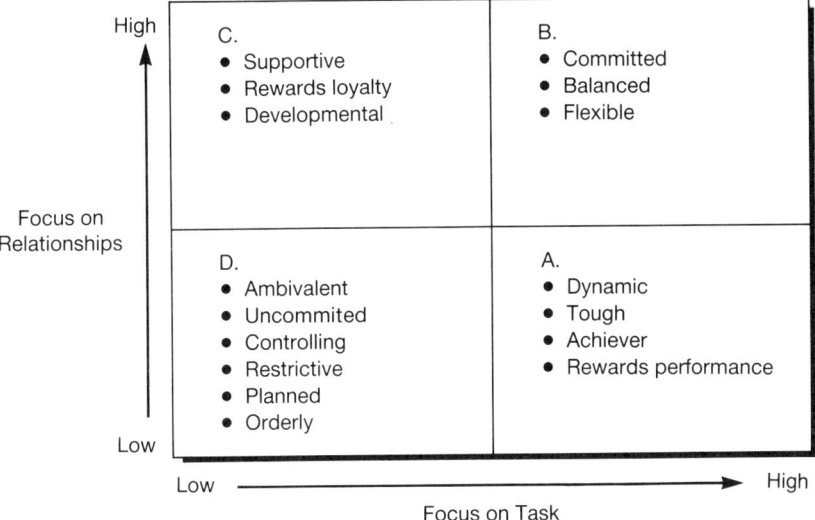

*Fig. 4.3 Tasks, relationships and leadership style*

In the readings in Step 3 below the various roles for the leader in setting up and working in a learning organisation will be explored. As we move on to develop possible visions for creating a focus on learning in your organisation then your leadership style will be seen to be a major factor in your thinking.

## CREATING A VISION OF THE LEARNING ORGANISATION

In Chapter 3, Step 1 it was suggested that this study into the learning organisation should have a clear purpose and a simple set of objectives. One of these objectives was to formulate a vision for the enterprise and identify the areas where opportunities for a focus on learning will arise. It is important to note that the word enterprise will be used increasingly in the book to describe the host organisation. The reason for this will become clearer as we proceed.

This section will also help to crystallise the picture of the future that you wish to create for the learning organisation. It has to start with your personal vision and will then need to be shared and shaped by the visions of colleagues. Unfortunately there are no standardised ways of creating a vision but there are some guidelines that will help.

First, some clarification as to what is meant by a vision. A vision can best be described as having an aspiration or wanting to realise some goal or end point. It must be something that you seek to achieve for both its intrinsic value to yourself and also for extrinsic values, i.e. values that others will recognise and want to subscribe to for the benefit, growth and survival of the enterprise. Linked to and supporting this vision will be an underlying sense of purpose defining what you stand for and value as a core set of ideas or beliefs, i.e. what you are striving to become.

In creating your vision for the learning organisation it is essential to forget about the problems and constraints that you can envisage that emanate from the here and now. Your focus must be on the future opportunities that can be realised and that you wish to achieve. To do this you will be starting to adopt what we will see later in Step 3 as the visionary leadership role. In Fig. 4.4. the way in which vision and sense of purpose are related and also the on-going nature of vision-building are illustrated, i.e. the vision is used to drive the organisation on and refreshes the underlying sense of purpose. The sense of purpose defines what the learning organisation is fundamentally trying to be and tends to include descriptions of how the vision is to be supported.

These notions of vision and sense of purpose are not easy to grasp and some examples may help. First a simple example.

VISION: *To be the first person to swim the Atlantic by the year 2000.*

SENSE OF PURPOSE:

- Being the best swimmer in the world
- Maintaining a 100 per cent level of fitness
- Setting an example for the youth of the world.

You may have found that example a bit extreme but let us provide some more respectable examples of vision leaving you to ponder on the underlying sense of purpose for each.

### Creating the Vision of the Learning Organisation 85

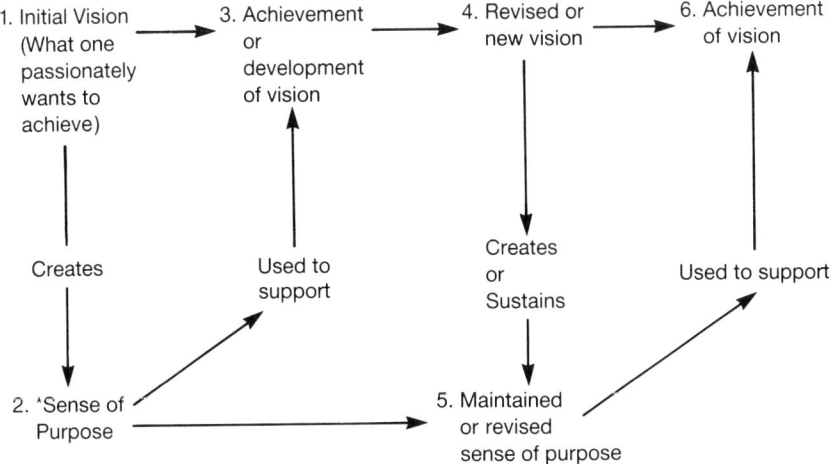

*Note that some may find it helps to think of sense of purpose as 'the mission'.

*Fig. 4.4 Links between vision and purpose*

VISION: *To establish a joint learning partnership with key customers within three years in both strategic and operational areas.*

VISION: *To operate an organisation with only two layers of management based on extensive use of knowledge based systems within five years.*

VISION: *To be able to measure and demonstrate the value of organisational learning in terms of operational cost savings and added value performance within five years.*

VISION: *To set up learning processes and facilities in all the major organisational functions such that learning is used as an explicit management tool.*

VISION: *To develop learning systems in the organisation that eliminate the need for all investment in management development and training.*

VISION: *To be able to sell services as consultants in organisational learning to major customers and suppliers within three years.*

There is nothing wrong with a learning organisation being focused on one vision. The underlying sense of purpose that this demands will in turn lead to clarity as to the key areas of learning that then need to be stimulated and managed. For example, if the vision is around an issue involving growth then the need to stimulate learning around areas involving people skills, markets, customers, funding, technologies, ethics, collaboration, etc. will quickly be identified. There are techniques for building vision such as brainstorming, use of imagery and looking at what other people are doing and copying or adapting their ideas. But the key is to discuss your personal vision with colleagues, remembering to ignore the constraints of reality at this stage, and finish up with a roughly shared view to which you and a number of colleagues can declare a commitment.

If you are still finding this vision building a problem then the following trigger questions may help:

(a) What is it that the enterprise is really trying to achieve in terms of its vision and where could a learning organisation vision fit in? If there is no obvious fit this might spring your thinking as to what really needs to be achieved by the learning organisation.

(b) What timescales are being considered for the learning organisation and vision? (It is possible to set a series of visions over, say, two, four and six years from now.)

(c) To what extent is the environment in terms of economic, social, technical, legal etc. a trigger for your formulation of vision?

(d) To what extent are ethics and morals important to your vision?

(e) What are your fundamental beliefs about the type of organisation and climate that the learning organisation could help to establish?

It is important that before you move on to the next step you record your vision or visions for the learning organisation and the associated sense of purpose. There will be an opportunity to revise these as the study proceeds and you continue the readings. But it is key that you undertake this creative activity which will later be seen as an invaluable step towards implementing the learning organisation.

LEARNING MODEL – STEP 2

## REVIEW OF THE ENTERPRISE (THE HOST ORGANISATION) STRATEGIC DIRECTION AND PLANNING SCENARIOS

In Step 1 the initial thinking around a vision for the learning organisation will have been carried out at the enterprise level or at that of a Division or Functional Unit. It is likely that a vision for the enterprise already exists if

### Creating the Vision of the Learning Organisation 87

not in writing then in the minds of the senior managers. At a Divisional or Unit level it may be necessary to enquire or seek out this enterprise vision. What becomes obvious at this stage is that the vision for the learning organisation (what you want to achieve for the learning organisation) is couched in different terms from those for the enterprise, Division or Unit. The learning organisation can now start to take on the form of a priming agent or enabling force for the enterprise.

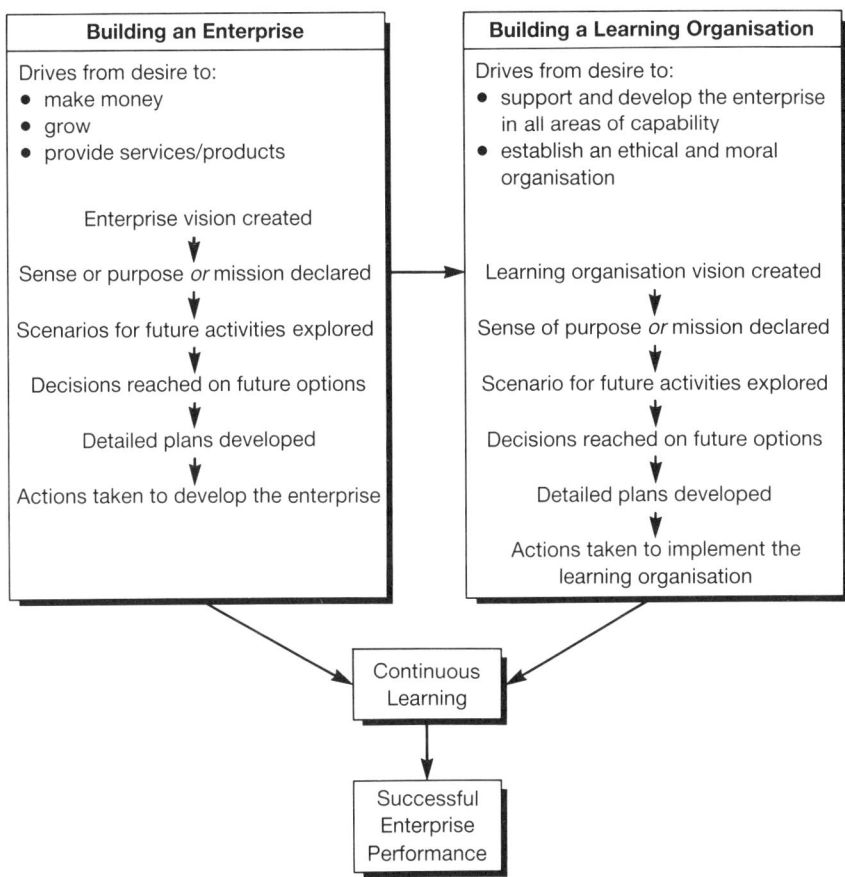

Fig. 4.5  Links between Learning Organisation and enterprise visions

This contrast between ideas around developing the enterprise and those concerning the learning organisation is shown in Fig. 4.5. The crucial point made in the figure is where the mission of the enterprise is shown as triggering the creation of vision for the learning organisation. In essence the

## 88 Implementing the Learning Organisation

learning organisation is a notion in its own right that uses all the processes and approaches in its development that would be seen in conventional strategic planning activities within an enterprise. The key point is that the learning organisation is being created in order to support the enterprise itself and as such will eventually merge into the enterprise activities. The strategic thinking and operational development of the learning organisation should therefore be carried out by the enterprise managers themselves in order to ensure commitment to the notion at the formative stage. In practice it will require a dedicated team and a champion to tackle the implementation and how to do this will be covered in Chapter 7.

The current approaches or processes used in the enterprise for creating strategic direction will provide a guide to their use for the learning organisation. If on the other hand these strategic processes do not exist, or are not used, then the learning organisation will need to initiate the process.

A typical enterprise strategic planning process should meet the following requirements and be used as a guide to setting up a strategic planning process for the learning organisation. The process requirements are:

- the process should be formal and laid down
- key participants in the process must be named
- the participants should set the tone for the process that they wish to communicate to others in the organisation
- the process should identify and interpret key strategic issues
- the outcome of the process should be a clear statement of strategic direction and capable of being articulated by senior and middle managers
- senior and middle managers should be committed to the outcomes and not merely compliant
- the process must be efficient in terms of use of management time
- the process cycle time should fit the nature of the environment in which the organisation operates
- the process should be creative and lead to successful innovations that benefit the organisation.

A first step in using this process to build the learning organisation will involve setting the visions created in Step 1 into a framework as shown in Fig. 4.6. This enables the relative attractiveness of the visions to be shown in terms of meeting the needs for learning in the enterprise and feasibility in the context of the enterprise's culture, history and environment. This initial assessment of visions helps to decide on which ones to pursue and initial thoughts on implementation strategies.

Ideally the same process should be completed for the enterprise visions and this will produce two parallel paths identifying areas of organisational learning that will eventually overlap and establish the learning organisation.

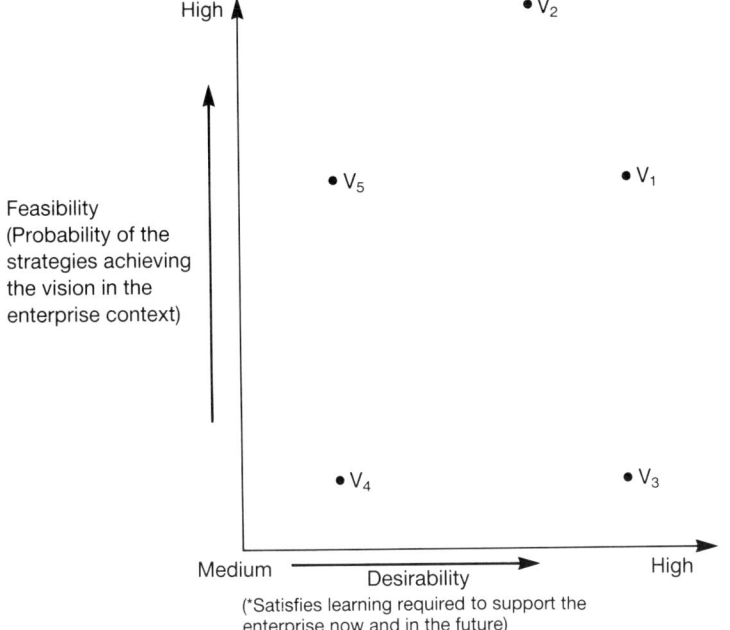

Fig. 4.6  Assessment of visions and mission for the Learning Organisation

This is shown in Fig.4.7.

By this stage an overarching vision and mission (sense of purpose) will have been created and this will be used to develop and sustain the notion of the learning organisation. What is needed now are some short to medium-term objectives that will help to test out your thinking on the learning organisation. These objectives should be quantifiable and thus capable of being used to direct and measure performance in the following key areas:

- identification of learning opportunities for internal client groups, units and or functions
- review and evaluation of existing learning processes
- identification and improvements in the processes required to operate and develop the enterprise.

Most of the information needed to help derive these objectives will have been identified by the review activities completed in Chapter 3 and from your work on visions for the learning organisation.

We have now taken on board the notion that the learning organisation adopts a clear identity and high profile in order to generate an interest and

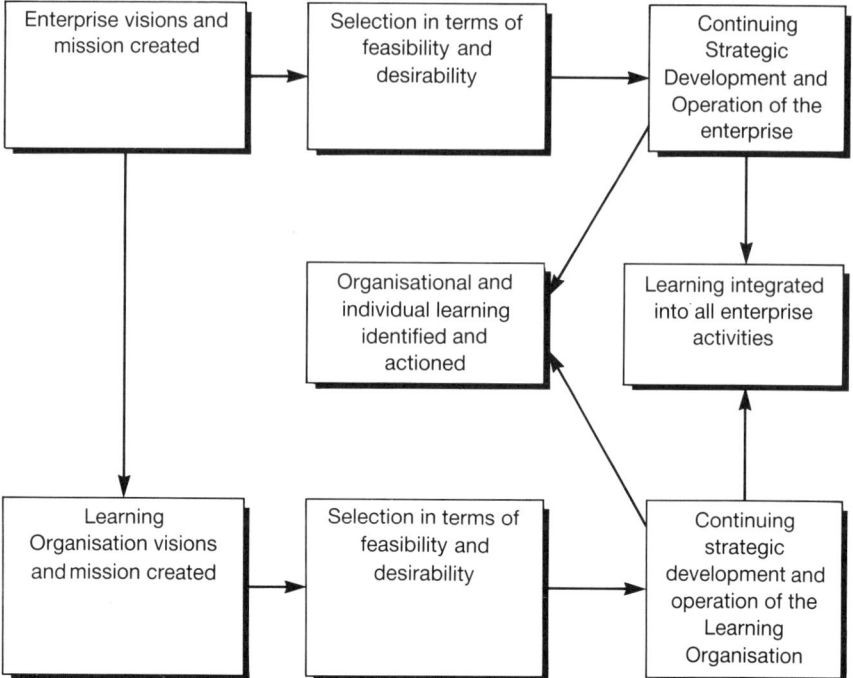

*Fig. 4.7 Strategic development of the enterprise and the Learning Organisation*

focus on learning within the enterprise. To be practicable this high profile learning organisation will have to fit into the existing formal learning patterns that have been established in the enterprise. These will usually be activities already identified by those responsible for management development and training activities.

## Management development and training approaches

It is in this area that conventional learning will be focused. Within organisations the management development and training activities can be considered as deriving from three perspectives which may all be present and active. The three perspectives are:

*The Corporate Needs:*

- derived from the Corporate Planning process where skills gaps are identified and met through recruitment, training and development.
- derived from Corporate views on key manpower succession and development of potential in identified managers.

### Creating the Vision of the Learning Organisation 91

- derived from major programmes involving culture change, organisational development, re-engineering and introduction of TQM etc.

*The Functional or Unit Needs:*

- team or functional development surrounding a work or project issue.

*The Individual Needs:*

- derived from an appraisal process, needs analysis or assessment centre activity.
- self-development programmes based on self-appraisal and supporting network activities.
- learning contracts where the individual and the senior are committed to a supported personal development programme and outcomes are measured in terms of competences.

It is important to note the extent to which these various perspectives are operating in the enterprise and to understand their links to any promotion or rewards schemes – either tacit or explicit.

Delivery of these development and training activities will include: on-the-job, off-site courses, private study, team development programmes and special projects conducted by task teams. A clear assessment of these formal approaches, their use, acceptance, scale and perceived value will provide a framework against which you can begin comparing your views on how to begin implementing the learning organisation.

## Power groups and existing change leaders

In considering any change it is important to determine the operation of power groups within the enterprise and who are the key change leaders. This will help to identify the way in which any change can be approached. The following questions should be used for this review.

1. To what extent is the enterprise directed by the Chairman, Chief Executive alone?
2. To what extent do Board Members either collectively, in groups, or individually, initiate and direct changes?
3. What use is made of external consultants to effect change?
4. Are task teams used to initiate and deliver change?
5. To what extent are briefings and mass communications used to initiate and direct change?
6. To what extent are changes derived from informal groupings?

## 92 Implementing the Learning Organisation

7. Are particular functions or specialist areas seen to initiate key changes?
8. How are the views of the various management levels obtained either to derive a change of direction or to test acceptance:
   (a) senior level
   (b) middle level
   (c) junior level
9. To what extent are the views of the workforce sought when considering a change?
10. How would you set about deciding upon and introducing a major change?
11. Who would you look to for support when considering how to introduce a major change?
12. Do you consider that you are skilled at introducing change?

The three reviews have now been completed and you should have formed much clearer perspectives as to:

- your own preferred leadership style and how this creates biases when considering implementing and managing major change programmes
- how the enterprise vision and the vision of the learning organisation need to be separate and how they will eventually integrate into one
- the way in which the enterprise approaches and values conventional learning, i.e. management development and training
- the use made in the enterprise of groups and individuals to introduce and carry out change programmes.

These perspectives will be used in Chapter 7 when considering approaches to implementation.

LEARNING MODEL – STEP 3

## READING TEXT AND REFLECTION

In this section three sub-topics are introduced to help promote reflection on the findings resulting from the above reviews. These readings will help develop your thinking and understanding about the behaviour of managers in organisations. It is important that you use the notions presented to reflect on the perspectives that you have formed and check out your thinking and arguments with colleagues.

- The areas covered by these sub-topics are:

- vision building and shared mental models
- new roles for the leader
- strategic planning and human resource development.

## Vision building and shared mental models

In Step 2, above, the visions and underlying sense of purpose for the learning organisation were created. These visions may have been the result of one person's thinking or created by a team. What this section sets out to explore is the way in which these visions can be developed and shared within the organisation. It will be argued that without shared vision the learning organisation is likely to run out of steam or even founder completely.

Organisations are made up of managers who hold a range of mental images about how the organisation works and how they themselves work. Ways of approaching and tackling day-to-day problem-solving and longer-term actions are based on these mental models. Sometimes these models surface and are made clear and explicit (usually when the manager is under pressure) and at other times remain tacit or subconscious. It is your mental models that will influence how you approach the creation of the vision and how you then set out to persuade others to support your vision and work at developing strategies and actions that will move that vision towards action and outcomes.

In considering your personality traits and preferred leadership style you will have highlighted some of the biases that will be influencing your approach to building and sharing your vision. It is reasonable to assume that within the enterprise there will be a wide spread of biases and well developed mental models. This is the basis or start point that must be taken into account in creating a vision that can be shared and owned. Exhortations and mass communications may cause an initial reaction but this will eventually be submerged among all the other messages within the enterprise and the excitement that managers are already experiencing in making things happen and solving problems. The mistake would be to believe you will be walking on to a stage to deliver your message to an expectant and naive audience.

To survive and grow the vision must satisfy two key criteria: it must stand up to close inquiry and survive the gut feel test. This latter test is vital and is based on the view that experienced managers at times appear to be making 'seat of the pants' or 'intuitive' judgements. What this really means is that they are using a complex mental process involving imagery, sensing, rapid analysis and pattern matching based on experience, to make what appear to be snap judgements. This ability to use intuition is a key attribute of the more successful entrepreneur or visionary.

If we take the first criteria of being able to stand up to close inquiry, we are automatically moving towards the idea of inviting managers to challenge the vision and the notion that changes are possible. This presents a dilemma for vision holders who hold mental models that will encourage them to employ advocacy or argument to win their case against allcomers. On the other hand those who favour appeasement and harmony will be prepared to compromise on their vision. There is no simple answer to this dilemma but there are some basic guidelines that might help. These guidelines are:

(a) The importance of seeking commitment from others as opposed to compliance.

(b) Many managers have never experienced commitment to an idea and may be ambivalent about themselves and the organisation (see preferred leadership style analysis in Step 2).

(c) If compliance is all that is really being sought then make this clear and above board. Commitment may have to be tackled via another route and develop over time.

(d) When engaging in close inquiry it is important to encourage people to surface (make explicit) the mental models or assumptions on which their argument is based; also to make your models clear. In this way the inquiry becomes a learning process.

(e) Be prepared to adapt and develop your vision based on inquiry and gut feel reaction from others but do this on the basis of your commitment to the new vision.

(f) Insist that any changes or developments of the vision are made on the basis of clear descriptions of the future organisation scenarios that are envisaged.

(g) Be prepared to confront those whom you feel are espousing a view based on 'what we say' as opposed to 'what we really do'.

(h) Be prepared for the process of vision building and sharing to take time.

These guidelines will help the process and should be used as a checklist for your own learning.

One of the issues that will surface early in the process is that of the pressure or tension that managers will feel between the vision plus underlying sense of purpose and their view of the current organisational reality. This tension can be destructive in that managers will either reject the vision as totally unreal or after an initial honeymoon period will lose interest and be swept up in the day-to-day challenges. This can be guarded against and overcome if the following two requirements are met:

### Creating the Vision of the Learning Organisation

(a) The vision must be based on the shared mental models of the managers and have inspired commitment from those key to its success.

(b) That the tension created by the vision and the realities of daily organisational life is used to encourage creativity and innovation that will lead to realising the vision.

One way of moving towards harnessing the opportunities that this tension provides is to set up teams that will focus on the learning required to implement the learning organisation. The overall approach by these teams should be to hold to the vision while enquiring and challenging the contradictions thrown up by their perception of current reality. The steps in the vision building process then become:

1. (a) Establish a shared vision and underlying sense of purpose based on inquiry and use of gut feel responses.
   (b) Share mental models that underlie the organisational thinking and behaviour.
   (c) Recognise that you and the other managers will have ingrained biases.

2. Seek to establish commitment recognising that expecting all managers to commit is unrealistic and probably unnecessary.
   Compliance may be acceptable particularly if the organisational culture encourages this response.

3. Identify the broad strategies that will be required to support the vision.

4. (a) Identify the power groups and where power and influence will be required to implement the learning organisation.
   (b) Some power groups may be informal others may be established but only be required to provide token influences.

5. (a) Maintain a sense of urgency behind the vision building and strategy thinking phase.
   (b) Set a timescale and clear milestones to record progress.

6. (a) Communicate the outcomes of the process but avoid exhortations which managers will probably take as a signal to switch off.
   (b) Use influence groups to communicate the progress of the process.
   (c) Build task teams from across the enterprise.
   Make it enjoyable.

7. Seek backers for the process across the enterprise and where possible with clients, customers and suppliers outside the enterprise.

## Implementing the Learning Organisation

8. Avoid the missionary tag by integrating the process into the daily working issues.

## New roles for the leader

In the previous sections your consideration of preferred leadership style and the need for someone to initiate or lead the vision building process have been explored. This section will bring these two ideas together and clarify what for many is seen as a series of new roles for the leader. In conducting this study into the learning organisation it is vital that the requirements for leadership are identified. From this it will be possible to determine whether this capability is recognised or available either within yourself or others. Learning how to be an effective leader in setting up the learning organisation may be a key first step. The learning also needs to be transferred to the wider enterprise as it is applicable to other innovative processes and change programmes.

In conventional terms the leader sets a clear direction using manipulation in a positive and helpful way in order to get people to work towards a shared and common goal. The leader is seen as having to be an authoritarian and deal with those who reject the vision and who behave in ways that are counter to the good of the enterprise, the managers and workforce. There are alternative roles or parts that the leader needs to fulfil. These are grouped for convenience under the two headings: visionary and designer, and developer.

*Visionary and Designer:*

1. Encouraging the creation of a vision and sense of purpose to which people can become committed.
2. Helping managers approach complex issues as an opportunity for learning.
3. Setting an example in the way in which sharing of mental models can help create a clear understanding of complex issues.
4. Inspiring managers to take risks and use the outcomes as opportunities for learning.
5. Encouraging managers to be creative in either innovative or adaptive ways.
6. Setting the tone and standards of behaviour for the enterprise.

*Developer:*

1. Encouraging managers to explore the boundaries and constraints that inhibit creativity.

## Creating the Vision of the Learning Organisation 97

2. Developing intuitive approaches and capabilities of the managers.
3. Helping managers learn how to take in the helicopter view.
4. Helping managers break out of rigid mind-sets.
5. Helping managers learn how to balance perspectives gained from day-to-day reality with a longer term vision and harness the tension that this creates.
6. Building committed teams that can work at creative tasks.
7. Helping to capture knowledge and understanding that is tacit and then making it explicit and transferable.
8. Promoting learning processes that will help create an enterprise that produces satisfaction for both stakeholders and employees.
9. Helping to identify the shape and culture of the enterprise.
10. Legitimising viewpoints.
11. Identifying and providing the support to key managers who will help influence the vision and strategies for the learning organisation.
12. Holding off pressures that are restricting managers from taking risks.

The above list can obviously only give a broad indication of the variety of roles required of the leader. It can be argued that in any enterprise there are many situations and jobs where the role requirement is nowhere near as wide or demanding as this list suggests. Remember that we are focusing here on the leader who is faced with tackling a major change programme. The existing enterprise may either have a culture which supports directive leadership or have introduced changes through management training programmes that encourage a more visionary and developmental leadership approach. This new leadership role is thus seen as being one that emphasises the ability to be a visionary and change agent.

Within the existing enterprise it is also likely that leadership is a term that tends to mean management. Here management is conventionally seen to include:

- the planning and budgeting of resources to achieve a targeted outcome
- organising, staffing and creating systems to guide activities and monitor progress
- controlling work and solving problems
- providing satisfaction to a range of stakeholders including the staff.

In executing this role the manager is expected to demonstrate sufficient leadership to meet the needs of achieving the tasks in hand. Leadership of a higher order tends to be seen as the requirement or prerogative of the more senior or high-profile managers.

In considering the feasibility of setting up the learning organisation it is important that these conventional roles of managers and the part that leadership is normally seen to play are understood. The leader of the organisation will need to be capable of carrying out the roles outlined above and appreciate the need for the more conventional management roles and approaches in order to make the enterprise work. The mistake would be to think that the fully integrated learning organisation should exhibit the new leadership roles at all levels.

All managers need to be aware of the use and purpose of these leadership roles but also be capable of determining:

- when they are important
- how they can be applied
- what they will produce
- whether they themselves have the skills, ability and interest to adopt the role or if it would be wiser to select someone else.

This indicates a key area of learning for most managers and should be noted as an important element in the development of the learning organisation. If this is not built into the learning then the likelihood is that strong conflicts will occur between the visionaries and leaders of the new learning organisation and the custodians of the status quo.

It is always important to remember that those representing the status quo have managed to create and sustain an enterprise that has survived and represents an opportunity for change. The temptation to see, or allow others to label, the learning organisation as a 'white knight' or 'evangelical force' should be resisted. The learning organisation is being presented as a way of supporting the enterprise in the execution of its vision and mission; separate initially in order to create a clarity of vision and purpose but eventually being integrated and merged as a set of practices and way of life for those in the whole enterprise.

## Strategic planning and human resource development

The case has been argued that the learning organisation should in the early stages be thought of as an organisation whose vision and mission derive from that of the enterprise itself. This suggests that the way it is introduced, its form and support will all depend on the way in which the strategic direction of the enterprise is currently determined. It has also been argued that a choice will need to be made as to whether the learning organisation is subsumed as a responsibility of the Directors and line managers or whether it is to be staffed by a dedicated team. This section aims to help develop your thinking in this area as it looks at the links between strategic activity and human resource management.

Bearing in mind that human resource management is seen as the conventional repository for developments in learning, it is suggested that consideration of the feasibility of implementing the learning organisation would have to address this issue of ownership, perceived relevance and the level within the enterprise to which the activity belongs.

In some enterprises the importance of HRD (in particular management development and training) has been emphasised by creating budgetary sanctions on departments that do not train and individuals who do not attend courses. Managers charged with HRD responsibilities thus set out to identify and secure their activities into the line activity of the enterprise. Typically HRD staff would be encouraged to engage in:

- understanding HRD and business links
- contributing to debates on organisation structures needed to support changes in the activities of the enterprise
- diagnostic work to gauge the skill base of the enterprise
- introduction of contemporary HRD practices
- debates that help translate the existing skill base into opportunities for the enterprise
- managing the changes and developments in the enterprise culture
- identifying pressure points that indicate the need to change the culture, organisational structure and practices and the skill base.

It could be argued that HRD is a natural focus and potential driving force for initiatives to set up a learning organisation. The apparent failure of this to happen can be attributed to three key factors:

(a) that staff engaged in HRD have become sidetracked into servicing the mainstream activity of the enterprise. Their efforts are centred on responding to demands from the managers and not having a clear vision.

(b) that the focus on learning and the learning organisation has only recently gained attention. Staff in HRD areas have ingrained mind-sets and ways of working that have not yet been able to make the necessary transformations.

(c) that the power around strategic planning and direction rests with the top management group who have learned to push learning to a lower level in the enterprise.

This presents a bleak and potentially cynical view of the HRD activities and those of the top management team. A closer look at some of the underlying structural causes of this phenomena may help develop a more constructive perspective.

The top management team engage in long-term direction and portfolio planning covering mainstream activities, policies and relationships between different parts of the enterprise. In this planning process they take into account the external and internal environment of the enterprise. Their tendency is to discount HRD for five key reasons:

1. There is no pressure or reactions from HRD/HRM areas to many of their plans and decisions, e.g. with the reduction in power of the Unions and in times of high unemployment.

2. They see no obvious connection between HRD/HRM and the plans and decisions they are making certainly not in the short term.

3. Issues surrounding HRD/HRM can easily be pushed down to lower levels in the enterprise which in turn leads to a variety of responses and hence a perception of lack of direct relevance.

4. Any pressure or constraint placed on the process from areas that do not wield power will tend to be ignored. (The areas of HRD/HRM are historically seen in this light).

5. Any issue that does not appear to have a direct economic or asset implications tends to be ignored.

If this view of the structural factors that mitigate against HRD/HRM are even partly accurate then some of the difficulties that the learning organisation visionaries will face become clear. The response by many enterprises to this problem has been to appoint HRM managers to main Board positions in order to recognise and enhance their power to influence the enterprise direction. The importance of the decision as to whether the learning organisation should be established as a separate group or integrated into the enterprise at Main Board and Director level becomes more urgent and crucial. The success of the learning organisation approach may in the final count hinge on getting this decision right in the context of the enterprise, its culture and history. There are a few precedents around on how to proceed and what appears to constitute current best practice, but not many examples of how to move into this emerging way of directing and managing complex enterprises.

LEARNING MODEL – STEPS 4, 5, 6

## FORMING AND TESTING PERSPECTIVES

This section provides the opportunity for some reflection on the organisational reviews and the above texts.

## Creating the Vision of the Learning Organisation 101

This chapter has taken a major step towards tackling the core questions surrounding the vision for the learning organisation and how the notion fits alongside the existing vision, purpose and strategic direction of the enterprise itself. The review of your preferred leadership style and how new roles for the leaders need to be considered have also been explored. The place of the HRM/HRD functions in the mainstream activities of the enterprise will have opened up the meaty question of where the learning organisation fits and choices as to form.

Based on these reviews and readings it should be possible to articulate your perspectives on:

- a vision for the learning organisation and the underlying mission or sense of purpose. Also how these will be developed and shared
- the vision and mission of the enterprise
- the way in which the learning organisation will be represented and articulated within the enterprise
- how the learning organisation vision and mission will be made to come alive in terms of key strategies and short to medium-term objectives
- the processes both formal and informal that will be used to develop and grow the learning organisation
- the key links between the enterprise and the learning organisation at both strategic and operational levels
- how the learning organisation will relate to and fit with the existing management development and training activities in the enterprise
- how the learning organisation will make use of existing power figures, power groups and change leaders within the enterprise
- the use that will be made of existing change processes within the enterprise when implementing the learning organisation
- the difference between the notions of compliance and commitment and their importance in implementing the learning organisation
- the significance of surfacing and sharing mental models as a fundamental approach to individual and team learning
- the impact of your own preferred leadership style on the design and implementation of the learning organisation
- the value and use that can be made of the creative tension that will build up between the vision and perceptions of current reality
- new roles for the leader as visionary and change agent, in the learning organisation and the place and contribution of conventional management.

Some of these perspectives may be important and appear more powerful than others. Remember that we are still only considering the feasibility of implementing the learning organisation and exploring various areas in order

## 102 Implementing the Learning Organisation

to build up understanding and confidence.

It is important that the mental models that you are using behind these perspectives are surfaced and checked out with colleagues. A technique that can be used is to prepare a short presentation (say, ten minutes and five slides) covering the main ideas that have been developed in the study, e.g.

- what triggered the study
- the purpose and objective of the study
- the enterprise vision and how the learning organisation vision provides support and integration
- how the learning organisation could be implemented and the timescale
- some potential barriers to implementation and how they might be tackled.

By making this presentation you can begin to test out your own perspectives and begin to build confidence and support for some of the ideas. The dangers of presenting a hard sell or setting yourself up as a missionary are obvious. If you have been working as task teams or in a team then presenting to other groups in the enterprise becomes less of a problem.

As a final point it is suggested that you make summary notes on your key perspectives and questions that still need to be addressed. Reflecting back on summaries of perspectives held at the end of Chapter 3 is also important. The key point is to note where there is a fundamental change or development of these perspectives.


LEARNING MODEL – STEP 7

## COMMENTARY AND LINKS TO CHAPTER 5

This chapter represents a major milestone in setting the vision and key strategies for implementing the learning organisation into the context of the enterprise. Where the study is being made at the enterprise-wide level then views of links between the learning organisation and the enterprise activity and processes should now be very clear.

Alternatively, where the study is at Divisional or Unit level there is a danger that discontinuities between the central organisation (area from which direction and control comes) or parent body will be highlighted. This needs to be watched carefully as, although some would see the tension between parent and child healthy, this tension can quickly become destructive rather than creative. Fig.4.8. illustrates how a Division or Unit that begins to engage in learning around vision and mission can quickly move to a viewpoint that encourages them to leave the parent. Where this happens there are often no winners.

### Creating the Vision of the Learning Organisation 103

|  |  | Division | |
|---|---|---|---|
|  |  | No clear vision and mission | Clear vision and mission |
| Corporate or directing group | Clear as to role for division | • Marginal player<br>– Replaceable<br>– Average performance | • Key player<br>– Essential to corporate success<br>– Excellent performance |
|  | Unclear as to role for division | • Ad hoc player<br>– Poor performance | • Non player<br>– Seen as threat to corporate success<br>– Average to poor performance |

*Fig. 4.8 Tensions resulting from divisional learning*

In Chapter 5 the focus moves on to look at the issues surrounding the introduction of these complex changes into the enterprise. The notion of organisational culture and how this can block organisational learning will be explored. It is an important chapter in that it will identify the ways in which the learning organisation can be introduced and developed.

# 5

# IDENTIFYING THE CULTURE AND THE OPPORTUNITIES FOR CHANGE

## INTRODUCTION

It is suggested that seven days are allocated to this topic over an elapsed period of seven weeks. An outline study plan is shown in Fig. 5.1. The approach will be to provide guidance on how to conduct each step in the learning model which consists of a review of how you see the enterprise culture and where this presents blockages to your own learning. This is followed by a review of the enterprise in terms of the existing culture, from the perspective of key managers, plus boundaries and blockages to learning. Finally a review of any previous change programmes their sponsorship and impact.

Checklists and proformas are provided to help focus your ideas. A series of selected readings covering development of an organisational culture and managing complex change are then used to help the reflection stage.

Finally an opportunity is provided to test out new perspectives that will have been formed before moving on to the next study topic.

LEARNING MODEL – STEP 1

### ENTERPRISE CULTURE AND BLOCKS TO LEARNING – A PERSONAL VIEW

The notion that each enterprise has a distinctive culture is commonplace amongst managers. What might not be so common is to attempt to establish a clear view of what the culture might mean for any one individual.

| Step in the learning model | Activity | Sub-topic studied | Study days |
|---|---|---|---|
| 1 | Analysis of the enterprise culture and blocks to learning | – | 1/2 |
| 2 | Review of the enterprise:<br><br>• Culture<br><br>• Boundaries and blockages to learning<br><br>• Previous change programmes | – | 3 |
| 3 | • Reading text and reflection | • Development of organisational culture<br><br>• Managing complex change | 1 |
| 4/5/6 | • Reflection and testing of views<br><br>• Recording views, ideas, perspectives and concerns | • Implementation plans and timescales | 2 1/2 |
| 7 | Reading text | • Commentary and links to next study topic | |

*Fig. 5.1 Study plan*

Obtaining this view is vital as it will influence the way managers approach identifying problems and making decisions and hence their approaches to learning. If the notion of the learning organisation, that is presented, is to strike any resonance with the managers then an understanding of the enterprise culture becomes paramount.

Most managers when asked to describe the enterprise culture would probably have immediate thoughts along the lines of 'the way it really is around here'. But they would most likely talk about it being bureaucratic, open, amorphous, like living on a roller coaster, like being in a machine, thrown together like rats in a sack, etc. Most of us like using such metaphors.

Some would talk about there being a dominant culture and a number of sub-cultures that have developed within Divisions, work units, disciplines and sub-groups.

People use rich metaphors to capture their perception of the enterprise and its culture as it allows them to build images and communicate their deeper feelings about themselves and their struggles. It is in many ways a very creative activity and can represent a key step in helping managers to move to a more conscious learning focus.

To tap into your views of the culture the following questions should be tackled and explored with a colleague. What metaphors would you use to:

- capture a mental image of the culture
- illustrate the most common management approach used
- caricature how managers have to behave if they are to be seen as successful
- describe the main power group
- illustrate the formal enterprise structure
- illustrate the rewards and sanctions in operation
- capture what the enterprise has learned to do that makes it successful
- illustrate what the enterprise needs to learn to do well
- describe how the enterprise responds to your need to learn

Your metaphors may start out with some fairly formal images but may become more exotic as you proceed. By reflecting on the meanings behind these metaphors you can begin to gain an insight into your view of the dominant culture.

As an additional check on your view it is helpful to reflect on a major piece of work or problem that you are currently tackling. Think of three metaphors that would describe the aspects of the culture that are influencing your approach to this piece of work. Then pick three metaphors that are contradicting or opposite to the ones you chose. Consideration of these contrasting metaphors and their underlying structures will highlight different aspects of your view of the culture.

This is in itself a learning opportunity but more so when you begin to link this view to the impact that it has on your approach to designing the learning organisation.

## Blocks to learning

We all experience blocks to learning. How these are interpreted and dealt with will depend partly on your view of yourself, the relative importance of the learning and your view of the dominant culture; in particular the power structure, controls, procedures and structures.

**Identifying the Culture and the Opportunities for Change** 107

| Step 1 | Step 2 | Step 3 | Step 4 | Step 5 Blockages to Learning | | | Step 6 Learning Strategies | |
|---|---|---|---|---|---|---|---|---|
| Key Areas | Measures of performance | Score (1-10) | Action to improve/maintain score | Tensions | Feelings | Org./Structural | Personal | Org./Structural |
| 1 | | | | | | | | |
| 2 | | | | | | | | |
| 3 | | | | | | | | |
| 4 | | | | | | | | |
| 5 | | | | | | | | |
| 6 | | | | | | | | |

*Fig. 5.2 Identifying blockages to learning*

## 108  Implementing the Learning Organisation

Everyone experiences these blocks at either a conscious or subconscious level and in the learning organisation it is vital that these blocks are faced and overcome. An effective way of reviewing blockages is to complete the proforma laid out in Fig. 5.2.

This involves the following steps:

**Step 1.** – Reflect on the six key areas in your current job that, if conducted to a high standard, will lead to your being successful.

These can be described in terms such as:

- maintaining an effective relationship with the major customers
- ensuring that the Production Organisation has the technology that will support all key production processes
- having a motivated and committed team
- convincing suppliers of the need for quality
- ensuring that all contract deadlines are met
- achieving targets in both profitability and investment return areas.

These should be written down in sufficient detail that they enable you to move to Step 2. Note that it may help if you write down against each area the types of outcomes that you would look for as indicators of success.

**Step 2.** – For each area describe the way in which you measure your performance. Remember that it is meant to reflect how you do this and not how your senior or others measure your performance. It may be that you may wish to do a comparison between your view of performance and that of your senior. They are rarely the same and can provide a key area for learning if you so wish.

Note that there is a tendency to write down what you do – avoid this and concentrate on how you measure performance, e.g.

Key area – to maintain an effective relationship with the major customers.

Expected Outcomes

- no contracts cancelled
- contracts extended
- changes to products and services readily accepted

Performance Measures

- the number of contracts cancelled as a percentage and the monthly trend
- the number of repeat orders from existing customers by categories of contract and size
- the time taken to reach agreement on a change and the cost recoveries as a percentage.

**Step 3.** – Give an estimate for each performance measure on how well you are doing on a scale of 1 to 10, ten being the top score.

Most people score themselves at around 7 or 8 for most areas. If you are scoring around 4 or 5 the next Step could be vital.

**Step 4.** – Reflect on what you have to do to either improve your performance or to maintain performance with less effort, time, resources and stress.

It may help to talk this over with a colleague and try to identify the things that you either need to learn about or need to learn to do.

**Step 5.** – Reflect on the blockages to your learning the things you identified in Step 4 above. These blockages fall into two categories.
- Personal blockages that present themselves as tensions such as: how to appear an expert when I lack up to date knowledge; how can I depend on staff that I do not have direct control over.
- Personal blockages that present themselves as things you feel such as: feeling anxious, feeling exploited, lacking commitment, disliking someone.
- Organisational and structural blockages where the processes, the rules, the policies, the rewards, the sanctions, the power groups, the hierarchy, your position, block you from learning.

**Step 6** – Pick one key blockage at a personal level and one presented by the enterprise organisation and structures and produce for each a strategy to explore and overcome the blockages.

As you work through the analysis you will need to go back over your key areas, performance measures and blockages to make connections and adjustments.

This exercise will have introduced you to a cornerstone of the learning organisation and a technique that can be used by both individuals and teams to identify blocks to learning, agree learning strategies and evaluate the emerging benefits. Before moving on to conduct the reviews of the enterprise it is important to reflect on the two reviews completed above and their relationships.

The review of your job and blockages to learning will have been heavily influenced by your view of the organisational culture. The strategies you will have identified, and might possibly pursue for your own learning, are in effect a form of self-development. Where organisations have relied on this self-development to promote a learning organisation there have been many failures to sustain the impetus. Empowering individuals in organisations where the hierarchy, power groups and in effect the culture are not supportive of learning presents formidable blocks to even the most intrepid manager. Disillusionment, apathy and withdrawal soon take over. This has been experienced by countless managers returning from training and development programmes who then perceive a culture that resists and blocks changes. An awareness of this phenomena has led to the growth of organisational development programmes, culture change programmes and business focused team development programmes.

The key to developing a learning organisation must therefore be to find ways of linking the individual's needs to learn how to master and create their own environment with the needs of the wider enterprise.

In studying the feasibility of implementing the learning organisation it is obvious that the existing culture will have been effective in creating and sustaining the enterprise performance. There is a widely held view that it is the task of those who drive the enterprise to ensure that the culture meets the current and future needs of the enterprise. In this book we are inviting you to view the existing culture from a perspective that inquires into its ability to promote and sustain learning. What we will be trying to determine is how the existing culture supports learning and how it may benefit from an improvement in its ability to accelerate the learning of both the individuals and the enterprise itself.

This is starting to move the notion of culture to the centre point in the design of the learning organisation. It is therefore important to undertake an initial review of this culture. It is also vital that before you move on to the next Step that you record your view of the culture, also the way in which this view impacts on your choice of learning strategies and the confidence you have that they will lead to improvement in your job performance and quality of life.

LEARNING MODEL – STEP 2

## REVIEWS OF THE ENTERPRISE

### Culture

In conducting this review it is important to decide how the information is to be collected and how it will be analysed. The aim is to capture a view of the culture as seen by the groups that are easily identified within the existing structure. The target groups should be those considered key to any support that will be needed at the early stages of implementing the learning organisation.

One way of collecting the information is, of course, by providing managers with proformas but this has its problems in that form filling when you are not really committed to an idea can be counter-productive. The suggestion is

### Identifying the Culture and the Opportunities for Change   111

that you enrol a number of key players into this review from the groups that represent those areas where initial learning organisation support may be required, e.g. corporate levels, operational levels, administration, human resource management, support services or from key team leaders and task group chairman. Having recruited your players, explain what is needed and how they will be involved in the review of their findings.

| Area | Questions | Comments |
|------|-----------|----------|
| 1 | What is seen as normal for senior/subordinate interaction? | |
| 2 | What slogans are used to tell new recruits how to view work? | |
| 3 | What slogans are used to impress customers about our group? | |
| 4 | What are the values underlying policy making and action towards staff and customers? | |
| 5 | What are new staff told to do if they want to fit into the group? | |
| 6 | How would new recruits describe the group after their first week? | |

*Fig. 5.3 Sub-culture of groups*

The proforma shown in Fig. 5.3. seeks fairly broad information and is relatively easy to compile and analyse. The information is grouped under six areas:

1. What is considered normal or acceptable organisational behaviour between staff at different levels, e.g. no-one questions the boss, everyone has a right to refuse, we want people to confront a silly request etc.

2. How do managers and staff describe what is seen as acceptable work behaviour, e.g. stay till the job is done, cut corners to get a result, using initiative is our hallmark, etc.

3. What does the enterprise pride itself on in terms of what it stands for in

the outside world, e.g. right first time, a centre of technological excellence, the customer is king, etc.

4. What are the key values that dominate policy making and actions towards customers and employees.

5. What are the key pointers that would be given to a new recruit that, if followed, would lead to their fitting in, e.g. get to know who holds the power, make sure that you demonstrate an area of expertise, never refuse to do a job, stand up and argue your point, etc.

6. How would a new recruit describe the enterprise based on first impressions and by talking to some of the key customers, e.g. a friendly and welcoming place, a sweat shop, a jumble of confusion and chaos, a friendly but scary place, a labyrinth full of experts and eager workers, a fun palace, etc.

The data can then be analysed using the proforma in Fig. 5.4 to focus on the views of the various groups. It is likely that these views will be widespread as sub-cultures rarely add up to a common enterprise-wide culture. This can be illustrated by checking back against your own analysis of culture derived from the use of the metaphor.

The statements gained from the reviews will have been based on certain sets of fundamental values or beliefs held by the group. If the group has been in existence for some period of time the beliefs will have become sets of basic assumptions that are used to guide decision making, action and behaviour.

| Group | Areas of group sub-culture | | | | | |
|---|---|---|---|---|---|---|
| | 1 | 2 | 3 | 4 | 5 | 6 |
| | Senior/ subordinate behaviour | Work norms | External values | Internal values | Group norms | Group style |
| 1 | | | | | | |
| 2 | | | | | | |
| 3 | | | | | | |
| 4 | | | | | | |
| 5 | | | | | | |

*Fig. 5.4 Comparing the sub-culture of the groups*

In a group that is new or one that is not working well together it is likely that the views will not be congruent with basic beliefs and could well represent rationalisations based on views developed in other cultures or on a speculative view about what they want to believe rather than what they really experience. At this stage it is important to stress that conventional wisdom states that new cultures cannot be imported into an organisation or group. The favoured approach is to move incrementally from the present culture to the new position.

## Boundaries and blockages to learning

The technique used to conduct the self-analysis of blockages to learning can be used by other managers in the organisation in order to gain a wider insight but this would be time consuming. The focus would also be on learning at the individual level whereas in this review we are looking for blockages at the wider enterprise level. The interest is on enterprise level learning. The implementation of the learning organisation will rely heavily, in the initial stages, on gaining support because it can demonstrate contributions at this level.

This review will therefore seek to establish information to help determine ways of tackling learning that will overcome these blockages to learning and hence provide a direct benefit to the enterprise.

The approach taken will be to consider both the external and internal environment of the organisation in terms of opportunities for learning that would benefit the enterprise, identifying perceived boundaries that would define and at the same time restrict these learning opportunities. We will then consider the blockages to seizing these learning opportunities that are created by the enterprise in terms of its culture. Finally, ways of bending these boundaries, prior to formal attempts to change them and strategies for addressing the blockages will be explored. Fig. 5.5. illustrates the approach to reviewing the external opportunities for learning. A list of opportunities is provided and you may wish to add to this based on your own situation. The boundaries and blockages need to be compiled. An example of how to complete this analysis is given below:

1. **Opportunity**
   (a) To learn from our major competitors.
2. **Boundaries**
   (a) The Top 3 in this country are known by name only plus limited background data.
   (b) The Top 1 in the world, based on those who are quoted in the same industry finance sector, is located in France.

## 114  Implementing the Learning Organisation

| Opportunity | Boundaries to opportunity | Blockages to learning | Way of bending boundary | Strategies for tackling blockage |
|---|---|---|---|---|
| Industry | | | | |
| Customers | | | | |
| Suppliers | | | | |
| Shareholders | | | | |
| Owners | | | | |
| Investors | | | | |
| Competitors | | | | |
| Technological developments | | | | |
| Research centres | | | | |
| Govt. bodies | | | | |
| Networks and collaborations | | | | |
| Social developments | | | | |
| Educational developments | | | | |
| Legal developments | | | | |

*Fig. 5.5  External opportunities for learning*

### 3. Blockages
   (a) No experience at conducting competitor analysis.
   (b) Not certain which sector of industry to focus on.
   (c) Not certain of the threat provided by the big players.
   (d) Worried that competitors may surface from other industry sectors.
   (e) Should we be looking at performance, processes or products/services?

### Identifying the Culture and the Opportunities for Change   115

4.  **Bending the boundaries**
    (a) Look at Top 1 in the world first and derive our approach from the findings.

5.  **Strategies to address the blockages**
    (a) Put together a team with a co-opted expert from a consultancy.
    (b) Complete a desk-based study of the industry structure and published information on one competitor.
    (c) Visit the Top 1 in the world and ask basic questions.

This does constitute a potentially large review of learning opportunities and at this stage it is advisable to select those areas that would provide an obvious pay-off to the enterprise. What is important here is to develop a way of thinking about opportunities for learning and how to approach boundary setting and strategies for overcoming blockages. Fig.5.6 illustrates the approach required for reviewing the internal opportunities for learning. A list of oportunities is also provided and you may wish to add to or amend this list. Some boundaries are suggested in the proforma such as the hierarchy

| Opportunity | Boundaries to Opportunity [1] | Blockages to Learning [2] | | Way of bending Boundary | Strategies for tackling Blockage |
|---|---|---|---|---|---|
| | | Cultural | Personal | | |
| Business Development | | | | | |
| Product/ Service Development | | | | | |
| Process Development | | | | | |
| Projects | | | | | |
| Change Programmes such as TQM | | | | | |

[1] Note that these boundaries will be created by: the organisational structures, hierarchy, functional disciplines, geographic locations, competences and skills and resources.

[2] Cultural blockages will be grouped under: senior subordinate behaviour, work norms, external values, internal values, group norms and style.

Personal blockages will be made up of tensions created by roles and position plus personal feelings.

*Fig. 5.6 Internal opportunities for learning*

and structure while blockages are seen as deriving from the dominant culture and more personal perspectives. Strategies for addressing these blockages will require a high level of creativity.

Having completed these two major reviews a clear picture should now be emerging as to how the culture, opportunities for learning and strategies for redefining boundaries and tackling blockages all constitute the main thrust of the learning organisation. Linking the enterprise level, team and individual learning now becomes a practical proposition.

## Previous change programmes

Most organisations will have experienced change programmes that have probably been described as:

- strategic in their focus where the stimulus has come from outside of the organisation
- operational where the trigger has been to improve aspects of performance
- organisational where the drive has been to create new structures, change the culture, introduce new administrative process and ways of working or to introduce new technology.

In considering the implementation of the learning organisation we are looking at a change programme that will have an impact on all three of the above areas.

Conducting a review of previous change programmes will provide an opportunity to understand the way in which the enterprise has learned to respond to and use such programmes. To guide this review a series of questions are presented below and it is suggested that key managers are sought as sources for this information.

For each change programme that has taken place over the past five years the following questions should be posed:

1. What was the name of the programme and was it primarily: strategic in focus, operational or enterprise-wide?
2. When was the programme initiated and completed?
3. Was it enterprise-wide or limited to particular divisions, functions, areas, etc?
4. What were the pressures and tensions that created the need for change?
5. What were the stated and the underlying purposes?
6. Who were the key sponsors?

### Identifying the Culture and the Opportunities for Change    117

7. How was the programme communicated and introduced?
8. Who were the key implementors?
9. Was the programme interpreted by managers as central to the core activity of the enterprise or as peripheral?
10. Was the programme interpreted by managers as being introduced in an incremental or a radical way?
11. How was the programme implemented, e.g. off-site training, on-job activities, task teams, using consultants, etc.?
12. Was the programme costed and what were the approximate costs incurred?
13. Was there any attempt to evaluate the effectiveness of the programme and if so what methods were used?
14. What were the key benefits and outcomes?
15. Was the programme deemed a success or a failure?
16. What critical incidents led to its success or failure?
17. What were the major lessons from the programme and have these been incorporated into subsequent programmes?
18. What other programmes are being considered?

This represents a rigorous review of previous change programmes and it is unlikely that reviews of this type have been conducted in the enterprise. There are many reasons for this ranging from:

- difficulty in determining a clear purpose for a change programme
- that the process of change produces effects that are subjected to an on-going rationalisation process, thus fudging the original purpose
- the difficulty of pre-determining the areas where resistance to change will be met and in detecting or countering it when it occurs
- the focus is rarely on learning and hence opportunities for feedback and reflection by both sponsors and users is not built into the process
- the failure to gain commitment to the change
- the low level of experience in change management within the enterprise.

Where an organisation has experienced a number of change programmes over the past few years there is a danger that saturation point may have been reached. Managers' enthusiasm for change can rapidly turn to apathy and then resistance. This occurs where the changes are perceived to be either not central to the mainstream activity, not being carried through to completion or trying to change a culture which has become the perceived reality and comfortable. The analysis of past programmes is therefore key to forming a view of what the enterprise has learned from introducing such programmes. This will pave the way for determining how best to introduce the learning organisation so that it is seen as:

- in tune with the key interests of the enterprise
- building on the existing culture and providing obvious improvements
- using a change model approach that appeals to the perspectives on change held by the power groups and the wider management
- not threatening previous change outcomes.

LEARNING MODEL – STEP 3

## READING TEXT AND REFLECTION

In this section two sub-topics are introduced to help promote reflection on the findings from the reviews. They are aimed at developing thinking and understanding about how to set about introduction of the learning organisation. The notions presented are used to encourage reflection on perspectives and as a basis for developing persuasive arguments to support the implementation approach. The areas covered by these sub-topics are:

- development of organisational culture
- managing complex change.

### Development of organisational culture

There are as many views about what organisational culture is as there are about what is a good leader. A definition of culture that most would support is where a group of people who have worked together for some time are behaving in a consistent way. This could obviously apply to a convict gang or to a group of scientists in a research centre. We talk about having a set of shared philosophies and common fundamental values. It is likely that the members of the group share beliefs about the way organisational life works and would have expectations as to how they want to be treated and how they would treat others. It would be relatively easy to identify what the group's norms for behaviour were as the myths that make these norms acceptable would be relayed through stories and shared humour. There would also be a clear indication of the use of rituals or physical demonstrations that would be used consistently by the group to induct new members, re-enforce group beliefs and maintain the power of the leaders.

## Identifying the Culture and the Opportunities for Change    119

This notion of a group culture that can be observed in organisations is very powerful. It is also attractive in that it suggests a way of explaining in one swoop how organisations really work and how by harnessing this culture the path to achieving the goals of the organisation would be secured. This notion poses some key questions for those approaching implementation of the learning organisation. Firstly, if culture is developed over time and represents the shared learning of a group then what stimulates or fosters this learning? Secondly, how powerful is the group culture in determining behaviours and what strategies are available to influence culture at group and organisational levels? In effect we are asking: how is organisational culture created and how can it be managed?

Many organisations by-pass these questions when considering a major change programme. The assumptions made are that the culture exists, can be easily described and that an ideal culture to match the vision of the enterprise can be articulated. Some examples of this would be where an organisation wishes to become more customer focused, more innovative, more service orientated, more flexible, more profit orientated, more ecologically sensitive, more employee centred, more quality conscious. The list is endless and to become more learning focused can also be intrepreted under this broad banner of a culture change. The problem is that many organisations have gone to great lengths to identify an appropriate culture in the sense of being one that matches the vision and mission of the enterprise and then either failed to influence the existing culture or achieve the desired enterprise outcomes. Some of course would claim to have achieved both or rationalise that it was just bad luck.

The central aspect to understanding how cultures develop and change would appear to be the main focus for this study of the learning organisation. Identifying and producing a culture to fit the vision and mission of the enterprise at some point in the future would perhaps lie in the realms of mystery and the occult. If we can concentrate on understanding the way in which learning plays a part in the formation and development of culture then this should provide a start point for any design of an effective learning organisation. It is possible to conceive of the learning organisation being used to create the environment in which a culture can develop that becomes fully integrated with the aims of the enterprise. So let us return to our two original questions:

- what stimulates or fosters the learning that creates the organisational culture?
- does the culture determine behaviours and what can be done to change the culture?

## Learning and culture formation

For a manager joining an organisation there is the immediate question of how to maintain personal independence in terms of behaviours, values, beliefs and assumptions held and how to integrate into the new group. If the manager becomes completely integrated then personal identity is lost whereas separation may have initial advantages but in the long run may lead to failure to harness the power of the group. Some managers wrestle with this dilemma on obtaining a major promotion and when joining groups where their expertise is less than the perceived group norm.

In inducting the new manager a cohesive and effective group will be attempting to help the manager integrate quickly in order that efforts can be focused on the external task of the group. In less cohesive groups where the individuals have not reached a state of integration themselves and are uncommitted to the goals of the group then the integration of the new manager will be a much slower process.

Many organisations use formal induction programmes to speed up this integration whereas others rely on individuals making their own links and learning about the culture in a less structured way. In the final count the new manager has to determine at a personal level the extent to which the group and organisational environment can be managed and mastered either through maintaining independence or through integration.

Individual personality traits also have a major influence on how the group culture develops. This effect was explained in Chapter 3. The tendency is for individuals to either influence or be attracted to groups that approach information gathering and processing in ways that suit their own personality traits. For example, those with a sensing-thinking (ST) profile will favour a bureaucratic organisational approach, where the information is gathered in a systematic way with procedures used to solve problems and a focus on the problems of today. Whereas for those with an intuitive-thinking (NT) profile will prefer a more project orientated or matrix way of working which would be found in research and development areas. This approach would favour the identification of patterns in data, be associated with risk taking in their thinking, a desire to reduce complex problems to simple ones and remain objective. This group influence can then be added to by considering the preferred styles that individuals use when identifying and tackling problems where creativity is needed and when adopting leadership and management roles.

One could argue that these personality characteristics are random within any one group but that does ignore two factors; firstly, that individuals may be attracted to groups in the first place because it appeals to their personalities and preferences and secondly, that once in a group some individuals are unaware of the effects or stresses that are being created by the mismatch between personality and the group norm. The tendency is for individuals then to learn how to handle or cope with these mismatches. This learning can be potentially disruptive to the group culture. Defensive routines are learned and conflict suppressed. Ideas are no longer challenged and creative learning with the associated personal risk that it brings is no longer a possibility. This learning can then be translated to the group itself which then internalises these approaches. For new members this style then represents 'the way it is around here'.

The group has thus learned to preserve social relations by hiding the thinking that is behind the views of the individual members. Compliance rather than commitment then becomes a characteristic of the group and thus lends itself to ready manipulation from outside forces or from a new entrant. The danger is that the organisation may be seeking or requiring commitment from the group and mistake their compliant response as one of commitment. This may be one of the major factors behind the failure of many organisational development change programmes. The paradox here is that the group culture that might best suit a rapidly changing environment may be one that appears to be challenging, lacking cohesiveness, disruptive and at times chaotic. Most of these characteristics would be ones that conventional management practice would see as 'anti-culture'.

Another major influence on culture is where the critical incidents or events in the history of the group have a major formative effect. If the response of the group to the event was seen in retrospect as successful in terms of reducing the anxiety of the group or leading to obvious benefits then this response will be institutionalised. Stories develop around, 'how it really was' and these provide a way for the group to see themselves as a reality and a powerful force.

New members to the group are told these stories and encouraged to demonstrate their support for the behaviour and values of the group. Over a period of time a group that experiences a number of critical incidents will use these demonstrations of group values to build boundaries as to who is considered a member of the group, what constitutes areas of authority and expertise and the role that the group plays within the wider organisation. In this way norms of behaviour and the underlying assumptions that support these norms are established.

This can be contrasted with a situation in which a group is brought together and has to respond quickly to an external threat or task. For example, a group on an outdoor training course will be lost and in an initial state of chaos over how to diagnose a problem, determine a course of action, take action, evaluate outcomes etc. The event is usually aimed at helping individuals find out how groups form. Their response is nearly always to seek a leader who will assume responsibility, represent authority and create the canopy under which individuals can pursue their own search for intimacy, support and security. The group in effect learns to deal with its problems, to achieve the goals and build a structure and way of working with which it is reasonably comfortable. Through a process of rationalisation over past critical incidents the group learns what constitutes successful practices and which problems and practices are to be avoided. This is a fairly clear way of learning but in areas where the outcome of an incident was not deemed a success or failure but say just partially successful then the tendency is to keep using the approach far beyond the point where an outsider would clearly see the inefficiencies and persistent failures.

This tendency to continue to use an approach to, for example: problem identification, analysis and decision making that fails to lead to success in many cases continues to be used by the group. The group has in effect institutionalised learning that only produces marginal results, only putting obvious failures under a process of critical review. Errors are in this way continually built into the group approaches.

This notion of learned approaches to problems by the group can be extended to the way the group learns to believe about itself, its place in the wider organisation, its capabilities, its influence based on past incidents. These are usually couched in statements such as: 'we really know how to get close to our customers', 'our engineers are able to design to a cost every time', 'we know how to run the business using finance from our customers', 'everyone in the organisation is dedicated to safety', 'we are seen by our competitors as the market leaders in the innovation of new products', 'our strength is in our ability to respond to technological change'. Assuming that these are statements of belief and not mere exhortations they will continue to dominate group thinking and behaviour until they either fail to gain response from the wider organisations or obvious evidence to the contrary appears. The group may choose to ignore or avoid this evidence for some considerable time, rationalising and explaining failure in order to avoid the conflict and changes that would then have to be made to what will have become a key feature of the group culture. The danger is that when the group accepts the information that shows their failure to perform and the decisions that might have led to the failure their response may be to determine never to engage in that area of business activity again. In the absence of any clear and agreed ways of capturing and reviewing the learning around these critical incidents the group is in a situation where learning takes place that may be counter to the longer term interests of the group.

Another and perhaps obvious factor that helps formulate the group culture is that of the actions of key individuals in the organisation. For example at the formative stages of organisations the founder provides

## Identifying the Culture and the Opportunities for Change    123

pointed messages as to what is expected, how the game is to be played and the sorts of behaviour that will be rewarded and punished. Senior managers will follow this lead and thus pass on the initial messages about this culture to the enterprise. Other managers will take a careful note of how actions are interpreted in terms of encouragement and criticism by the senior figures and quickly learn the appropriate responses.

Groups within the enterprise learn how to survive and manage themselves within this system of apparent cultural requirements. In the early stages of forming an organisation this entrepreneurial or style dictated from the centre will provide an effective response from the various groups or functions within the enterprise. But as the enterprise matures, its external environment changes and the founder members become more remote from the daily action, then the original culture becomes separated out from the organisational forms and personal systems that have been created. The original culture will then continue to exist in the behaviours and values of the managers unless it clashes or conflicts with the way the structures need to operate. For example, where a founder instils an open management style with risk-taking associated with high rewards and instant punishment this will eventually clash with an enterprise that becomes bureaucratic and functionalised. Then the founder will either resort to breaking the enterprise into smaller parts and reviving the original culture or seek someone who can support the new bureaucratic structure and promote the relevant culture.

The final area in our exploration of the factors which stimulate learning that results in culture formation is the one of rewards. There are various types of rewards available in enterprises and ways in which they are allocated to individuals and groups. It will be obvious that these rewards have a major influence on how the culture is created. The most obvious reward is financial which can include salary, bonus incentives, stock and share options and tangible benefits such as cars and expense allowances. Other areas include: the job itself in terms of the extent to which it offers opportunities for personal growth satisfaction and promotion; the status provided by the job and the wider opportunities for fulfilment that it provides and finally by providing a career path. These rewards are used to provide incentives for individuals and give an indication of where behaviour is consistent with the organisation's cultural norms and work outputs.

The culture itself can therefore have an influence on the reward system because the culture embodies the beliefs and values of the power group and key members. Examples of this would be where an enterprise had a culture that was dominated by profitability and growth with profit centre managers working on a percentage share profit scheme or another enterprise where scientific deduction and breakthrough were dominant.

A problem arises where the dominant culture transcends an enterprise in which a number of sub-cultures exist. Within these sub-cultures the dominant reward system can have threatening and disruptive effects. An example of this would be in a hospital where the power group culture may have swung from patient care and total community provision towards one favouring profitability and cost reduction.

The reward systems also affect the culture in terms of the type and calibre of staff that the enterprise is able to attract and retain. Many talented younger people will be attracted to an enterprise that offers rewards and the opportunity to be challenged and stretched. Those that offer less attractive reward packages may find that they attract individuals who are not looking for commitment to an ideal or vision and will accept a low reward for a low risk and non-challenging work environment.

In summary we have looked at six areas that can be seen to foster the learning that creates group cultures. These are:

**1.** *Social integration:* where a manager learns how to integrate into a new group and makes trade-offs between maintaining personal identity and relating to the group norms.

**2.** *Personality and learning from previous cultures:* where personality traits and style preferences towards creativity and leadership influence adaptation. Seeking a working structure that is comfortable.

**3.** *Developing defensive approaches:* where individuals and groups learn how to hide the thinking behind key ideas. The paradox of wanting groups to be chaotic and confrontational while seeking cohesiveness on work approaches.

**4.** *Critical incidents:* the use of rationalisations on historic events in order to develop best practice for the group. The danger of continuing to use outdated and inappropriate models.

**5.** *Impact of the founders and key leaders:* how the culture promoted by the founder may become inappropriate as the environment and the enterprise itself changes.

**6.** *Impact of reward systems:* how financial, job, status and career aspirations are used as reward areas and how this influences culture.

By focusing on the formation of culture it is possible to isolate these six areas and see how they help formulate ideas on implementing the learning organisation. Culture is the obvious focus for considering change and tackling the second of the two original questions will demonstrate what can be done to bring about changes in the culture.

## Changing the culture and the behaviour

If we are to consider changing the culture and the consequences on behaviour of the group it would help to understand what the culture enables the group to do. In this way any ideas on how to introduce changes and their effects can be made on a sound basis.

Culture provides two basic functions for the group. It enables the group to address and manage the task of mastering the external environment in which it operates and manage its internal affairs in a way that suits the members and the tasks in hand.

From the external environment there will be many signals and pressures that have to be interpreted and acted upon in both proactive and reactive ways. For example, a decision on the type of client or customer to be sought, how to respond to challenges from another group for resources or opportunities to do work. The group response will usually be focused on actions and decisions from the nominated leader or head of the group but what we are arguing here is that this response is dominated and influenced by the group culture itself. These influences will include sentiment, feelings, attitudes, beliefs, assumptions, ways of working and established levels of expertise and competences. The function of the group culture when adapting to this external environment will therefore be to provide:

- a shared understanding about the primary task of the group and the functions that it is to carry out
- agreement on the climate and atmosphere that will be created within the group
- agreement on the goals being sought
- agreement on how the talents and resources of the group are to be harnessed, managed and controlled
- clarity as to how success and achievement are to be measured and the value that will be attributed to these measures.

It will be obvious that the above functions of the group culture are almost directly translatable to those of the wider enterprise. This perhaps points up why many culture change programmes only address the last item, namely, the measurement of future performance, e.g. the determination to treat every customer like a shareholder in the company. By bypassing the other functions of group culture the spotlight for change is made too narrow. An understanding of the wider aspects of the functions of culture for an enterprise or group is therefore crucial.

Some sub-functions that the culture will provide are just as important to the members. These will include provision of a common language that will accelerate the interchange and development of ideas and ways of working;

definition of the boundaries of responsibilities and the rules that will govern the formal working of the group and the interfaces to other groups; the authority and power that the group can exert over other groups and how this is to be used; the style and climate that is to be maintained in order to promote the effectiveness of the group in areas such as: creativity, critical debate and exchange of ideas, learning, personal development and discipline. Finally a sub-function would be to help the group members cope with and learn from their experiences both within the group and outside the group.

In an active culture group members will be constantly questioning, testing and developing these functions and sub-functions. The degree of activity will depend on three key factors:

- the boundaries that the group perceives both external and internal to the enterprise in terms of key stakeholders and power groups
- the degree to which the group is setting out to master its external environment and the degree of success experienced
- the extent to which the internal environment is satisfying the members at both group and individual levels.

This suggests a need to seek a fit between the group culture and its environment so that the group can achieve mastery of that environment and hence satisfaction of stakeholders and group members.

This places culture at the heart of a successful learning organisation with the notion of the learning organisation subsuming all the groups and hence cultures within the enterprise. Anyone wishing to introduce strategies or place unacceptable demands on an enterprise that has a unified and cohesive culture will face severe difficulties if these demands are not in resonance with the dominant culture, e.g. introducing a group bonus scheme to a department of top class sales representatives or proposing a scheme in a hospital where the consultants are to become cost centre managers. If, on the other hand, the culture is not cohesive and key parts of the enterprise has cultures that conflict with others then change will be easier to introduce. The problem will then be to identify and maintain the new cultures that emerge. Let us consider some ways in which attempts are made to influence cultures.

The most common method is for the Corporate leader to espouse some top level values. These are then interpreted and used by managers along with a change programme made up of training workshops and task teams to implement the required changes. The new culture is then seen to have been introduced. A variant of this is where a new leader is appointed and having reviewed the performance of the enterprise decides to introduce a change of culture and hence performance. In an enterprise that has developed strong culture features such as leadership style, where authority and power lie and

## Identifying the Culture and the Opportunities for Change   127

how the outside environment is to be managed will all be understood and supported. If this enterprise is surviving and adapting well in this environment then the new leader will find it difficult to introduce changes. If on the other hand the enterprise is already in trouble or envisages major problems on the horizon then it will be easier to stimulate changes. It is likely that the managers will not have been committed to the existing culture and hence will respond quickly to a new style, a new message or a new vision. These changes will then be implemented by familiar techniques such as:

- training programmes both on and off the job
- changes to working practices
- restructuring and enrichment of jobs
- introduction of a more participative management style
- mass and continuous communication of the new vision and corporate messages
- job rotations
- changes to the reward system
- development of task teams around new products and services
- restructuring
- collaboration and takeovers
- replacement of key job holders
- introduction of new technology
- divestment of work groups and structures.

These change strategies can be seen to hit at the features of the culture but not directly at the way in which culture develops. The resulting changes in behaviour may only be sustained if the messages and behaviours are constantly reinforced.

There are, of course, alternative and less drastic ways of affecting culture changes. These rely on:

- changing behaviour rather than underlying perceptions and mental models. This is appropriate where the required change is simply dependent on changes in behaviour. This behaviour can then be easily sustained through the use of sanctions and rewards
- making a more creative use of the existing culture. This can be useful where a re-orientation to how the groups perceive themselves will provide the required change.

In the next section we will explore the ways in which the complex changes involving culture and other aspects of group behaviour can be managed.

## Managing complex change

There are two fundamental perspectives that will determine how the management of change in an enterprise is approached. Firstly, a view based on certainty where the present position is deemed to be known and the future desired state can be described with some confidence. The second is where the present state is seen as unacceptable and it is not clear as to the desired future state or at least there is a high level of uncertainty around the vision.

Most managers would argue that the certainty perspective is the one that should be sought after if the change is to be implemented successfully and the goals achieved. Strategic change programmes and organisational development programmes support the certainty approach and would identify the following features as being characteristics of a successful programme:

- the identification of clear goals and objectives that are supported by the majority of those in the enterprise
- having a content and coverage that is seen as feasible in the current environment
- one that fitted the time constraints and other pressures on the enterprise
- having the support of the power groups
- staffed by competent people
- having scope for the use of creativity that would lead to successful innovations
- encompassing activities such as: participation, good communications
- making use of the existing structures and being linked to the accepted reward systems.

With the certainty view the factors that will influence the success of the programme are deemed to be well understood as are the processes that need to be used. In managing in this environment the use of conventional project management and rational logical approaches dominate. The strategies and approaches to introducing change are legitimised through the use of project task teams, regular use of key management processes and an emphasis on the maintenance of the purposefulness of the activity. This is represented by the use of organisational rituals such as reporting, briefings and presentations.

Depending upon the style of the change leader and the culture of the enterprise various approaches to overcoming any resistance to the changes will be used. Encouraging participation and enlisting support are the most common approaches along with in-depth counselling on major blockages. In some enterprises this leads to the use of conventional negotiation and

## Identifying the Culture and the Opportunities for Change 129

formulation of agreements. Finally the use of explicit and implicit coercion is not to be ruled out.

As can be seen this certainty approach does combine the rational-logical and the empowering-the-individual approaches to managing change. It does also focus clearly on changing the culture if and where it is seen as necessary. The change leader using this certainty view can be seen as moving through various stages in the programme.

**Step 1.** – Where the leader determines the extent to which the steps required to achieve the vision and mission will conflict with the current accepted strategies. This is where the degree of change to existing mind-sets of the key groups is assessed and tested.

**Step 2.** – Here the leader sets out to challenge the existing mind-sets. This may take the form of promoting the potential threats that are being faced, focusing on the competitive weakness of the enterprise, playing on old concerns or successful performances in the past. This step is the most difficult as it is attacking conventional wisdom and it is easy to create a high level of alienation or worse to cause the majority of the members to switch off.

**Step 3.** – The culture is now under direct challenge and this is managed through introducing changes to the power structure that are deemed acceptable. These changes can take the form of appointing task teams or forming multi-disciplinary teams with leaders who are committed to the changes.

**Step 4.** – By this stage most of the culture changes will have been initiated and resistance overcome.
Formal changes to the structure can now be made, systems introduced, training instituted and reward systems legitimised.

This certainty approach is well documented and fits neatly into conventional and well-tried methods of managing change. The approach works well at both the strategic and the operational change levels.

Where the uncertainty perspective is taken then the approaches are perhaps less familiar. Here the present position of the enterprise in relation to the external environment is less certain and the internal culture perhaps more fluid or varied. Due to the turbulence experienced in this environment the idea of there being an end goal is not seen as being a realistic one and the means by which change can be made are not obvious. This may sound like a situation of utter chaos but for many managers this is probably the reality even if it is not explicitly recognised and stated. Most managers see their role as being to bring order to chaos and will either do this by using conventional management approaches or by rationalising that it is only a temporary phenomenon. Alternatively when faced with uncertain conditions over an extended period of time managers will tend to adopt a risk and change avoidance posture.

Many enterprises have taken on board and accepted the reality that their situation is uncertain and have evolved ways of introducing change programmes. These approaches are characterised by their exploratory nature. The future is seen in terms of desirable domains and broad directions rather than quantifiable goals. A range of short-term goals are established and the most promising ones then pursued as the direction becomes clearer. Core teams are established and encouraged to adopt flexible and creative approaches with an emphasis on discovery and boundary breaking. The managers are encouraged to adopt temporary structures and hierarchies that are broken down when the discovery has been made.

The skills of the change leader now become paramount as the focus is on problem finding not problem solving. The idea of teams building and sharing maps that can illuminate the way forward and be changed is encouraged. Leaders and team members are given the opportunity to talk out their concerns and conflicts and helped to resist settling for 'it's either this or that' philosophies. The notion of living with paradoxes is thus encouraged, for example where a manager was wanting control yet valuing the ideas that freedom generates. In effect the change leader is encouraging the acceptance of chaos as a feature of growth and change as opposed to seeing this as a threat; the skill being to be able to put temporary boundaries around this chaos that can be used to pull out the learning that will inform future action. This uncertainty approach does make extensive use of the power of informal groups and requires a leadership style that does not readily integrate with the more conventional management role where direction and control are paramount.

This mix of roles, the visionary architect and the directive manager is often resolved by appointing two people as the change leaders. They need to recognise and value each other's approaches and welcome the creative opportunities that will result from the tension that the roles create. There is that awful story where a visionary and a conventional manager find themselves stranded in a cave in deepest Africa. They become hungry and decide to allocate roles. The visionary offers to go out hunting for food. His approach was to sit on a branch overhanging the pathway then jump on the back of a lion that walked underneath. Grabbing the lion's ears the visionary directed the lion, at speed, into the cave. Jumping down lightly he said, 'Well, you skin this one while I go and find another'. This story, perhaps, points up the difficulties of the uncertainty approach and the need to keep a firm hold on the overall requirements of the enterprise stakeholders and the quality of life sought after by the managers and employees.

## Identifying the Culture and the Opportunities for Change 131

Organisations that find themselves in very turbulent situations have evolved ways of using informal groups to explore changes and test out solutions while encouraging the majority of the employees to concentrate on securing a degree of stability and order. The innovations and changes that evolve can then be integrated into the orderly structure. These are known as 'skunk' works and are common in so-called high tech industries. It is conceivable that their use could be effectively employed in what might appear to be more stable or potentially moribund enterprises. Fig. 5.7 illustrates these two approaches and how they both rely on learning.

In summary we have explored ways in which complex change programmes can be approached. The external context in which the change is being considered is obviously vital as is the cohesiveness and strength of the dominant culture. The notion that managers will strive for rationality and logical approaches to managing change has been offered and the dangers of diagnosing certainty when uncertainty exists have been highlighted.

Conventional management skills and approaches have been seen to be essential to successful implementations where the current positions, causal links and future position are relatively certain. The learning that underpins this approach favours project management, empowering staff and the use of politics and power. Where the present position is uncertain and turbulent conditions in the external environment make the prediction of a favourable future unrealistic then a more exploratory approach is recommended. The learning associated with this approach favours visionary leadership, encouraging the use of creativity, networks and informal groups. The importance of some underpinning of conventional management processes in this approach is also recommended in order that the benefits that are identified can be captured and realised.

## LEARNING MODEL – STEPS 4, 5, 6

### FORMING AND TESTING PERSPECTIVES

This section provides the opportunity for some reflection on the reviews and the above texts.

The focus of this chapter has been on gaining an insight into the prevailing culture and identifying where blocks to learning are being experienced. By gaining this insight you will be in a position to gauge the cohesiveness of the dominant culture and where the sub-cultures differ within particular Divisions, Departments and functions.

The review of external and internal opportunities for learning at the enterprise level, the blockages to learning and strategies for tackling them

**Certainty Approach:**

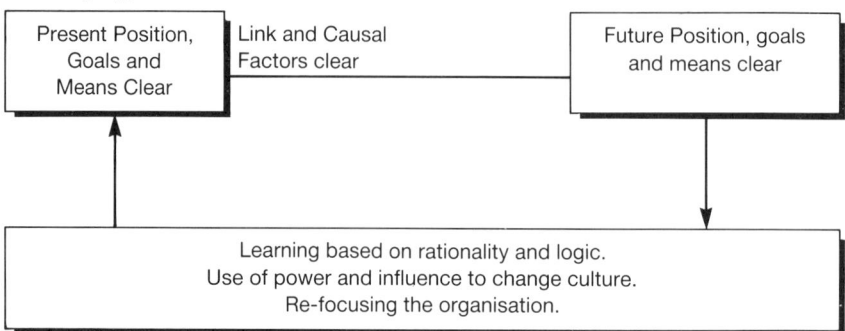

**Uncertainty Approach:**

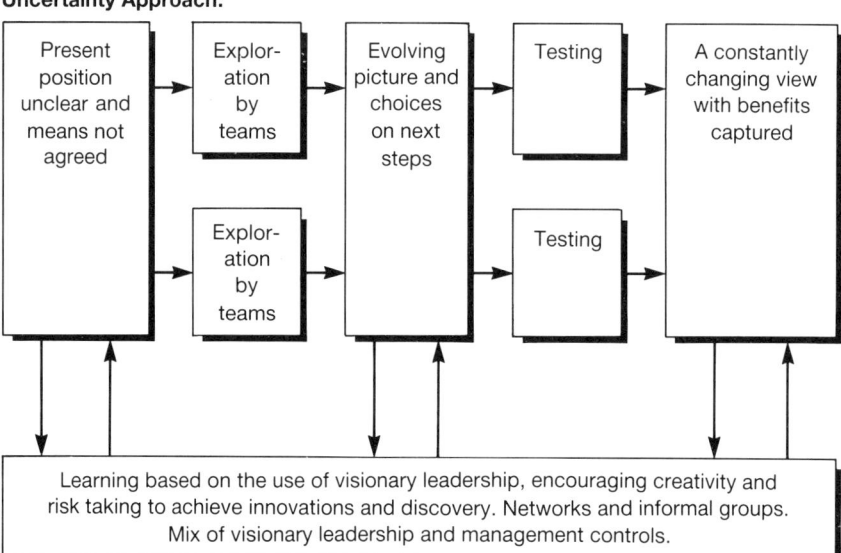

*Fig. 5.7 Managing complex change*

will have provided some links back into the culture. The review of the previous change programmes and how they were introduced and managed also provide a means of testing the degree of culture clash and areas of fit when considering implementing the learning organisation.

The first reading text has addressed the ways in which culture is formed and how change programmes often fail to tackle the key determinants of

## Identifying the Culture and the Opportunities for Change    133

culture. Culture was seen to be at the centre of group and individual learning and therefore a key to the learning organisation. The second text was on managing complex change and highlighted the consequences of adopting a certainty approach to change programmes as opposed to one where uncertainty dominates.

It is vital that any notions around implementation of the learning organisation take note of these differences. Where the environment is deemed to be turbulent and futures uncertain, a more exploratory and emergent approach was argued as being more appropriate. The learning and skills for both perspectives were stressed as being of the highest order and in many cases the exploratory approach may well be set within a framework that provides opportunities for capturing benefits as they appear.

For the learning organisation it will be important to assess the impact on the culture and the extent to which a balance needs to be struck between setting clear short-term goals and using rational logical – project management based approaches and using a more open and exploratory approach. Identifying medium-term objectives and seeing the future in terms of desirable domains or areas of interest rather than certainties that can be quantified.

Based on these reviews and readings it should now be possible to articulate perspectives on:

- your view of the existing dominant and sub-cultures
- where blockages to your learning occur that are related to your job and performance
- what action you can take to overcome these blockages at a personal level and at an enterprise level
- what the dominant cultures and sub-cultures are within the enterprise
- how easy or otherwise it is to recruit group leaders to help capture these sub-cultures
- the external and internal opportunities for enterprise level learning and strategies for tackling these blockages
- the use made of previous change programmes and the problems or opportunities this provides for ideas on implementing the learning organisation
- how cultures form and where learning takes place
- how to tackle a culture change programme in your particular setting
- the way in which perspectives as to certainty or uncertainty can influence approaches to managing complex change programmes. Also the skill and learning needed in both types of programme
- how a complex change programme can be introduced into your enterprise. Also what you need to learn if this implementation is to be successful.

### 134  Implementing the Learning Organisation

These are all quite complex perspectives and it is once again important that you attempt to capture them in diagram or note form. Some key questions will no doubt have been raised by this chapter and these should be highlighted and tackled with a colleague.

Your perspective on how to tackle change in your enterprise should by now be much clearer. The opportunity exists but the task involved may appear enormous. If you find this a daunting prospect then recognise this as the tension that needs to build up between your vision and your perception of current reality. Avoid the temptation at this stage of lowering your sights or rationalising about current reality. This tension is the key to your making the creative leaps that will be required in an area as important as that of building the learning organisation.

LEARNING MODEL – STEP 7

## COMMENTARY AND LINKS TO CHAPTER 6

This chapter will have crystallised your thinking about introducing changes in the context of your own enterprise. The important point is to be clear about how learning pervades all enterprise activities. At times learning is explicit but often hidden in the culture and subtleties of thinking and behaviour. We are now moving to a position where the learning in the previous chapters is reaching a point where we can start putting it all together.

But first we need to focus on what could be the main success or stumbling block for implementation. Chapter 6 looks at the part played by key stakeholders. These are the people, groups, functions, other divisions, external organisations and investors who have to be satisfied if the enterprise is to be allowed to survive, change and grow.

# 6

# ASSESSING THE BENEFITS

## INTRODUCTION

It is suggested that three days are allocated to this topic over an elapsed period of three weeks. An outline study plan is shown in Fig. 6.1. The approach will be to provide guidance on how to conduct each of the steps in the learning model. This will begin with a review of the outcomes and benefits that you are seeking from the implementation of the learning organisation. This is followed by a review of the key stakeholders internal and external to the enterprise and by identifying their primary requirements for performance and outcomes from the enterprise and how these are evaluated. Opportunities for using the learning organisation to support or satisfy these requirements will then be explored. Finally, arguments and ways of using cost benefit models to support proposals for implementing the learning organisation will be developed. Checklists and proformas are used to help focus these reviews.

A series of readings then help the reflection stage, providing an opportunity to test out perspectives before moving on to Chapter 7 where the learning from the study is put together.

LEARNING MODEL – STEP I

### OUTCOMES AND BENEFITS BEING SOUGHT – A SELF ANALYSIS

In Chapter 3 various purposes and objectives for this study into implementing the learning organisation were considered. There were four key objectives:

- to produce an overview of the strategic and operational activities of the current enterprise
- to understand the vision of the future that is driving the enterprise
- to determine ways of moving the enterprise activity to a learning focus
- to determine how the major stakeholders can benefit from the learning organisation.

| Steps in the learning model | Activity | Sub-topic studied | Study days |
|---|---|---|---|
| 1 | Self-analysis of the outcomes and benefits being sought | – | 1/2 |
| 2 | • Review of the organisation:<br><br>• Key stakeholders and their requirements for performance and outcomes from the organisation.<br><br>• The measures used to evaluate the performance and outcomes both formally and informally.<br><br>• Opportunities for the learning organisation to support or satisfy the stakeholders.<br><br>• Preparing cost benefit arguments. | – | 1 |
| 3 | • Reading text and reflection | • Influencing values<br><br>• Models for evaluating change programmes | 1 |
| 4/5/6 | • Reflection and testing of views, ideas, perspectives and concerns. | – | 1/2 |
| 7 | Reading text | Commentary and links to next Chapters | |

*Fig. 6.1 Study plan*

In this chapter we are focusing on the fourth objective and will begin by exploring your views on the outcomes and benefits that you will be seeking. This will help to prepare the ground for exploring the views of the key stakeholders.

From the work done in Chapter 3, Step 1, on vision building a clear view of what you passionately want to achieve (the vision) and what you will fundamentally try to become (the mission) will have been developed for your view of the learning organisation. This vision may have been developed by a team or task group in which case the vision will have a shared base. The challenge is to determine links between the vision and the outcomes and benefits being sought. Outcomes and benefits have been deliberately separated in order to help focus on the extent to which the learning organisation will be able to claim a lead or support role in their achievement.

## Outcomes

Outcomes should be capable of being observed, tangible and measurable (such as behaviours, changes in working practice, reduction in times to complete activities etc.). Everyone in the enterprise should be able to recognise and describe these outcomes and how they came about. They should also have a degree of permanence over timescales of say 24 months. These outcomes should also be recognised by those outside of the enterprise and hence capable of being used to support the development of both an external and internal image of excellence. Some examples of outcomes from the implementation of the learning organisation might include:

- retention rate in key resource areas improved by 20 per cent per annum
- strategic planning cycle time reduced by 50 per cent and manhours involved reduced by 30 per cent in year one
- customer service enquiry response time reduced by 15 per cent in year two.

If the learning organisation is allocated a key role in any of these outcomes it does not mean that other factors are absent or of less importance in influencing the outcome.

So where an outcome for the enterprise was stated as: return on investment, turnover, development and launch of new products or service, the learning organisation could certainly act in a support role but not be credible as a lead body. This distinction of roles for the enterprise leaders and for the learning organisation leaders in the formative stages is vital. As the learning organisation develops and links more closely to the vision and mission of the enterprise then this distinction will become blurred.

## Benefits

Benefits tend to be less tangible and more attributable to changes in mind-sets, mental models held, perspectives and values. They are therefore more easily described at individual, group, function, divisional and corporate levels. For example:

1. *Individual benefits*
   (a) to be able to engage in a more open dialogue on ideas and concerns
   (b) to have the opportunity to influence the culture and direction of the group.

2. *Group benefits*
   (a) to have a means of structuring the ways in which work is obtained and implemented
   (b) to exert a greater influence on the way in which we relate and work with other groups.

3. *Divisional benefits*
   (a) to be able to identify areas in our client relationships that threaten our contracts and performance
   (b) to be more responsive to the need for changes to policy and work practices
   (c) to improve our internal communications
   (d) to be able to absorb technological changes more quickly and with less trauma.

4. *Corporate benefits*
   (a) to be able to work more effectively as a top team
   (b) to be able to interpret messages from the external environment
   (c) to know how to link policy making to action in the organisation.

Using the descriptions above as a guide you should now be able to identify the outcomes and benefits that you are seeking in implementing the learning organisation. The following questions should therefore be addressed:

1. What outcomes are you envisaging from implementing the learning organisation at: a) a personal level, b) at a Division or enterprise-wide level?

2. To what extent do you consider these outcomes to be obtained with the learning organisation acting in a lead role or a support role? Prioritise these outcomes in terms of your enthusiasm and their link to your vision for the learning organisation from Chapter 3 Step 1.

3. What benefits are you envisaging from implementing the learning organisation at a) a personal level, b) at a Division or enterprise-wide level? Prioritise these benefits in terms of your enthusiasm and their links to your vision for the learning organisation from Chapter 3, Step 1.

**Assessing the Benefits** 139

| 1. Outcomes sought at a personal level | Learning organisation role | | Personal priority based on vision for the learning organisation | | |
|---|---|---|---|---|---|
| | Lead | Support | H | M | L |
| | | | | | |
| | | | | | |
| | | | | | |
| | | | | | |
| | | | | | |
| 2. Outcomes sought at the enterprise level | | | | | |
| | | | | | |
| | | | | | |
| | | | | | |
| | | | | | |

*Fig. 6.2 Personal outcomes*

The proforma in Figs. 6.2 and 6.3 will help capture your personal views on outcomes and benefits.

Having completed this personal review it is useful to revisit and if necessary revise your vision and mission statements. It may be necessary to extend the number of visions being considered and put them on a timescale based on a prioritisation of outcomes and benefits.

LEARNING MODEL – STEP 2

## REVIEW OF THE ENTERPRISE

### Key stakeholders – performance and outcome requirements

In order to survive, grow, change and prosper an enterprise has to satisfy to some degree or other what are known as its stakeholders. Stakeholders are those individuals, groups or organisations who have a vested interest in the enterprise for reasons that are at times explicit and at others more tacit.

| 1. Benefits sought at a personal level | Learning organisation role | | Personal priority based on vision for the learning organisation | | |
|---|---|---|---|---|---|
| | Lead | Support | H | M | L |
| | | | | | |
| | | | | | |
| | | | | | |
| | | | | | |
| | | | | | |
| 2. Benefits sought at the enterprise level | | | | | |
| | | | | | |
| | | | | | |
| | | | | | |
| | | | | | |

*Fig. 6.3 Personal benefits*

The stakeholders are those that can either add to the success of the enterprise by supplying political power and influence, financial resources, human resources, physical resources or other means of support and co-operation. They can include customers, suppliers, subcontractors, fund holders, expertise groups, professional and other institutions. In some cases these will range from Governments and International bodies to institutions representing the workforce. For others considering a Division in a company then the key stakeholders may be the Board or the Financial Director at one extreme and Divisions that act as collaborators on projects at the other. It is likely that some stakeholders may not be immediately obvious whilst others may not themselves be aware that they are stakeholders until they become dissatisfied with their evaluation of the performance of the enterprise. Addressing the following questions will enable this vital review to be completed.

## Stakeholders (external to the enterprise)

1. Who provides the finance that is used for long-term investment?
2. Who provides medium-term financing?
3. Who provides financing for the operation?
4. Which other groups can influence long, medium and operational financing?
5. Which groups can provide external influences in the following areas:
   - technology
   - technological innovation
   - product and or service provision
   - manpower requirements, skills and standards
   - professional standards
   - the structure of the industry
6. Who are the major clients, customers or users of the enterprise? (By major users is meant those that individually account for more than 10 per cent of the enterprise annual output or services).
7. Who are the other clients, customers or users?
8. Who are the major subcontractors used by the enterprise? (By major subcontractors is meant those that account individually for more than 10 per cent of the total subcontract work).
9. Who are the other subcontractors?
10. Who are the major suppliers of goods and services? (By major is meant those that individually supply more than 10 per cent of the total goods and services).
11. Who are the other suppliers of goods and services?
12. What external collaborations, coalitions or joint ventures exist?
13. What are the legal trading entities of the enterprise?
14. Are there any user groups or bodies that can exert pressure on the enterprise?

## Stakeholders (internal to the enterprise)

1. Who within the hierarchy provides or controls the investment decisions?
2. Who determines the medium and long-term strategy and direction for the enterprise?
3. Who sets and controls the Operational Strategy and direction?

## 142 Implementing the Learning Organisation

4. Who sets and controls the operational budgets?
5. Who sets and controls the overhead budgets?
6. Who are the members of the power group or dominant coalition?
7. Who sets the standards of behaviour and tone for the workforce?
8. Who would be seen as the custodian or guardian of the image for the enterprise?

For each of the groups or companies named above identify a named individual or key figure who is the main source of influence (see Fig. 6.4.) Some

| External stakeholders: | Area of influence |
|---|---|
| | |
| | |
| | |
| | |
| | |
| | |
| | |
| | |
| | |

| Internal stakeholders: | Area of influence |
|---|---|
| | |
| | |
| | |
| | |
| | |
| | |

*Fig. 6.4 Key external and internal stakeholders*

| Definition of Stakeholder: | | External | |
| --- | --- | --- | --- |
| | | Internal | |
| Named individual or known contact point: | | | |
| No. | Outcomes required from the enterprise | Current level of satisfaction | | |
| | | H | M | L |
| 1 | | | | |
| 2 | | | | |
| 3 | | | | |
| 4 | | | | |
| 5 | | | | |

*Fig. 6.5 Outcomes required by stakeholders*

of these external and internal stakeholders will be more important than others. A proforma for detailed analysis of each of those deemed important enough that withdrawal of their patronage would severely hamper the growth and survival of the enterprise is provided in Fig. 6.5. These proformas should be used to analyse what each one requires from the enterprise, in terms of outcomes.

## Outcomes and performance measures

Outcomes, as explained earlier, should be capable of being observed, tangible and measurable. Conventional formal measures include those that are based on:

- financial ratios and budgets
- output quantities, customers serviced etc.

## 144  Implementing the Learning Organisation

- service response times
- errors and error rates
- stock and inventory levels
- benchmarking against key competitors
- human resource management criteria such as staff turnover, recruitment ratios, absenteeism, etc.
- time taken from product concept, through to design and production
- value of sales orders and contracts

Many of the outcomes required by key stakeholders will be amenable to standard setting and performance measures of the type outlined above. But for some outcomes what might be termed informal measures are often used. The informal measures are often implicit and intangible, sometimes being viewed as psychological benefits. An example of this is where a stakeholder (say, a key Divisional Managing Director) sets a formal performance measure for the number of customer contracts renewed each year but sees this as a demonstration of the professionalism and dedication of the product sales managers. Another example would be where a client places a contract for a service that is measured in terms of service response time but who sees the service as offering a high quality and technologically leading edge response. A final example might be where a hospital was providing reassurance to clients by the way in which they were received and dealt with whereas the administration might be using patient throughput and costs as formal measures of performance. The concern at this point in the analysis of the stakeholders' requirements is to give an emphasis to the more intangible or informal measures that they may be using. The task is to identify both the formal and informal measures and ensure that these are addressed. We will see in Step 3 below how it may be important to influence these informal measures through addressing the values held by these key stakeholders. The proforma shown in Fig. 6.6 will help focus on these performance measures and the role that the learning organisation can play in providing stakeholder satisfaction.

It is likely that much of the information required in the above reviews was not available or obtainable. Much will depend upon the extent to which the enterprise has, in the past, been explicit about its stakeholders. In many enterprises the more senior or front-line executives will probably see their major role as handling the external stakeholders. Where the enterprise is well established then the links and relationships may have reached the point where outcomes and performance are at times kept in the realms of mythology; downturns being talked up and excellent performances being expressed as the norm. To gain an insight into how the learning organisation can support the formal measures may be easy but to discover the informality

| Description of Stakeholder: | | | External | |
| --- | --- | --- | --- | --- |
| | | | Internal | |
| Outcomes required | Description of Performance Measures used by stakeholder | | Learning Organisation Role | |
| | Formal | Informal | Lead | Support |
| | | | | |
| | | | | |
| | | | | |
| | | | | |
| | | | | |

*Fig. 6.6 Outcomes and performance measures*

may require learning of a very high order. For those enterprises where the stakeholder management approach is less well defined then the learning organisation will be able to contribute by providing this focus and demonstrating how stakeholder satisfaction needs to be focused on both the formal and informal measures.

The reviews will have provided a much clearer focus on the personal outcomes and benefits that you are seeking from implementing the learning organisation; also a view of the key stakeholders in the enterprise, both external and internal, the outcomes that are sought and how performance is measured and evaluated. It is now possible to identify the areas in which the learning organisation can either take a lead role or support other initiatives in the enterprise in order to satisfy the key stakeholders.

## LEARNING MODEL – STEP 3

### READING TEXT AND REFLECTION

In this section two sub-topics are introduced to help promote reflection on the findings resulting from the review work in the previous step. The important point is that they will help develop your thinking and understanding about the way in which influence groups can be used to help develop the learning organisation, also to consider how to prepare an argument in support of the implementation of the learning organisation and to evaluate the benefits.

The areas covered by these sub-topics are:

- influencing values
- models for evaluating change programmes

### Influencing values

People use their idea of values (the ideas and thoughts to which individuals place significant meaning) to evaluate the outcomes of their efforts. Where an enterprise has stakeholders ranging from shareholders, investors, executives, managers and workers there will exist a wide range of values. Although variety might be the spice of life in some walks of life, in an enterprise it is the variety in the values held that creates the complexity. For example, a traditional hard-nosed business executive might value bottom line performance and capturing market share, whereas an executive with values biased towards society might favour creating a network of co-operating firms or an ecologically sound set of products. This is not to say that the two cannot exist in harmony.

When individuals in an enterprise share values then decisions at the top will be recognised and reflected in a concerted response at operational levels; for example, at British Airways the focus on 'the Customer as King', provided a guide for action at all levels. In other settings providing a friendly workforce, creating a responsive and caring climate all echo the drive for identification with a set of common values. These values help individuals in decision-making, selecting priorities and basic behaviours.

It is not unreasonable to envisage situations where stakeholder groups have different objectives and needs for the outcomes of their investment and or efforts, e.g. investors seeking short-term returns while managers are looking for longer-term investments and hence pay back periods.

When this occurs attempts to negotiate around desired outcomes usually address the underlying values attached to these outcomes. In this way stakeholders seek to persuade other groups that their best interests lie in supporting a higher set of values or that their best interests can be met by supporting the other group's values. This, when carried to an extreme will result in stakeholders in an enterprise eventually sharing a set of high level values to which their own values have been subsumed. This notion of values suggests that they are fundamental to the way individuals view their lives.

The enterprise therefore needs to demonstrate support to a set of values by the way it presents an image, leads, manages, controls, rewards, punishes and behaves. With the learning organisation the suggestion is therefore that success will depend on the extent to which the values being promoted, e.g. risk taking, openness, support, networking, etc. are reciprocated in the wider enterprise. In particular, the resonance of the values of the learning organisation with the way in which the enterprise operates and the values held by key stakeholders both internal and external to the enterprise.

The learning organisation will thus need to set out to promote a set of values. These will need to be recognisable in their own right from those that already exist. They need to be sustainable over a period of, say, five years taking into account the changing nature of the external environment of the enterprise. It is also important that they are realistic in terms of being achievable when taking into account the existing enterprise structure and the key players involved. It would be disastrous to set out with unrealistic aspirations towards values based on today's situation and to underestimate the danger of them then becoming lost in the enterprise noise.

Values such as empowerment, creating a learning climate, a determination to achieve continuous improvement etc. may fail to meet the criteria of realism, significance and durability. There are some values that could be identified within the enterprise and encapsulated in the learning organisation process. These might include:

**Professional values** such as integrity, honesty, the preparedness to stand by the agreements made with suppliers, customers and contractors.

**Commercial values** such as supporting the legal and safety regulations, fair dealing with competitors, selecting suppliers and subcontractors on the basis of merit. Providing quality goods and services that meet the real needs of customers while staying within the trading standards and regulations would also underpin these commercial values.

**Operational values** in terms of promoting a quality engineering service, rewarding innovation and creativity, supporting development of individuals, responding to customer demands in a caring manner. This area could also include values that focus on the way individuals are treated within the enterprise, e.g. creating a family atmosphere, supporting and developing colleagues, etc.

These values can be used to support the vision and mission for the learning organisation and develop an insight into what it might mean for individuals working in such an environment. The values can be seen as forming a strong link between human values and the purpose of the wider enterprise. For many managers there is an urgent need to derive meaning from their work. Linking their work to a higher purpose is something that can help support the corporate direction initially and eventually help create the direction for the learning organisation. If the links are not established then the decline in the clarity and purpose of the enterprise in the eyes of the stakeholders and influence groups will accelerate.

The management effort required to introduce and carry through even a minor change to either a product, service or process, let alone changes to structure or culture are enormous. Unless managers believe in the purpose of the enterprise and recognise that their values will be respected and supported, they are unlikely to produce the effort required. The commitment to produce and sustain the effort derives from the values held and the level of associated loyalty and enthusiasm that can be achieved.

To deliver an approach that attempts to identify and harness such values requires a high level of managerial skill and appropriate leadership. It requires great skill and commitment on the part of the leaders in the learning organisation to explain where and why trade-offs have to be made between competing stakeholders. Failure to face up to the debate and failure to identify the values underlying the demands of the various stakeholders will encourage middle managers to lapse into mistrust, disillusionment and cynicism. The learning organisation does not offer a solution to these complex challenges but does offer the opportunity to discover and explore how values can be harnessed to the overall benefit of the enterprise.

## Models for evaluating change programmes

Change programmes are expected to produce outcomes and benefits to an organisation. Various models are used to evaluate such programmes and an appreciation of these will help to frame arguments for implementing the learning organisation.

The simplest evaluation model is based on the notion that an input causes an output. This is the magic box model where there is no inquiry into what is inside the box as long as changes in the input appear to produce changes in the output, for example, a change programme whereby managers are put on a training course with a survey of their attitudes taken before and after. Some people will argue for the output to be validated by use of a control group but the reality is that a positive outcome leads to continuation of the programme. Failure sometimes leads to cancellation. This approach is used

## Assessing the Benefits    149

even when the managers and the sponsors are well aware of the complexity of the factors involved in the change and the tenuous cause and effect links.

The second level of complexity for evaluation models is that described in terms of cost-effectiveness and cost benefit. The cost-effectiveness model is similar to the magic box approach but here assessments are made as to the effectiveness of various optional approaches to implementing change based on the assumption that outcomes from various options can be measured on a common scale. Thus the effectiveness (measured in whatever terms) of an approach can be compared to an alternative approach either in terms of being less cost or by producing a greater amount of the change; for example, a change programme that involved training internal mentors who would then help introduce a change of working practices to other managers could be compared to one where the managers were provided with an incentive scheme to encourage them to change their working practices. This approach to evaluation of the change still assumes simple cause and effect relationships and that the outcomes can be measured in a way that is both valid (in that it measures the phenomena, e.g. behaviour being sought) and reliable (in that the process if repeated would produce the same effect).

These models have historically been confused by the use of quasi statistical approaches and ideas imported from other disciplines, namely the sciences and sociology. Where the changes are known to be complex there is usually some attempt to quantify and therefore justify the programmes using statistical measures. A more common model that became famous through both the construction industry, large engineering projects and then information technology programmes is that known as the cost benefit model.

With this model the benefits from a change programme are calculated on the basis of either cost displacement (cost savings) or added value. Sometimes both benefits are measured. The method still allows for comparisons between alternative approaches but is more usually used to win an argument or persuade an audience. Although attractive at first glance this cost benefit model does present some practical as well as theoretical difficulties.

On the practical side it is necessary to calculate the costs of a planned programme and then to list the benefits in similar monetary values allowing that benefits (like pay-back calculations) will occur over time (say, two or three years) and these have to be discounted back to present value. For example, a change programme where the management time and other costs were calculated at, say, 100,000 monetary units, then this would have to be compared with benefits of, say, labour hours savings of 50,000 monetary units per annum over five years and value added benefits (e.g. more contracts gained, higher sales revenue, lower cost of services, etc.) of 500,000 monetary units per annum in year two and 700,000 monetary units in year three. Discounting these benefits back to present value then allows a comparison to be made with the costs.

Large ratios of benefits over costs are used to persuade audiences that the change programme is to be supported. An approach often used to increase the benefits side of the equation is to derive a large list of perceived benefits to which value can be apportioned, e.g. getting more business, producing a better quality product or service, being more professional than our competitors, attracting higher calibre staff, reducing staff turnover, etc. The theoretical considerations with this approach are the same as those with the magic box model, i.e. control groups and complexity of the cause and effect relationship. Fig. 6.7 illustrates these three models.

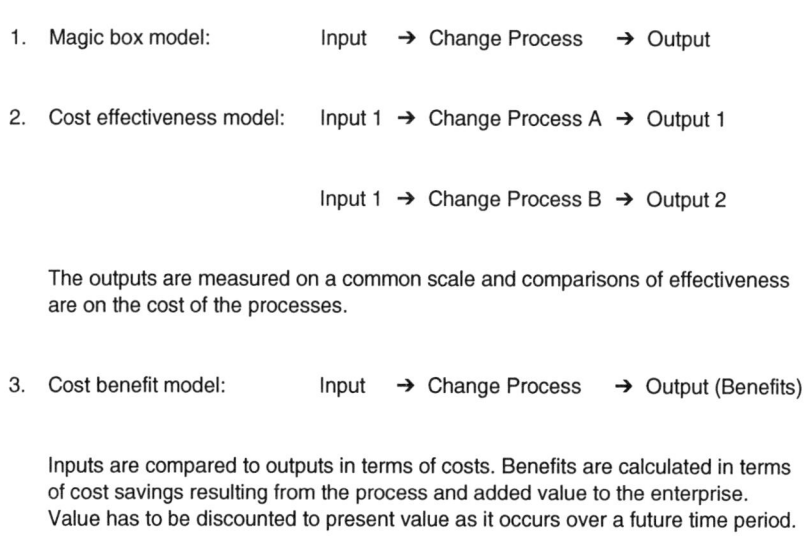

*Fig. 6.7 Models for evaluating change programmes*

For the type of changes envisaged with the implementation of the learning organisation it is obvious that the above models would lack an element of credibility amongst experienced managers. The cost benefit model does in some way provide a means of getting managers to focus on the nature of the benefits that they are envisaging from the learning organisation. Saying that the learning organisation will make the enterprise more competitive or provide more examples of successful innovation or create a more open and responsive organisation will help focus the mind on what these statements actually mean. The desire to put a monetary value on these benefits is reasonable in that where a cost in terms of external investment or management time is to be incurred then a comparison with other investment options should be made; particularly where the alternative options can be seen to more obviously lead to achieving the desired outcome.

For the learning organisation to argue that it is outside such hard-nosed investment criteria is a bit tenuous. Another basis for argument needs to be found. It also points up the fact that the learning organisation is not something like culture change where a desire to achieve a response in terms of behaviour from an organisation becomes an act of faith. It could be argued that with a sufficiently powerful sponsor then an act of faith could be a sufficient determinant for action. But the view of the learning organisation being presented is that it hits at the very bedrock of the enterprise activity. The learning organisation should be seen as contributing directly to enterprise ambitions and outcomes in the short term as well as the long term. Where an enterprise culture dictates that its ambitions and outcomes are evaluated in monetary or other quantifiable terms it is important that the learning organisation is evaluated in similar terms; or at least its contribution to those outcomes is evaluated.

This leaves only one model for the learning organisation to use. This is the process model where the decisions of the policy makers are seen to trigger off a process which leads to outcomes. The evaluation is carried out in two ways. Firstly, to understand whether the intended process for creating the change was actually carried out and the quality and application of the agents of that process. Secondly, to determine the extent to which the process itself contributed to the outcomes or whether there were other factors involved. Where the outcomes sought by the policy makers are not achieved then either the policy decisions are changed or the process itself is reviewed and revised. This process model is shown in Fig. 6.8. It is possible to attribute costs for this process model to both the process itself and value (in monetary terms) to the outcomes, thus providing both a focus on the policy makers' ambitions, the process mechanisms and the outcomes.

Chapter 7 will provide an opportunity to look at the practicalities of this approach. Where the learning organisation is envisaged as starting off working jointly on areas of concern to the enterprise one approach would be to use a series of mini process models to evaluate both costs and outcomes. In this way confidence is built up in both the enterprise and the learning organisation as to the value of these joint exercises.

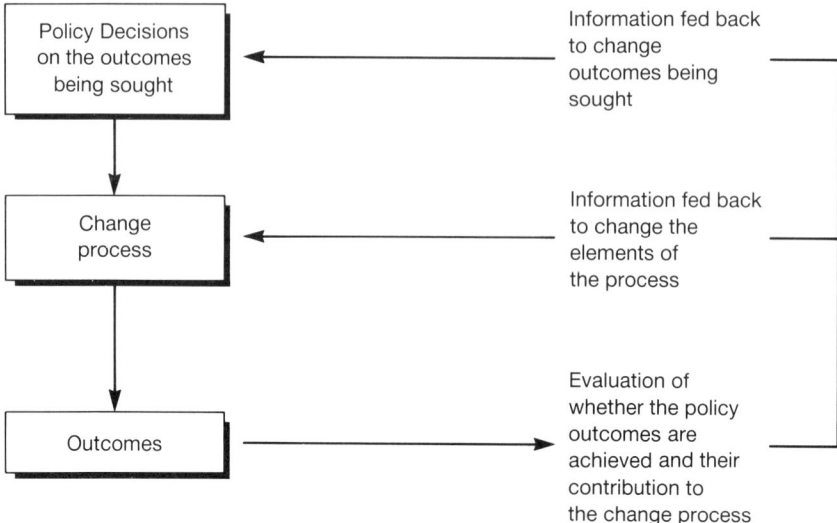

*Fig. 6.8 Process model*

LEARNING MODEL – STEPS 4, 5, 6

## FORMING AND TESTING PERSPECTIVES

This section provides the opportunity for some reflection on the review and the above readings.

There is nothing more powerful than the drives that result from having a vested interest in the outcomes of an activity. By identifying your own interests in the learning organisation, in terms of outcomes and benefits, the links to earlier views on vision and mission for the learning organisation should now be much clearer.

An appreciation of the outcomes and benefits sought by key stakeholders in the enterprise is vital to successful implementation of the learning organisation. Determining who are the key stakeholders, possibly by name, both external and internal to the enterprise will no doubt have generated a wide list. It should have been possible to identify those that are key and to consider both the formal and informal measures that they use to determine whether the enterprise is performing to their satisfaction.

Formal measures such as return on investment, error rates, benchmarking against competitors, etc. are those that are perhaps more easily identified. But just as important are those informal or less tangible measures that border on the subjective, political, psychological.

The extent to which the learning organisation is able to identify and address both the formal and informal measures used by stakeholders is obviously a key to success. The learning organisation has a role to play in helping to satisfy these external and internal stakeholders' demands and aspirations for the performance of the enterprise. In some cases the learning organisation can play a lead role and in others one of support. It is also likely that in some areas it has no role to play at all. It may be important to stop at this point and reflect on how thinly the learning organisation is to be spread in terms of satisfying stakeholders and link this view back to your ideas on implementation and the image that needs to be promoted.

A major role for the learning organisation could be in this very area of highlighting stakeholders' requirements. In many cases stakeholder satisfaction (e.g. from shareholders to the workforce) may be the key to survival and success of the enterprise. Where the enterprise is well established how to provide this satisfaction may have reached mythical levels. In many instances this area will be handled by senior executives who are using a mixture of style, intuition and years of experience. If the learning organisation is to have a role here it will need to be played very carefully and perhaps best presented as an aid that senior executives can use to assess change in the external environment that may impact on stakeholders' perspectives and values.

The first reading text addressed the question of how values (ideas and thoughts to which individuals place significant meaning) play a key part in influencing the way individuals and groups behave and take action. It was argued that in an enterprise where there is a wide range of held values then strategic and operational decisions will require a trade-off to be made between these values. One way of handling this trade-off where one group would perceive a threat or challenge to their values is to appeal to a higher set of values, e.g. society, the community, the ecology, etc. Where an enterprise espouses such values then it is important that the management approaches and styles are seen to be in support. If this support and demonstration is not seen to take place then the values will become self-defeating and cynicism will set in.

When considering implementation of the learning organisation it is important that the values promoted match or link in a clear way those held by the wider enterprise. The suggestion is that the learning organisation thus sets out to promote a clear set of values that are recognisable above the enterprise noise level, are sustainable over a reasonable time period and are capable of being realised in a tangible way. It was suggested that these values should support the vision and mission of the learning organisation and cover three broad areas: professional values, commercial values, operational values. The management time and effort involved in identifying and implementing the learning organisation is not to be underestimated. The commitment required to generate and sustain this effort was argued as being best pursued through the identification, influence and support of these deeply held values.

The second text focused on the ways in which change programmes are evaluated. The question was raised as to why there is a need to evaluate a change programme in hard terms such as costs or management time. Furthermore, why is there a need to measure outcomes when the whole idea of the change borders on the philosophical if not the metaphysical. It was argued that people do use models to evaluate the outcomes of effort and this is mainly done to either justify their arguments and therefore continue to gain patronage or where alternative strategies and hence options for investment of effort exist. Being aware of these models helps to either make arguments for investment in the learning organisation or counter criticisms built on a faulty premise.

If faith in a cause (e.g. a culture change programme) is sufficient for implementation to begin then one has to be very careful before taking the hard-nosed evaluation approach. There are perhaps two views. Firstly, that something as obviously important as organisational learning should be introduced and supported. That as the outcomes are not obvious then any attempts to evaluate their worth in relation to investment in time and money for implementation would be pointless. So the decision could be just to go ahead and do it. The second view, the one being promoted here, is that the notion of the learning organisation is key to the success of the wider enterprise. Therefore if the wider enterprise is measured in terms of costs, management and intellectual effort then why should the investment in the learning organisation be treated differently. By making the learning organisation justify itself and show how it contributes to both formal and informal enterprise performance measures, its profile is raised and its importance justified.

Before making any decisions as to which viewpoint to adopt it is important to consider two factors. The dominant culture in terms of its use of hard or soft measures of performance and the extent to which the approach to evaluating costs and outcomes from the learning organisation can be sustained. Many enterprises are quite happy to allocate an overhead budget to developing the capability of the staff and the enterprise that can vary from 1 per cent to 10 per cent of the total revenue turnover per annum. If this is the case then where support and commitment to the ideas behind the learning organisation can be obtained this act of faith approach may be the best route to take. In these circumstances arguing a cost justification approach for its own sake would appear to be inappropriate.

On the other hand, where the culture favours or even dictates hard measures and cost justification arguments then the learning organisation would need to follow this pattern. If this is the case then the argument needs to be well thought out and when made should be both realistic and achievable in the context of the enterprise and what is being sought. Based on the above reviews and readings it should be possible to articulate your perspectives on:

- your own ambitions for the learning organisation in relation to its vision and mission
- how it is important to differentiate between formal outcomes and less tangible benefits when considering the learning organisation
- the enterprise stakeholders both external and internal, their requirements for outcomes and benefits
- where the learning organisation can act in a lead or support role in satisfying the requirements of the key stakeholders
- the part to be played by values held by key stakeholders in implementing the learning organisation
- the values to be promoted by the learning organisation and how these link to those held in the enterprise
- how change programmes can be evaluated
- the importance and relevance of cost justification of change programmes
- the arguments to be made in support of implementing the learning organisation in your enterprise

These perspectives will help focus on the arguments needed when seeking support for implementation of the learning organisation. By now the perspectives from previous chapters will begin to link and in many cases overlap. This is to be expected and is an important realisation as part of the learning process in which you are engaged.

LEARNING MODEL – STEP 7

## COMMENTARY AND LINKS TO CHAPTER 7

Previous chapters have addressed all the issues that are key to understanding how to approach implementation of the learning organisation. A great deal of ground will have been covered in a relatively short space of time and no doubt many areas will have suffered through lack of information or apparent lack of relevance from your standpoint. In Chapter 7 all these parts will be brought together and guidance will be given on how to take the next steps. As you proceed through the chapter it may be worthwhile revisiting some of the earlier chapters where it becomes obvious to you that either some key learning points may have been missed or where you have second thoughts as to their relative importance.

# 7
# IMPLEMENTATION

## INTRODUCTION

This chapter provides a framework for summarising the outcomes from the feasibility study and offers strategies for implementing the learning organisation. The sections covered are:

- putting it all together
- making it work

It has been pointed out that two major assumptions have to be made when attempting to describe the notion of the learning organisation. Firstly, that an organisation can be viewed as an entity that can learn as a result of individuals learning. The learning being captured in formal ways through policies, procedures, practices and rules. Learning is also represented in terms of the culture and what can be described as agreed ways of behaving and the existence of commonly held sets of values.

The other major assumption is that through learning the organisation is able to survive and grow in an ever changing external environment. The notion of the learning organisation thus relies very heavily for its understanding on this view of an organisation being an entity that is capable of demonstrating learning through adaptation and changed behaviour.

There are two commonly held views of how the notion of the learning organisation can be used to help in this process of adaptation and growth. Firstly where the learning organisation is used as a tool in the hands of the senior management group; being used to shape and direct policy and strategy through culture changes and innovative approaches in order to change direction and emphasis in the enterprise. Conversely, where the learning organisation provides a climate, culture and structure within which individuals can feel empowered and engage in programmes of continuous development and self-improvement.

The experienced manager will recognise that these need not be either/or views and they can often co-exist. The difficulty arises when attempting to move from these theoretical and often philosophical considerations to implementation and action. Implementation of the learning organisation as with any change programme, calls for a high level of commitment in order to sustain the impetus needed to overcome the many learning blockages. Commitment, it is argued, comes from identifying deeply held values and beliefs about organisational life and linking these to the purpose of the enterprise at the level being considered. These views as to whether the learning organisation is a tool for the Corporate body to use or an opportunity to empower individuals at all levels is a major factor in determining approaches to implementation. The feasibility study outlined in the previous chapters has attempted to bridge the gap between these two views on the basis that both have a lot to offer and that they can co-exist.

It is very tempting to be prescriptive about how to set about implementation of the learning organisation. There are some general guides as to best practice, that have been gleaned from both academics and practitioners but it is obvious by now that there is an abundance of good advice but not many rules. The implementation problem is itself incredibly complex and culture-dependent. Being alerted to this problem the feasibility study therefore set out with the broad aim;

- to determine the need for and clarify how to set about implementing an approach to directing and managing the organisation with a major focus on learning in its widest form.

The four key objectives of the study supporting this aim were:

1. To describe the current enterprise in terms of the:
   - environment
   - historic and forming events
   - key measures of performance
   - pressures for change both internal and external
   - opportunities for growth and development
   - current learning processes.
2. To formulate a vision for the learning organisation and identify opportunities for learning within the enterprise.
3. To identify how to move to a learning focus.
4. To describe how key stakeholders can benefit from this focus on learning and how to evaluate the benefits.

In the sections below the outcomes of the feasibility study are reviewed in order to help structure the findings in such a way that approaches to implementation become clear. Guidance is then provided on how to make the implementation work and to reap the benefits.

## 158 Implementing the Learning Organisation

While completing this task of putting it all together it is suggested that you refer back and forth to Chapter 8. In this chapter a series of examples of how various organisations are focusing on learning are presented. The value of these examples is where they provide a stimulus or trigger to your own deliberations. For those readers with a creative style that is predominantly adaptive this will be enormously helpful. For those with a more innovative style these examples may provide the stimulus to help you break new ground. They have been presented for this purpose and while bearing in mind that not all good practices are transferable the examples should provide a powerful aid to your learning.

## PUTTING IT ALL TOGETHER

### Consensus on what is a learning organisation

*The academics*

In Chapter 1 the various views and beliefs around the learning organisation were explored. One of the more favoured views was that of an enterprise where learning is focused at all levels and linked to the purposes and objectives of those groups that constitute the wider enterprise.

The notion of an enterprise gradually transforming itself from one state of ability to learn to another is a model used by many to support this idea of change through learning. Hence characteristics such as participation, altering the way people think, open management style, etc. are quickly attributed to the notion of a climate or culture in which organisational learning can be encouraged and achieved. Pedler, Burgoyne and Boydell offer eleven characteristics of the learning organisation which they cluster into five main areas. Their model suggests that:

**(a)** Strategy, policy formulation, implementation and evaluation in the enterprise should be highly participative and structured as learning processes.

**(b)** Information exchanges inside the enterprise should be made on a client to customer basis and alternative reward systems established.

**(c)** Structures should be set up for both business and individual development to take place.

**(d)** Customers should be involved in joint learning programmes.

**(e)** Learning from mistakes and opportunities for self-development should be available to all employees.

Burgoyne has also made strong arguments for linking management development activities much more closely, to the development of the learning organisation. In this way the cumulative capabilities of the staff are harnessed in order to provide an input to corporate policy formation and illuminate the policy-forming process. The emphasis here is on maximising the opportunities for learning arising from the business activity.

From America, Peter Senge offers a view of a learning organisation where everyone is encouraged to develop their abilities in key areas. Firstly the ability to perceive their actions and decisions as being part of a set of interconnected system of events. Being capable of scrutinising their own mental models and developing patience as a step towards personal mastery. Finally the ability to help build shared visions and contribute to team learning.

These views on what is a learning organisation go part way towards explaining the philosophy and do provide a great deal of insight into how individuals can put themselves into a position or state where they can contribute to the purposes of the wider enterprise. The difficultly arises when trying to decide how to approach implementing the learning organisation. It requires a lot more than the understanding or even acceptance of the philosophies and notions outlined by the academics.

## *The consultants*

Consultants who are engaged in the area of managing complex change have a host of labels and approaches that are used with their clients. Some of the more prominent are those in the fields of Organisational Development and Culture Change. Here an enormous amount of experience and expertise based on practical experience has been built up by the consultancies in areas that focus on learning. For the learning organisation in particular a number of guidelines can be set down:

(a) individual development must be linked to developments within the enterprise and corporate strategies (without these links learning will either founder, be downgraded or not be transferable and hence not valued).

(b) the development of management processes is central to the growth of learning in an enterprise. (Evidenced by the emergence of business process re-engineering consultancies).

(c) that reward and incentive systems must be built into the learning organisation.

At McKinsey the notion of the 7-S framework identified variables which must be considered when developing an enterprise. These are:

- Strategy
- Structure
- Skills
- Systems
- Style
- Staff
- Shared Values

These variables are used by many consultants to help focus and implement organisational change programmes.

The creation and management of knowledge as a tangible facet of organisational learning has also been adopted by McKinsey within their own consultancy practices. Personal networks have been set up to accelerate the rate at which knowledge about successful practice is captured and transferred within the organisation. Promotion and reward systems being linked to this new knowledge-based learning approach.

The main focus for the consultant is that of client satisfaction and the drive for demonstration of a positive contribution to the purposes and objectives of the enterprise. Their approach is thus to promote the use of structured change programmes and the observance of a set of basic change principles. These change principles would tend to follow a pattern of vision building and objective setting, followed by a stage of planning the transition with intermediate goals to sustain commitment and finally execution where the changes are embedded into the enterprise processes and behaviours. The consultant's use of this top-down approach to change programmes derives from the fact that the brief is agreed with the Corporate client. Although there is often a high degree of management and staff participation in setting up the brief and involvement in the implementation stages.

## The practitioners

With large corporations the label of the learning organisation is rarely used for a change programme. The example given in Chapter 1 of the Xerox Corporation was deliberately chosen to emphasise the role that the Chief Executive takes in major change programmes. The Xerox example did show how creativity and learning were harnessed in the programme as a means of achieving some specific corporate and operational capabilities. Areas where learning had to be undertaken were identified and actions then taken to ensure that behavioural changes followed. The Xerox programme was in many ways purposeful, fast moving and linked the purpose of the wider enterprise to the learning requirements of the enterprise in order to effect change.

This type of programme would perhaps represent the framework for an

Organisational Development Programme that emphasised learning. The extent to which this learning focus can be sustained without the continuing stimulus from the Chief Executive remains to be seen. Other practitioner programmes that have used the learning organisation label could easily be interpreted as having promoted either management development programmes, work focused training initiatives, organisational development or culture change programmes. Many of these programmes are initiated from the Human Resource functions. The virtue being that this is the conventional repository of those interested and capable of initiating and implementing such programmes.

The disadvantages are that in many cases the Human Resource function is not directly linked to the line operation and does not have a power position at Corporate or Business Policy-making levels. This is not always the case but in general represents one of the major factors holding back the wider acceptance of the notion of the learning organisation and its implementation.

An obvious example of this ambivalence as to where to host a change programme is that where Total Quality Management programmes are introduced. Typically, a consultancy or outside agency will be chosen to introduce a change programme that incorporates massive requirements for managing organisational learning. A senior member of the Board then being appointed to oversee the implementation.

This does pose the question as to where the focus for the learning organisation should reside within an enterprise. Is it something to be incorporated into the hearts and minds of all managers and employees, or something that is driven from the top as a means of achieving some clear and identifiable benefits for the enterprise stakeholders. The recommendation is that both are correct and desirable. The reality is that the top group must set the direction using whatever perspectives and ambitions that they can muster; that the managers and workforce should be given the opportunity to make their best contribution to the success of the enterprise wherever possible. Also that a focus on learning at all levels is key to both of the above groups being successful and that the enterprise should be structured to encourage learning that will lead to demonstrable rewards and benefits to all those involved. A broad definition of the learning organisation but one which offers opportunity for all.

## Personal style preferences – your bias during design and implementation

### Personality

The personal reviews, covered in Chapters 3 and 4, illustrated the influence of personality, creative style and leadership style on your approach to implementing the learning organisation.

Personality was explored in terms of traits which influenced the approach adopted in problem solving. Four personality types were highlighted:

STs  Systematic decision making with hard data.
     The focus being on the problems of today.
NTs  Stress is on analysis but takes leaps into the unknown. Their interest is in simplifying complex problems. Tend to be impersonal.
SFs  Emphasise people's opinions, seek harmony. Focus on short-term problems.
NFs  Stress their judgement and experience.
     Emphasis is on broad themes.

You will have identified your own type from the review in Chapter 3 and this should point up some potential weaknesses and biases that will be present in your thinking on the implementation of the learning organisation. You will also by now have validated your initial self-analysis by undertaking an objective test through a registered agency.

If your type is ST dominant then your weakness will be that you will tend to rely on standard approaches to the learning organisation and reject suggestions for a new or novel approach. During the review stages of the study you will have been highly analytical and found it difficult to cope with or accept data that was ambiguous. As far as implementation is concerned your approach would tend to be risk averse and emphasise the short term. When considering evaluation of the benefits of the learning organisation for the stakeholders, your approach will tend to be to reject evidence that does not conform to your original preferences and beliefs.

This analysis does present a fairly daunting picture for an individual contemplating undertaking the implementation of the learning organisation. On the other hand it does suggest that you could be a very powerful antidote to someone that was operating in a totally high risk, and non-systematic way. The ST dominant type, as will become clearer when we look at implementation strategies, is enormously valuable when required to make proposals and support hard-nosed demands for short-term performance and contributions from the learning organisation.

If your type is NT then your weakness will be to adhere to beliefs which have been developed through experience with other change programmes. During the review stage of the study you will have been looking for patterns in the data and will have demonstrated a tendency to over complicate what might have been a straightforward set of issues. When thinking about implementation your time horizon will have been on the long term and you will have been seeking opportunities to be innovative. For the evaluation of outcomes your approach would be to seek to adopt methods that suit your own preferences.

This is an encouraging profile where the complexity of the enterprise and perhaps its open culture lend themselves to the system thinker and innovator. The danger being that the more straightforward and obvious approaches may be missed.

For the SF type the tendency will be to spend too much effort on consultation, favouring the discussion perhaps more than the ideas. During the review stage the temptation will have been to seek data from discussion with others and emphasis will have been placed on data that has a higher emotional content. Thoughts on implementation will favour the short-term pay-off and priority given to solutions that are acceptable to others in the enterprise. At the evaluation stage the learning organisation will have been described as producing outcomes that will be given wide approval by others in the enterprise. This presents a much more people-centred approach and will make the introduction of any changes more acceptable to a wider audience. The difficulty will arise where the dominant coalition or power group are at odds with the more widespread feelings and views in the enterprise.

The NFs will have a tendency to use imagery and vivid examples to illustrate their views on the learning organisation. They will reject standard problem-solving approaches. During the review stages the tendency will have been to reduce areas of uncertainty by using personal judgements and rely heavily on the use of analogies to explain their meanings. As implementation approaches the tendency will be to be very innovative and seek solutions that will provide a best fit to the culture and the enterprise activities. The approach to evaluation of outcomes will be to favour the use of imagery rather than hard data.

These four types all have their part to play in developing approaches to implementing the learning organisation. The two important messages to be made from this are that:

- your personality will bias your approach
- you will need a team view in order to cover all possibilities.

## *Style*

Two key areas of style have been covered in the personal reviews. First, your style preference when faced with a situation where there is a need to be creative. Styles being described in terms of your tendency to prefer adaptive approaches or those that can be described as innovative. Second, your preferred style when acting in a leadership role.

Implementing the learning organisation will place a high demand on your ability to be creative when determining approaches and solutions to the numerous open-ended problems that will arise. From the review in Chapter 3 you will have a view as to whether your preferred style will be to adopt an adaptive approach. This involves building on existing ideas and practices, incrementally moving from the present to some future position. Alternatively, your preferred style may be to seek original solutions in attempting to bring about radical changes to the status quo. Both approaches are creative but your style preference may at times be an enormous asset, at other times extremely counterproductive. Being aware that those working with you have their own style preferences will help to ensure that the best solutions are reached. Implementation will require that all three stages of the innovative process are used. Creative style needs to be matched at each stage to the issues being faced, i.e. at the ideas stage; when communicating and seeking support from the enterprise and finally when ensuring that the learning approaches are integrated into the behaviour of the managers and staff.

Your preferred leadership style will also have a major impact on how you approach implementation. In Chapter 4 various styles were identified. A Style A manager will identify strongly with the enterprise purpose and pursue the implementation as a task to be achieved. To be successful this style relies heavily on both the strength and energy of the individual and the organisational power that they can call on. This type of manager will find it difficult to continue to persuade others unless the outcomes and benefits are immediate and obvious. The Style C manager will not be seen as in tune with the purposes of the enterprise and its culture. The preference will be for a team approach and where possible to avoid conflict and confrontation. In situations where the environment is fairly stable then this management style will be ideal. But where the implementation requires confrontation and where dominant ideas need to be challenged then this style preference is less appropriate. The Style D manager will not be happy with, and not ideally suited to, the prospect of managing the implementation. This style being relevant at later stages where routinisation and procedures need to be created and operated. The Style B manager would prove ideal for the implementation task. Preferring to work with groups in sharing ideas and prepared to understand the basis of any conflicts, by not seeking to demonstrate or attract power this style of manager will not be seen as a threat to the dominant coalition or power groups. The balance between the task of implementation and forming and maintaining relationships will be in good hands.

If you find that your preferred style is not ideally suited to the implementation task there are two ways forward. One is to get someone else to lead the implementation programme with your role being to bring your other strengths to bear. The second approach is to go ahead and lead yourself but to be acutely aware of how your style is going to have an influence and take time out to check when the bias is becoming counterproductive. For most managers this is the situation often being faced. Knowing your biases risks all the dangers that introspection brings but benefits from the enjoyment of knowing when the solution to the problem lies in your own hands.

## Lessons from the reviews of the enterprise

The feasibility study has involved a very extensive review of the existing enterprise. In this section some of the key areas will be summarised in order to help focus on the implementation task. A model showing how the key areas of the review link together is shown in Fig. 7.1.

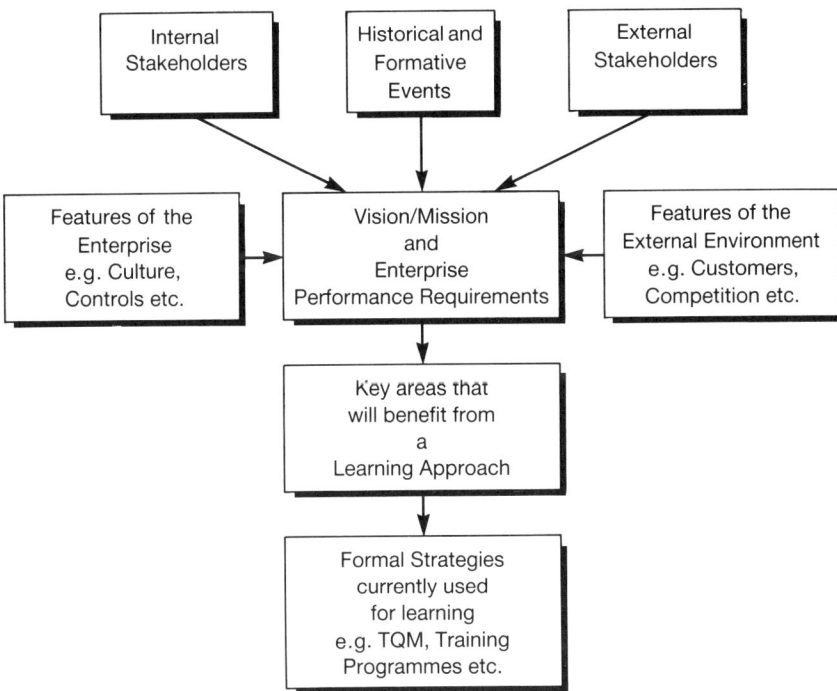

*Fig. 7.1 Linking key review areas*

## Stakeholders

In Chapter 6 the notion of stakeholders existing both internal and external to the enterprise was introduced. From a personal viewpoint you were invited to explore the outcomes and benefits that you are seeking from implementation of the learning organisation and to link this with your declared vision. The point being emphasised here is that outcomes can often be made explicit such as: to improve customer service response times by 15 per cent or to reduce new product introduction costs by 20 per cent in year two, whereas benefits tend to be just as important but much more intangible, e.g. to be able to maintain an open dialogue on new ideas, to have a better relationship with other groups in the enterprise. Both outcomes and benefits need to be declared, explored and confirmed if the learning organisation is to provide any real value to the wider enterprise.

The stakeholders external to the enterprise will have been identified and their areas of influence determined. This idea of a wider enterprise encompassing financial supporters, customers, suppliers etc. is key to the success of the learning organisation. They will all place explicit demands on the enterprise for outcomes in performance terms. There will also be some less explicit or informal demands being made and performances assumed. Failure to perform in these informal areas is often the key reason for stakeholders withdrawing their support.

In thinking about the learning organisation it is easy to forget that the existing managers will already be aware and responding to these external stakeholders. They will also have acted to close any performance gaps that have arisen. What this review will have produced is a clearer view of where a greater focus on learning could help identify and close any performance gaps. The role for the learning organisation is then to act in either a support or lead role to the enterprise.

The reviews of the internal stakeholders were more clearly aimed at finding out who were the groups or individuals within the enterprise that would have to be persuaded that the learning organisation is of value. By identifying who these groups are and what they are currently seeking from the enterprise it is possible to identify, once again, where a support or lead role from the learning organisation would be appropriate.

## The influence of historical and formative events

This review in Chapter 3 was aimed at identifying those key events in the history of the enterprise that could be noted as major learning events. Some of these events will have been due to acts by owners or leaders of the enterprise and others by external events such as mergers, failures or successes of major ventures or product and service innovations. The objective was to gauge the extent to which the current purpose and direction of the enterprise was still being driven by these historic events. The notion being that these past events become internalised through stories and slogans to the point where they become myths then reality. The perceived reality is then acted upon and used as a yardstick to make decisions and evaluate the efforts of the enterprise.

Where a myth becomes out of date and fails to be relevant in the current environment then attempts have to be made to unravel the myth before new learning can be incorporated. The task is first to clarify the myths, check their relevance to the current environment and future vision then either re-enforce or begin to unravel their mystery.

## Vision/mission and performance of the enterprise

In Chapter 3 the notions of the enterprise responding and attempting to be reactive in a changing external environment was explored. Establishing a top level vision (the aspirations associated with achieving some goal) and mission (the sense of purpose and what the enterprise wants to become) are accepted by most managers as the first steps in determining direction, policy and objectives for an enterprise.

The reviews in Chapter 3 started below these top level statements of purpose. The approach taken was to pick up the impact of those driving the vision and mission on the workings of the enterprise itself and thus identify the links to learning. For example, where changes were being made to the strategic position of the enterprise in terms of the markets, services, delivery channels, etc. Also where changes to the operational activity were being made, e.g. structural changes, investments in technology, relocation, changes to processes and controls, etc. This approach emphasises the particular way in which the learning organisation is being presented.

The role for the learning organisation is seen as deriving from the vision and mission of the enterprise. It is key therefore to be aware of what the enterprise is trying to achieve and identify ways in which the learning organisation can either support or at times lead in activities that will promote the growth and development of the enterprise. The way in which the vision and mission for the enterprise is used to create the learning organisation was developed in Chapter 4 and is covered more extensively later in this section.

In Chapter 3 the key functional and business areas and the associated formal measures of performance were identified. Opportunities for learning that are built into the management processes supporting these performance measures were then highlighted. The more unstructured and informal opportunities for learning were also explored. By focusing on informal measures of performance as well as the formal it is possible to identify areas where learning that is tacit (taken for granted) can be made more explicit and shared with others in the enterprise. This highlights a possible key activity for the learning organisation.

## *The features of the external environment*

In Chapter 3 the review of the external environment considered the opportunities and threats to the enterprise arising from the market place, technologies, resources, competition, etc. As the learning organisation will provide a support to the enterprise in these areas it is important that the scope for learning is identified. The potential for learning in these areas is enormous and to have an impact the learning organisation will need to focus and prioritise these opportunities.

## *Features of the enterprise*

In Chapter 3 the review of the enterprise focused on two key areas. The functions carried out and the management processes. The emphasis was on identifying opportunities for the learning organisation to make a contribution in these areas. The key functions such as marketing, operations, customer relations and administration were considered in terms of their primary purpose being either external or internal to the enterprise and the potential for learning to support that purpose. The analysis of the management processes essential to the functioning of the enterprise was aimed at establishing where these were clear in terms of how the process operated, the clarity of purpose and whether the focus was short or long term. By reviewing these management processes (e.g. operational planning, decision making, information exchange, investment planning, etc.) the scope for the learning organisation to help focus and accelerate their operation will have been made clear.

In Chapter 5 the way in which the culture can be used to promote learning was explored. The need for the learning organisation to be in tune with the culture is paramount. Where the learning organisation is seeking to change the culture over time to a learning focus then the start point must be the culture that exists now.

## **Key areas providing opportunities for learning**

The overall purpose in conducting the reviews was to look for opportunities where the learning organisation could provide a support role to the enterprise. The assumption was made that the performance of the enterprise could benefit from a focus on learning in the various functional and process areas.

A study of the external environment highlighted areas that would provide either opportunities or threats to the future of the enterprise. The features of the enterprise, in particular the key functions and the management processes provided an insight into the heart of the enterprise and the way in which formal and informal measures of performance could be used to identify opportunities for learning. The importance of recognising the part that the dominant and sub-cultures play on learning was also emphasised.

These reviews will have made it possible to identify a number of areas where the learning organisation can make a major contribution to the enterprise.

These areas are where the:

- external environment creates a major opportunity or threat to the enterprise
- historical perspectives are preventing key organisational groups or key individuals handling present challenges effectively
- formal management processes are either out of line with the current purposes and future direction of the enterprise or are not operating effectively
- informal management processes need to be made more explicit and informal performance measures made formal
- enterprise objectives and performance measures are not being achieved
- expectations and performance requirements of the external and internal stakeholders are either not clear or are not being met
- performance measures for the various functional areas are not being achieved
- opportunities for growth and development of the enterprise are not being identified or seized
- dominant or sub-cultures are not conducive to the success of the enterprise
- leadership and management style is not conducive to the success of the enterprise.

As suggested earlier, the management will be aware to some extent of these areas and the need to close the performance gap. In many cases this will have led to actions that incorporate a large element of learning.

In Chapter 4 the way in which the enterprise uses management development and training approaches to close the performance gap were explored. Some will have been derived from an identification of corporate needs while others will have been at Divisional, Unit or focused at the individual level. Establishing the links between these learning activities, rewards and enterprise outcomes was argued as being essential to success. A review of the impact of previous change programmes was covered in Chapter 5. The danger of an avalanche of change programmes on an enterprise is that their effect becomes lost and downgrades their use as an opportunity for learning.

The changes arising from the learning organisation activity therefore need to:

- be in tune with the interests of the enterprise
- build on the existing culture
- provide obvious improvements
- use a change model approach that appeals to the perspectives held by the dominant power group and middle management
- not threaten previous change outcomes.

Where an enterprise is already heavily involved in major change programmes such as Total Quality Management (TQM) it is essential that the learning organisation is in tune with the key benefits that are being sought.

## MAKING IT WORK

This section provides guidance on how to approach the implementation of the learning organisation. It assumes that you have completed the feasibility study in the previous chapters and have decided to proceed with planning and actioning an implementation programme for the enterprise.

It will be obvious by now that moving the enterprise to a focus on learning is more than just another culture change programme. With a focus on learning the opportunities for development and growth of the enterprise are enormous. A three-stage programme is therefore recommended to ensure that the enterprise can feel its way towards the future and evolve an approach that fits the particular context in which the enterprise operates. The three stages are:

**Stage 1.** (6 months) – An exploratory stage where the learning organisation supports and works with the enterprise in key areas.

**Stage 2.** (12 months) – The development stage involving wider training of managers and task teams, focusing on applying the approaches and setting up of processes to support learning across the enterprise activities.

**Stage 3.** (12 months) – A consolidation stage where collaborations with the wider enterprise are established and the notion of learning integrated into all the enterprise activities, direct pay-offs from the learning being built into the enterprise reward and incentive schemes.

The various stages are described below in terms of major activities, suggested approaches and where relevant some health warnings.

It should be emphasised that for your particular requirements some of the suggestions given below may be either less of a priority or not appropriate. Where this occurs it is important that you note your difference of opinion and the reasons why. In this way you will be able to evolve an approach which has been tested against that offered below.

## STAGE I – EXPLORATION (6 MONTHS)
### SETTING UP THE STAGE

*State of the enterprise*

An enterprise can be categorised as being in one of three states: stable, undergoing controlled change or turbulent. This may be a question of perspective but the analogy of the cruise liner moving gracefully to her next port as opposed to the kayak surviving in white water conditions should illustrate what is meant. These states determine the condition and hence trigger point for the learning organisation. Let us look at some of these alternative states and their influence on thinking about how to approach the learning organisation during this exploratory stage.

In the stable state triggers would be around issues aimed at improving the way the enterprise operates and is managed. There could also be a growing concern as to whether the stable state would continue. The learning organisation is unlikely to be seen as a major influence or force where these stable conditions persist. The role would tend to be limited to creating a focus on improvements in management and working practices, also in helping the management to develop the ability to detect changes in the external environment and manage the subsequent impact on the enterprise.

Where the enterprise is undergoing controlled changes, such as acquisitions, restructuring, moving into new products and services, altering the way in which the service is delivered, etc. there will be much more scope for the learning organisation. The management will have already detected and be responding to events in the external environment by introducing short-term and longer-term change programmes. These will include programmes that could include a major Total Quality Management (TQM) programme, culture change, process management improvements and changes in work processes. The choice is enormous. This is probably the state in which the majority of enterprises find themselves. The learning organisation will be looked at in terms of either helping to fit into the changes that are already in motion, acting as a focal point for change programmes or developing the ability of managers and the workforce to respond to change, etc. There will be no exclaims of 'Eureka' from managers who are steeped in change programmes when the notion of the learning organisation is raised. For many the notion will be lost in the background noise of the enterprise activity, for others it will appear as a nice idea and no more.

The learning organisation will therefore have to fight its corner and justify its demands on the intellect and time of the managers alongside all the other notions. This emphasises once again why it is so important to have completed a thorough review of the enterprise and to have thought through all the arguments before putting the notion of the learning organisation on to the line.

Where the turbulent state exists it is likely that fire fighting, intuition and rapid response action is the basis on which the enterprise functions. Decisions will tend to be made with apparent informality and there will be little support given to rational and logical approaches to planning for future events. The learning organisation will be viewed in terms of its use in overcoming major problems that the enterprise is tackling. It will be valued in terms of its potential for helping to grow the enterprise in order to meet performance targets, solve problems, manage the chaos. For the enterprise in a turbulent state the interest in the learning organisation will also be around whether it can provide a short to medium-term fix and if it can be used to move the enterprise into a more stable state. In effect looking to the learning organisation in terms of providing quick fixes now and medium to longer-term stability.

A learning organisation approach that only offers longer-term benefits is unlikely to receive any backing in this type of environment. It may be allowed to start but would quickly be stopped when high levels of turbulence were experienced. This ability of the learning organisation to be able to provide both short-term and longer-term benefits is key to its success in all but the most stable of enterprise environments. There are many contenders for the resources and time of the enterprise custodians and this pressure should heighten the desire and need to be clear as to what the learning organisation can offer, how it will operate and the benefits.

## *Assigning responsibility*

Assuming that the state of the enterprise has been considered, the time comes to make some key decisions as to who will drive the learning organisation. There are seven major options or choices:

- to lodge the learning organisation with the Chief Executive's office
- to appoint a Chief Executive to lead the learning organisation with a support team

- to lodge the learning organisation in the Human Resource Directorate function
- to appoint a multi-disciplinary team (from various functions) led by a Board Member to introduce the learning organisation
- to lodge the learning organisation with the Director of the Total Quality Management programme
- to invite all the Divisional or Unit Managers to explore their own way of introducing the notion of the learning organisation into their activities
- to engage a consultancy to introduce and develop the notion of the learning organisation.

It may be that the decision will be made on the basis of politics and expediency but the success of the learning organisation could well rest on this first decision. Whichever option is taken it will be necessary to complete some costings and set up a budget. For the exploratory stage it is suggested that the budget should be made on the basis of an overhead allocation with any specific projects costs (the idea will be made clearer later in this section) chargeable from the particular function or department where there is a clear accrual of benefits.

## *Establishing the vision, mission and objectives*

Successful leaders are considered to be those that are able to articulate an overarching vision for their enterprise and be clear as to the underlying purposes and beliefs. The vision for the learning organisation will have been developed during the feasibility study (Chapter 4) as a means of supporting the vision and mission of the enterprise. It was suggested that the vision can best be described as an aspiration or realising some goal or end point.

The vision must be one that has both intrinsic value to the leader and extrinsic values that others will recognise and want to subscribe to for the benefit of the enterprise. Linked to this vision will be an underlying sense of purpose describing what one stands for and values as a key set of ideas. Some suggestions for vision for the learning organisation were given in Chapter 4. Two of these were:

- to establish a joint learning partnership with our customers within three years in both strategic and operational areas
- to set up learning processes and facilities in all the major functions such that learning is used as an explicit management tool

The key here is to decide on the vision or set of visions that will guide and inspire you through this exploratory stage and set the direction for the subsequent stages.

## 174  Implementing the Learning Organisation

By also describing the sense of purpose you will have clarified what the learning organisation is fundamentally trying to be and show how the vision is to be supported. For example, the sense of purpose supporting the first vision statement given above could be:

- being the first business in the industry to achieve this
- setting an example in the market place for excellence

Identification and clarity as to the vision and mission for the enterprise itself is a key task at this stage. Most enterprises will have broad statements in this area and have a set of declared strategies and objectives for one year to two years in the future, the learning organisation needs to be in tune with these objectives. The model shown in Fig. 7.2 illustrates how the activities of the enterprise and those of the learning organisation are in some areas combined and in others separated. In this exploratory stage this coming together on a project basis where a problem is to be solved is vital.

There are two obvious strategies for the learning organisation to pursue at this stage. The incremental approach where the learning organisation comes alongside the enterprise and helps to support or initiate action to address

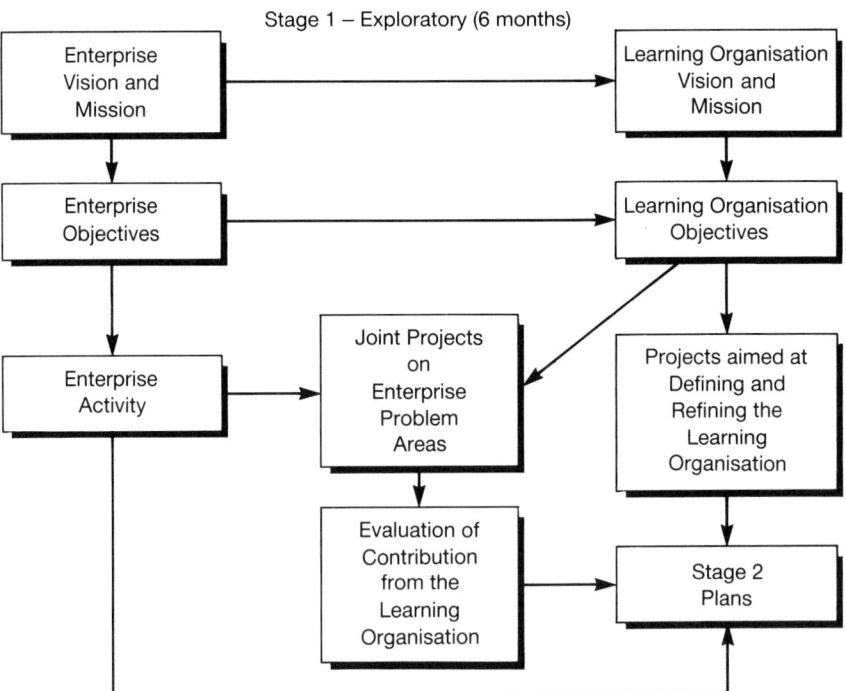

*Fig. 7.2 Matching the learning organisation to the enterprise*

Implementation 175

and solve enterprise problems. Alternatively, the approach whereby the learning organisation sets out to make a major change to the way the enterprise operates and behaves. The former approach is recommended and constitutes a broad strategy for the learning organisation.

Objectives need to be set for the learning organisation in this six months' exploratory stage. These should be grouped under two headings. First, objectives that stem from an analysis of where there are gaps between the enterprise targets and performance. It is here that the learning organisation can provide support. These must be quantifiable in terms of measures that would be recognised in the enterprise terms, e.g. quality, delivery, service response times, costs, learning curves, time spent, new ideas generated, problems solved and solutions implemented, etc. Second, objectives that are concerned with the definition of the learning organisation itself, e.g. identifying the value of techniques used, determining the requirements for the development Stage 2, transferring the notion of the learning organisation to all key managers, etc.

One danger here is that of stifling the learning organisation at this exploratory stage, in areas where some freedom and risk taking is key to success. There will be areas where the contribution of the learning organisation is clear, obvious and rightly quantifiable and accountable. In others a greater degree of freedom may be essential.

Where the emphasis is on exploration a rough guide is to allocate, say, 40 per cent of the budget to accountable project work for the enterprise with clear targets set on benefits to be achieved. The balance being used to develop the notion of the learning organisation and prepare for Stage 2. In this way a creative tension will be set up between the purposes and short-term requirements of the enterprise and the longer-term ambitions of the learning organisation. By maintaining and using this tension those charged with the success of the learning organisation will be able to derive a sense of purpose and drive. This will be communicated to the enterprise managers and help put the notion of the learning organisation higher on their agenda.

## The learning organisation in operation

### Areas for Action

The first step is to determine the areas in the enterprise activity where the learning organisation can provide support or take a lead role. The task is to produce some early winners to demonstrate the contribution that the learning organisation can make and begin to gauge the scope of a total coverage programme for the subsequent stages.

The areas for direct application of the learning focus, at this stage, can be grouped under four headings:

1. **Enterprise wide** (i.e. with organisations that co-operate with but are outside the enterprise such as suppliers, customers, etc.)
2. **Strategic levels** (i.e. policy making, direction funding, etc.)
3. **Operational levels** (i.e. the functions and routine activities)
4. **Process levels** (i.e. the way in which the enterprise gathers information, communicates, plans, decides and communicates).

The reviews, in Chapter 3, will have helped to identify the potential areas for this application. These reviews should be incorporated into the proforma provided in (Figs. 7.3, 7.4, 7.5, 7.6) to focus on those areas that will be suitable for this exploratory stage.

The criteria to be used in selecting an area for short-term action are:

- the extent to which the area is recognised by the power group as important to the enterprise
- how clearly defined is the area and how would a learning focus be used?

| Area | Obvious to power group | Clearly defined | Learning focus will produce an outcome | Outcome obvious within 6 months | What percentage of resource required | Will the learning focus be demonstrated | Go/No Go |
|---|---|---|---|---|---|---|---|
| Customers | | | | | | | |
| Suppliers | | | | | | | |
| Investors | | | | | | | |
| Industry collaborators | | | | | | | |
| Government | | | | | | | |
| Influence groups | | | | | | | |
| Statutory bodies | | | | | | | |
| Professional groups | | | | | | | |

*Fig. 7.3 Potential enterprise applications during the exploratory stage*

| Area | Obvious to power group | Clearly defined | Learning focus will produce an outcome | Outcome obvious within 6 months | What percent-age of resource required | Will the learning focus be demon-strated | Go/ No Go |
|---|---|---|---|---|---|---|---|
| Strategic planning | | | | | | | |
| Policy making | | | | | | | |
| Corporate Structure | | | | | | | |
| Succession Planning | | | | | | | |
| Joint ventures | | | | | | | |
| Collabora-tions | | | | | | | |
| Finance and investment | | | | | | | |
| Acquisitions | | | | | | | |
| New directions | | | | | | | |
| Change programmes | | | | | | | |

*Fig. 7.4 Potential strategic applications during the exploratory stage*

- can a result or outcome be achieved within the six months exploratory period?
- will tackling the area demand more than 40 per cent of the resource of the learning organisation?
- will it provide an opportunity to demonstrate clearly how the learning focus can be used?

This analysis will have identified, say, two or three areas where a learning focus will produce some obvious outcomes and areas where applications need to be planned for subsequent stages. By adopting this approach the learning organisation is beginning to act as a business and the model

| Area | Obvious to power group | Clearly defined | Learning focus will produce an outcome | Outcome obvious within 6 months | What percentage of resource required | Will the learning focus be demonstrated | Go/ No Go |
|---|---|---|---|---|---|---|---|
| Technology | | | | | | | |
| Organisation and structure | | | | | | | |
| Problems | | | | | | | |
| People | | | | | | | |
| Facilities | | | | | | | |
| Controls | | | | | | | |
| Quality | | | | | | | |
| Service | | | | | | | |
| Purchasing and inventory | | | | | | | |
| Design | | | | | | | |
| Innovation | | | | | | | |
| Resourcing | | | | | | | |

*Fig. 7.5 Potential operational applications during the exploratory stage*

illustrated in Fig. 7.7 will help focus on the various elements of this business that should be set up during this exploratory stage.

## Elements of the learning organisation business

### The markets and services

The model shows how services that the learning organisation provides must be derived from a clear identification of the needs of the external and internal stakeholders and those who are considered as being part of the wider enterprise, e.g. competitors. These needs will have been identified

| Area | Obvious to power group | Clearly defined | Learning focus will produce an outcome | Outcome obvious within 6 months | What percent-age of resource required | Will the learning focus be demon-strated | Go/ No Go |
|---|---|---|---|---|---|---|---|
| Business planning | | | | | | | |
| Operations planning | | | | | | | |
| Human resource planning | | | | | | | |
| Investment planning | | | | | | | |
| Project planning and management | | | | | | | |
| Communications | | | | | | | |
| Quality standard setting | | | | | | | |
| Decision making and problem solving | | | | | | | |
| Control | | | | | | | |
| New Ideas creation | | | | | | | |
| Performance reviews | | | | | | | |
| Environmental scanning | | | | | | | |

*Fig. 7.6 Potential process applications during the exploratory stage*

180  Implementing the Learning Organisation

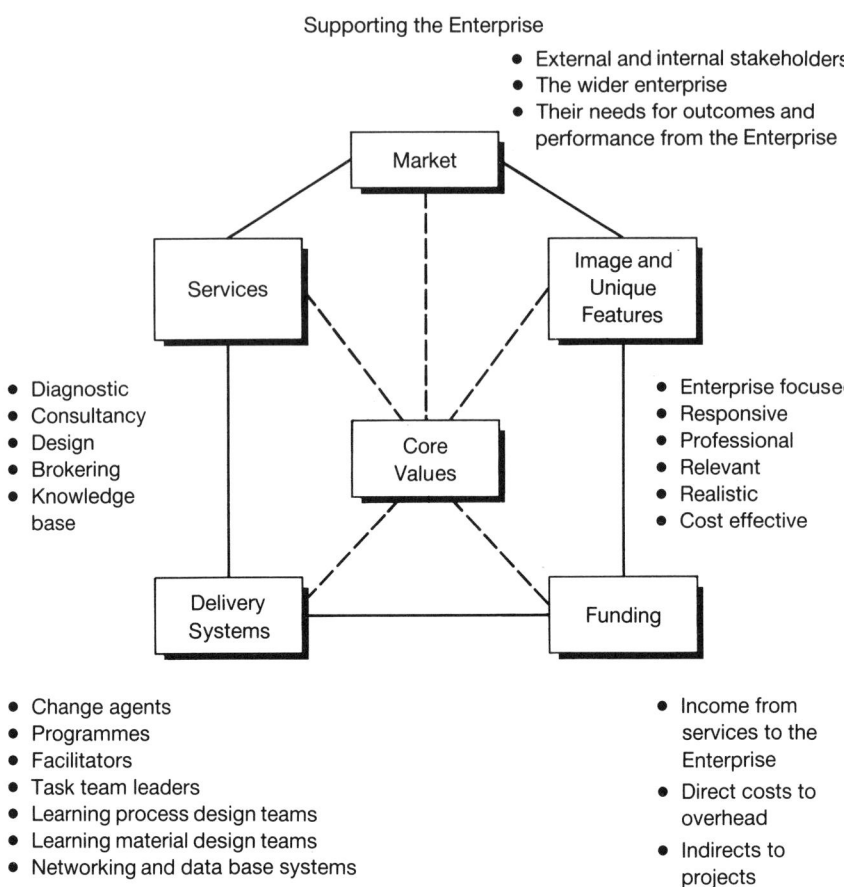

*Fig. 7.7 Elements of the Learning Organisation*

during the reviews in Chapters 3 and 6 along with their expected outcomes, benefits sought and both the formal and informal performance measures used. Discussion and observation will have also provided some assessment of where gaps between expectations and performance exist. Based on this analysis the services that the learning organisation can provide should be determined. These will typically include:

**(a) Diagnosis:** Where the problem owner is helped to explore the circumstances surrounding the problem or issue of concern. Various problem exploration techniques would be provided. These could range from idea generating techniques to group facilitating approaches. The emphasis is on helping the client to use and benefit from these approaches.

**(b) Consultancy:** This could be either process consultancy where the client is given direct help in designing and setting up processes that emphasise learning in order to address a problem. The process could involve people or ways of tackling a contract or specific work issue. Alternatively, the consultancy could involve giving specific advice concerning a decision to engage in some training or development activity.

**(c) Design:** Here the service could involve the design of an approach to diagnosing or tackling a specific problem or issue. For example, where the client wanted to improve or change the way a part of the operation was being carried out or where the managers were not being sufficiently creative in relating to their customers.

**(d) Brokering:** Where the service was to introduce managers to external consultants or to innovations and new technology developments from other organisations. Also helping managers to cross some of the boundaries either between the internal functions or outside the enterprise.

**(e) Knowledge base:** Here the service could be to provide a central source of data for managers in the enterprise on both learning-related issues and issues relevant to the enterprise. This could extend to providing a means of transferring both good practice and local knowledge around the enterprise.

*The delivery system*

This will depend very much on the context in which you are setting up the learning organisation and the capabilities that can be provided from within the learning organisation itself. Where resourcing and capabilities become a limiting factor it is recommended that managers from within the enterprise could well have the required talents. This introduces the idea of how you intend to deliver these learning organisation services.

One obvious way is to recruit the talent either from within or make outside appointments. The other is to act more in a brokering or agency role and either co-opt managers from within the enterprise to work on specific projects or to hire in external consultants. The decision as to which way to go should be made with a clear view as to your vision for the learning organisation and what form of organisation is required to achieve the objectives of firstly the exploratory stage (six months) and then the development and consolidation stages. A good compromise is to have, say, two key internal, highly talented and politically astute permanent learning organisation members who are respected within the enterprise and co-opt in managers from the enterprise to lead projects. External consultants can then be used for their specific contributions or where additional power and new thinking are required. In this way the notions behind the learning organisation will be more easily networked across and to the wider enterprise. It does, of course, depend very much on your ambition, confidence, willingness to take risks and the budget.

The types of areas and problems that the learning organisation chooses to work on will, of course, dictate the types of talent and skills required. In the exploratory stage it is likely that the emphasis will be on providing assistance in the form of simple or goal-directed learning and acting as a facilitator. This could include:

- helping managers use problem-solving techniques that are systematic, rational and logical; the approaches typically found in total quality programmes. These are well documented and include problem definition, brainstorming, cause and effect diagrams, use of weighting and criteria matrices, paired comparison, charting and analysing data, Pareto analysis, Delphi techniques, force field analysis, etc. The emphasis will be on encouraging rigorous thinking and challenging existing assumptions and mental models
- encouraging managers to use pilot programmes and adopt incremental, trial and error approaches to learn how to make breakthroughs and changes
- helping managers revisit past projects or decisions as a way of learning the factors that made for success as well as failure. Identifying those things that have been learned and internalised but now need to be unlearned
- creating networks and demonstrating how learning from other areas and disciplines can help to short cut the learning process. Learning from sources that have not been considered as either valuable or accessible, e.g. customers. Getting managers to question cosy habits that may be detracting from their own efficiency and effectiveness
- helping managers to learn how to cascade understanding and knowledge down and across the enterprise. Particularly making use of best practice in briefing, reporting and communicating plans and directions to key players in the enterprise
- encouraging managers to value the creation of new knowledge and learn how to apply this quickly to the benefit of the enterprise.

The various roles that those involved in promoting the above activities will need to be able to adopt are:

- as change agents
- facilitators
- designers of programmes that encourage learning
- task team leaders
- network managers

- learning material designers and producers.

## Funding

The funding during this exploratory stage should be allocated from the overhead budget. The direct costs attributable to any specific projects should be charged to the originating group and the benefits or outcomes that can be clearly identified to the activity should be highlighted. In this way the learning organisation will be seen as making a direct contribution to the enterprise. This may require some fairly creative ways of presenting the outcomes and the cost benefit model described in Chapter 6 can be used to provide a clear means of evaluation. Other measures of outcome can include:

- the learning curve model where the time to complete an activity reduces with the number of items serviced or results from major introduction of a new operational facility or technology
- straight cost and time savings
- internal and external benchmarking against such factors as: customer satisfaction, design criteria, inventory, procurement and competitors' performance
- the speed and fidelity with which knowledge and understanding are transferred within the enterprise
- the use of half-life curves where the time taken to achieve a 50 per cent improvement in a specific performance measure is used. This is a clear measure of the rate at which learning is taking place and can be applied to performance in areas as diverse as product design to time taken to get products to markets and defect rates. The technique involves plotting the time measured using a linear scale on the horizontal axis and the measure of interest on the vertical axis using a logarithmic scale. These half-life curves can also be used to make comparisons between groups and demonstrate the rate at which learning is taking place.

The health warning with these measures are that they do help to focus on the tangible outcomes of the learning activity but they are less applicable to more complex learning where mind-sets and basic values are involved. For example, where through involvement in a learning activity an individual or a team begins to think and act in a different and more effective way.

## The image

By concentrating on measuring the outcomes of their efforts those leading the learning organisation will begin to project and establish an image within the enterprise. This is a key element in building towards a learning organisation. The image should reflect a:

- focus on the purpose of the enterprise
- professional attitude in the way learning is presented and valued
- concern to provide a response to the managers in the enterprise and the stakeholders that is both relevant, realistic and sensitive to the situation
- determination to seek and demonstrate cost-effective solutions to problems and issues
- desire to build a learning capability in the enterprise by pursuing this focus on learning in all enterprise activities.

## *The core values*

Development of this image will be dependent on those involved being able to identify and hold to a core set of values and beliefs about the learning organisation. These beliefs will need to be reflected in the way in which they approach the managers and deliver their services. This is one of the foundation stones of the learning organisation and will need to be used to progress into the subsequent implementation stages where the learning organisation will cease to exist as a discrete activity, the notion being embedded into the enterprise culture itself by the end of the consolidation stage.

In summary it is recommended that implementation is approached as though it were to become a service activity within the enterprise. Then as the notion spreads within the enterprise to move to a gradual change of culture whereby the need for a separate identity will become redundant. In order to ensure that this change takes place it will be necessary to have determined a series of strategies for each element of the learning organisation business model. These stratetgies are best determined by those involved in the implementation but some examples are given below to illustrate the idea:

1. **Area – Markets**
Strategies:
   (a) To focus during the exploratory stage on those internal clients that will provide the greatest support for subsequent stages of the implementation.
   (b) To build up a set of expectations with clients both internal and external to the enterprise that will create a market demand pull for services.

2. **Area – Services**
Strategies:
   (a) To concentrate in the exploratory stage on perfecting the match between clients needs and the provision of diagnostic and consultancy

services.

**(b)** To define the other services in such a way that they become easily recognisable by the clients and can be readily selected for problem applications.

**3. Area – Delivery Systems**
Strategies:
   **(a)** To create a small core team of highly skilled facilitators.
   **(b)** To perfect tools, instruments and techniques in the area of diagnostics.
   **(c)** To build up a network of internal managers and external consultants to support the delivery of the services.
   **(d)** To seek investment support for building up a database of enterprise knowledge and good practice.
   **(e)** To identify and promote ways of measuring and evaluating the outcomes of investment in a learning focus towards problems and issues within the enterprise.

**4. Area – Funding**
Strategies:
   **(a)** To use the overhead budget as a way of focusing the attention of the senior management on the activities of the learning organisation.
   **(b)** To buffer high risk and exploratory areas of learning from tight management controls.

**5. Area – Image**
Strategies:
   **(a)** To project a professional and responsive image through the use of all media and documentation.
   **(b)** To demonstrate the cost benefits to be gained from the use of a learning focus within the enterprise.
   **(c)** To produce and promote a learning organisation newsletter.
   **(d)** To provide an incentive and reward scheme for those involved in learning organisation linked projects.
   **(e)** To build up a network of other organisations who are engaged in learning-focused developments.

**6. Area – Core Values**
Strategies:
   **(a)** To declare a set of core values and beliefs that resonate with the enterprise and support the vision and mission of the learning organisation.

Fig. 7.8 illustrates how the strategies and actions should be summarised.

These strategies should be linked to a set of plans and objectives

| Area: | | | | | |
|---|---|---|---|---|---|
| Broad strategies: | Target objectives: | Key resources | Key actions | Timescales | Leader/ team |
| | | | | | |
| | | | | | |
| | | | | | |
| | | | | | |
| | | | | | |

*Fig. 7.8 Exploratory stage – key areas, strategies and actions*

covering the exploratory six month stage. The plan should also project into both the development and, where possible, the consolidation stage. As the programme develops and the learning gathers momentum it is likely and desirable that the vision will become more focused and the strategies and plans more specific. It is important that key lessons are captured during this early stage as they will prove invaluable to clarification of actions and plans for subsequent stages. The planning of this exploratory stage is illustrated in Fig. 7.9 as a series of work packages.

## Gaining support and commitment

In order to build up momentum and establish a presence in the enterprise for learning it is important that the support of the key stakeholders and the dominant power groups in the enterprise is obtained. This will obviously have been influenced by your decision on sponsorship and how the learning organisation will be configured and located within the enterprise.

In the majority of cases it is unlikely, and perhaps undesirable, that the Chief Executive becomes involved directly in the implementation activities. But it is vital that the Chief Executive is seen as totally committed to the programme and acts to ensure that ways of matching the learning organisation to the enterprise are clarified and implemented. This means that those charged with implementation will have to identify the group or groups that are going to be the major stakeholders.

In Chapter 6 the review of the key stakeholders in the enterprise was

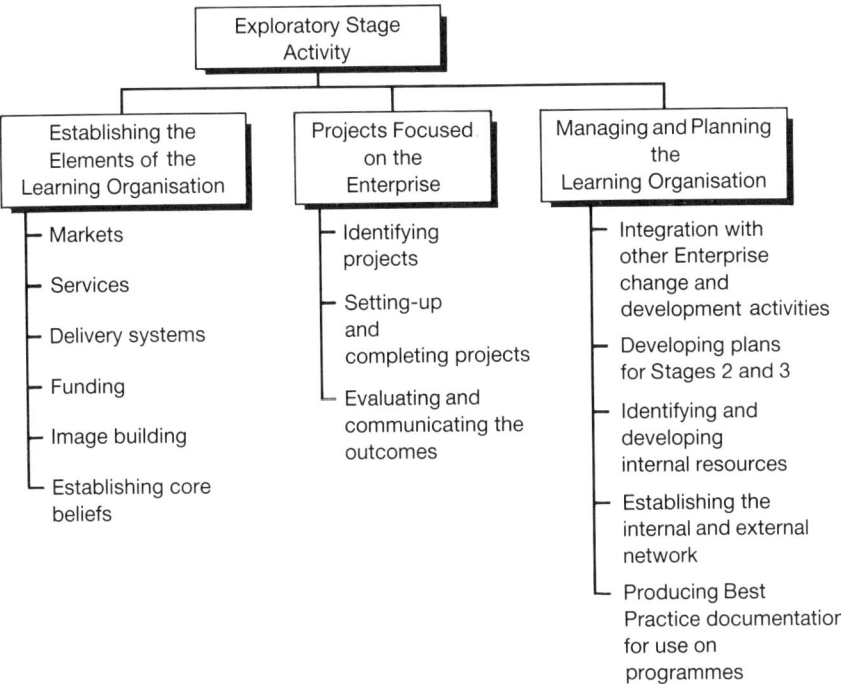

*Fig. 7.9 Exploratory stage – work packages*

completed and it is suggested that the list of internal stakeholders should be used at this stage. In subsequent stages the external stakeholders and those forming the wider enterprise will be key to spreading the learning approach but at this stage the essential action is to secure local support. This choice of internal stakeholders should be made using the following criteria:

- being influential members of the power group or dominant coalition
- prominent in setting the Operational Strategy and direction
- part of the longer-term strategy and policy forming group
- able to influence overhead budget allocation
- committed to the higher level ambitions and visions for the enterprise
- able to influence the behaviour and tone of the key managers in the enterprise.

During this exploratory stage it is essential that the outcomes from the learning organisation activities are communicated clearly and effectively to the chosen stakeholder groups. In doing this it will be necessary to strike a balance between the expectations and needs of the groups that are involved in the early problem solving projects and these stakeholders. In many ways the outcomes sought will be identical but the levels and perspectives being used to evaluate the outcomes are likely to vary, e.g. where an early project is aimed at improving the clarity and effectiveness of the existing management processes in the enterprise, the stakeholders may be concerned with the way in which major problems were identified whereas the managers may value the quality of decision-making and the reduction in time wasted at meetings. This need to balance expectations will come as no surprise to most managers but here we are seeking some early successes and support.

## Leadership and influencing the managers

In order to widen support within the management it is important to decide at this early stage on the style of leadership that will be presented. This is the point where those charged with implementation have to demonstrate, through their behaviour, a determination to create a climate in which experimentation and learning can be seen to produce startling outcomes in enterprise terms. Here the values being promoted such as risk taking, openness, support and networking will have to be demonstrated and justified. The readings included in Chapter 6 emphasised the importance of identifying values that would stand out and be clearly recognisable to the managers in the enterprise.

These values must meet the criteria of realism, significance and durability. Some examples were given in Chapter 6 that included:

- professional dealings with suppliers, customers and contractors
- commercial practice in terms of fair dealings with competitors, meeting customers needs while staying within regulatory standards
- operational dealings that rewarded innovation and creativity and the development of individuals, etc.

These values will need to be developed and encapsulated as the notion of the learning organisation takes shape.

It is recommended that values such as empowerment, creating a learning climate, continuous improvement, etc. are not introduced to the enterprise culture at this early stage. For many managers they are wildly out of tune with their view of organisational life and the day-to-day realities. Many change programmes have foundered due to an attempt to impose a change of culture or language before the benefits of the change have been explored let alone demonstrated. A more incremental approach to change is recommended as the way to success. A major danger is where the Corporate group quickly identify with the notion and then expect the enterprise managers to pick up the ideas and embrace both action and benefits. This more often than not leads to tears.

## Implementation 189

The leadership during this exploratory stage should emphasise the role of the visionary and designer. When approaching project work the emphasis should be on helping managers recognise the value of adopting a more learning-focused approach by setting an example in the way perspectives and mental models need to be surfaced and at times challenged. Leadership should also encourage managers to be creative in seeking ways of tackling problems and help them to recognise the strengths of both innovative and adaptive approaches.

The approach to projects should follow the basic steps shown below:

- concentrate on the problem definition stage
- seek to determine the background information, sources of pressure, outcomes favoured and perspectives held by those involved. Emphasise the use of metaphors to surface mental models
- determine the degree of certainty with which the favoured outcomes can be achieved and the major areas of risk
- determine whether the way forward is best served by adopting a rational, logical or a more innovative approach
- where there is a high level of uncertainty surrounding either the problem definition or solution encourage exploration and testing of ideas by small informal groups. This will encourage creativity and innovation around ideas
- pursue implementation only when agreement has been reached on how to measure the success of the outcomes being sought.

While working on projects the managers involved should be encouraged to identify areas where their thinking or acting are restricted or inhibited. These areas will include:

- a lack of knowledge or understanding about a topic, process, activity, etc.
- where a degree of tension is experienced that might appear as a paradox, e.g. how can I be expected to maintain the system when I am not given technically qualified staff or how can I advise the customer when my information is out of date, etc.
- where the manager feels exploited, undervalued or not committed to the project. The feelings will be the blockages to action
- where the rules, organisational structure, power groups, rewards and incentives are restricting and have a negative influence

The proforma in Chapter 5 should help focus on this learning process. The leader should use these identified areas to encourage both individuals and teams to seek ways of overcoming these blockages. This may involve a mixture of:

- open and critical debate aimed at sharing and testing perspectives and mental models

- self-directed learning and exploration
- off-job training
- informal task groups exploring blockages and testing solutions

All of these learning based activities should be aimed at producing a more effective solution to the project outcome being sought. There will be some internalisation and behavioural changes resulting from the learning, e.g. in how future problems are tackled but at this early stage the drive should still be to achieve a measurable outcome in enterprise terms that is recognised and valued.

## Linking to what already exists

In most enterprises there will already be a series of activities in place that when put together constitute elements that support the notion of the learning organisation. At this exploratory stage it is important that those who promote these elements should not see the learning organisation as either a threat or an irrelevance. These activities will range from appraisal schemes, structured training and development activities, major programmes such as Total Quality Management and culture change programmes.

The learning organisation will need to find and evolve a relationship with these activities and determine in which areas it can best contribute and those where it can establish a unique and distinctive role. The review in Chapter 4 will have identified the existing management development and training approaches at Corporate functional and individual levels and the major change programmes being undertaken. During this exploratory stage the learning organisation, as has been pointed out, should focus on enterprise related projects and as such this should present little conflict with the status quo.

In parallel with this a study of the wider applications for the learning organisation will quickly identify areas and opportunities where:

- existing development and change programmes have failed to deliver
- no attempt has been made to identify or clarify the need
- approaches based on a learning focus have not been considered
- the process of clarifying the needs is an opportunity for learning
- the learning organisation offers a unifying approach
- the existing approaches are out of tune with the turbulence being experienced by the enterprise
- the existing approaches are out of tune with the dominant or sub-cultures within the enterprise.

It is important that due attention is given to any areas of potential overlap or perceived threat from other parties within the enterprise who have been pursuing learning albeit under a different label. Coalitions and joint working should be the order of the day during these early stages. It would be a mistake to have the notion of the learning organisation lodged at the Corporate level and only being seen as relevant to broad strategic changes. The notion of the learning organisation is much reduced unless it is allowed to cascade down, across and outside of the enterprise. Therefore activities such as competence-based training, assessment centres, learning contracts, self-development, team building, quality improvement programmes, etc. are all building blocks and part of the learning organisation.

One way to begin building this unifying and overarching vision of the learning organisation is to begin to specify and develop an information database that enables managers to tap into opportunities for learning. This can then be extended in later stages to include best practices in areas such as project management, customer relationships, external benchmarking, etc.

## Summary for the exploratory stage

The condition of the enterprise in terms of being stable, undergoing planned change or in a state of turbulence will provide the main trigger or stimulus during this stage, the major learning opportunities arising where planned change or turbulence exists. The need to sell the notion and benefits of using a learning focus to address the needs of the enterprise will therefore be paramount as there will be competition from other approaches and ideas on how to operate and grow the enterprise. In many cases the enterprise managers will be looking for short-term fixes to problems and medium-term solutions to the perceived chaos. The learning organisation will in these conditions be flawed if it only offers longer-term benefits.

The need to gain support and commitment from the Chief Executive is seen as crucial in all cases. It is recommended that the core staffing level of the learning organisation should be kept small (say two to three people) with the ability to call on external consultants and use the enterprise managers on projects as appropriate.

The budget should be set at a realistic level and preferably be part of the enterprise overhead with costs for specific projects attributed to the group that benefits from the outcomes. The danger arises where the growth of the learning organisation can be stifled by placing on it either budgetary controls which are restrictive or setting too high an expectation on outcomes.

The importance of the need for a clear identity for the learning organisation cannot be over stressed. This identity should derive from the vision and mission statements and the close link to the vision and mission of the enterprise. The objectives for the learning organisation should be based on studying key areas where there are gaps between the enterprise targets and performance. These will occur in areas ranging from the wider enterprise (involving suppliers and clients) to internal management processes.

It is recommended that the learning organisation should be considered as a business in order to focus on its growth. Using the classical business model of markets, services, delivery, funding and image with associated strategies to encourage its development. This will help identify the services that are needed to be delivered and the types of skills that those driving the implementation will need to demonstrate. Getting support from key managers and power groups will be vital in the early stages as will communicating successful outcomes of projects throughout the enterprise in order to gain credibility and acceptance that the learning organisation is more than a notion.

Setting an appropriate visionary leadership style and demonstrating the commitment to a clear set of values will play a key part in establishing the learning organisation within the minds of the enterprise managers. The core team will need to be capable of delivering a wide range of learning processes and the ability to act as a facilitator will be crucial. Being able to bring to managers detailed and effective approaches to problem diagnosis and solution and explain how to overcome blockages to learning.

Finally, the need to form alliances and working relationships with training development and those engaged in major change programmes in the enterprise will enable the learning organisation to integrate into the enterprise activities.

## STAGE 2 – DEVELOPMENT (12 MONTHS)

The work in Stage 1 will have established the key elements of the learning organisation and have ensured a level of credibility through success of the project work. In Stage 2 five areas are highlighted as ways of progressing the development. These are to:

- identify and support enterprise based projects that can benefit from a learning focus
- continue developing the elements of markets, services, delivery systems, funding, image building and core values
- design and introduce a range of work-focused events and programmes where the emphasis is on the learning process
- create the climate in which a culture focused on learning can develop
- link reward and incentive systems to achievements in learning.

The work packages for this stage are illustrated in Fig. 7.10. The emphasis given to these areas will depend on the particular circumstances in which the implementation is being carried out. These areas are considered to be of a

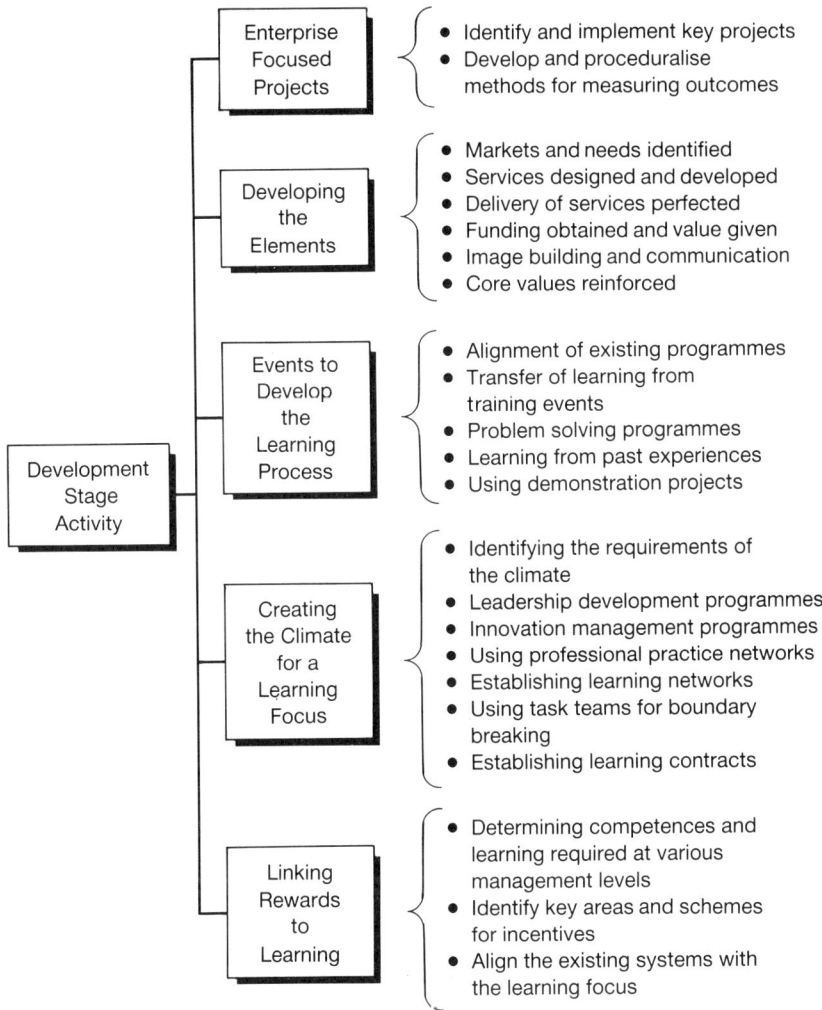

*Fig. 7.10 Development stage – work packages*

generic nature and to help you to decide on specific applications. Some guidance is given on how they might be applied in a typical enterprise.

## Enterprise-focused projects

It is vital that projects addressing key issues in the enterprise continue to be used to both demonstrate the value and perfect the learning-focused approaches. These approaches are described in the exploratory stage as are some of the methods used to measure outcomes.

An attitude of experimentation and the use of unstructured, as well as structured, approaches to the diagnostic, idea generation and idea evaluation and selection stages should be encouraged. With most projects there will be three key stages through which the team will need to progress; problem analysis, generating ideas, evaluating and selecting ideas. There are a range of techniques and approaches that can be used in these stages and these are outlined below.

The problem analysis stage will often require a redefinition where new perspectives are brought to bear. The trick is to move away from the initial perception of the problem using divergent thinking and other techniques to spring the mind into new ways of seeing. There are some well documented techniques to help in this such as:

- boundary examination where key words in the problem statement are underlined and hidden assumptions identified. These are then considered in terms of their implications. From this a new problem definition is developed. In this way the boundaries are explored and the problem re-defined.
- goal orientation where a general description of the problem is made and questions are posed such as: what do I want to accomplish? what is stopping me and what constraints must I accept to solve the problem? The problem is then redefined.
- the classical five Ws of who, what, where, when and why?
- decision tree analysis where the symptoms of the problem are used to derive the underlying causes or factors. These are given weightings and then options for solutions derived with advantages and disadvantages for each option spelt out.

The second stage is where ideas to solve the problem are generated. Some of the more popular techniques used are:

- brainstorming where a verbal generation of ideas is collected from a group in either a nominal (private) or shared process. Brainwriting on the other hand is used where ideas are written down and then shared. In this way problems associated with the status of group members and inhibition can be overcome
- assumptions reversals where the major assumptions about a problem are written down then each assumption is reversed, thus stimulating a new set of ideas
- creative imagery where mental images are allowed to flow freely around the problem. Then these images or pictures are captured and described and new insights to the problem generated.

The final stage is where ideas are evaluated and selected. Some of these techniques are best suited to problems that are well structured and thus lend themselves to rational and numerical ordering of alternatives. These would include linear programming, decision theory, game theory and risk analysis, all of which rely to some extent on the use of probability theory. For the more unstructured problems the solution may require use of techniques that rely on creativity. The more popular techniques are:

- simple advantage – disadvantage evaluations where various alternative decisions are rated using an agreed set of criteria. An additional step is to give weights to each criteria.
- screening of ideas through various filters such as: financial viability, resources available, match with existing organisational processes, timescale etc.
- categorising ideas under the headings simple, hard, difficult, the degree of difficulty being related to expenditure of time and money for implementation. This technique is best used where these criteria are dominant or where a quick grouping of ideas generated from a brainstorming session was required. The grouping would indicate levels of complexity.

Some of the more popular and well-tried problem solving techniques include:

(a) Kepner–Tregoe method where the problem is defined as a divergence from a known norm. The problem being analysed in terms of what is distinctive about the problem and what changes have occurred prior to the problem being noticed? What is distinctive about the frequency of occurrence and the size and growth of the problem? It is mainly used for closed problems where something has gone wrong and relies on rigorous and systematic problem analysis.

(b) Value engineering where teams study alternatives to, say, reducing costs without altering quality, worth or reliability. The team then initiates and supports implementation of ideas arising from the study. The various stages of the process include: fact finding, analysis, creative idea generation, evaluation and decision making. The key is to seek new and original ways of defining and reframing the problem statement and encouraging boundary breaking and lateral thinking. The two key concepts used are those of value (to the user) and function (what the object is required to do). The functions are divided into basic, secondary and supporting types as related to the end user. The components of each function are then aligned with their associated costs. An analysis is then made between the cost of providing these functions and hence value to the user. The design and processes associated with each component is then analysed in terms of reducing cost while maintaining

## 196  Implementing the Learning Organisation

quality and reliability, etc.

(c) The Delphi technique where consensus from a panel of experts is used to define a problem and reach a consensus decision. This involves formulation of a question by the final decision makers that can be clearly understood by the panel of experts. The number of experts depends on the breadth of solutions being sought (say 30 experts). A questionnaire is sent out stating the broad problem and requesting examples of possible solutions.

A second questionnaire is then sent out based on analysis of the first response and focuses on: areas of agreement/disagreement, clarifies meanings, seeks priorities. A third questionnaire then seeks to summarise all the responses and seeks votes on the potential solutions. This method is used where the experts are widely dispersed and reduces the problems associated with group and peer pressure. The disadvantage is the loss of social interaction and problems associated with meanings.

These approaches to problem solving will require the use of a skilled facilitator and care should be taken to select approaches that are seen by the participants as realistic. The key to the success of these activities is to ensure that the benefits of using these problem-solving approaches are recognised and that they translate into a measurable outcome. The methods of measuring these outcomes described in the exploratory stage should be used and new measures established, e.g. learning curve models, straight cost and time savings. benchmarking against customer satisfaction and design times, the speed with which knowledge is transferred and the use of half-life curves around specific performance measures. These methods of measurement should be proceduralised where possible in order to ensure that their use is adopted throughout the enterprise.

### *Developing the elements of the Learning Organisation*

The activities stated in the exploratory stage should be clarified and developed. Typical changes to strategies for the various elements might include:

**1. Markets**
   (a) To focus on stakeholders or clients external to the enterprise in order to widen the scope for learning activities.
   (b) To identify the medium and longer-term capabilities that will be required by key internal groups and functions. To then align the services to these learning needs.
   (c) To continue to focus on all levels of the enterprise activity
   (d) To form close alliances with potential champions within the enterprise.

## 2. Services
(a) To continue to provide and perfect the diagnostic and consultancy services but increasingly formalise, document and proceduralise the approaches and techniques.
(b) To emphasise the role of brokering as a way of discouraging the managers from over-dependency on the core members.
(c) To establish a knowledge data base which managers are able to use and help build up.

## 3. Delivery Systems
(a) To formalise and document tools, techniques and approaches to problem solving.
(b) To establish key managers in the learning network both internal and external to the enterprise.
(c) To maintain a core team with increasing use of internal managers as facilitators and project team managers.

## 4. Funding
(a) To ensure that project savings and measurement of benefits from learning attract a high profile.

## 5. Image
(a) To emphasise the benefits both internal and external to the enterprise of the learning focus.
(b) To demonstrate areas where the core competences of the enterprise have been enhanced through using a learning focus.

## 6. Core Values
(a) Continue to promote values that are in tune with the vision and mission and support those of the enterprise.

## *Events to develop the learning process*

It is suggested that a number of events or programmes should be designed and implemented in order to create a strong foundation for a learning focus in the enterprise. These events can be grouped into three areas. Making best use of existing training events, setting up new training programmes and introducing some high profile demonstration projects. It is important that those training and development activities already in place in the enterprise are aligned with the more learning-focused approaches.

For well-established organisations it is likely that training and development is based on a mixture of needs analysis, appraisal schemes, assessment schemes and where the work itself is used to generate specific training requirements. A review should be made of all these activities in collaboration with those responsible for their operation. The review should focus on:

- how functional and managerial competences at each job level are linked to the programmes
- the links between the appraisal and needs analysis process and the programmes
- the key objectives for each programme
- the extent to which learning is built into the programme process
- the extent to which learning outcomes from programmes are measured

The result of this review should be a clear description of any gaps that exist between the generic learning needs of the managers, functions or operational groups and the existing training and development provision. It will also enable a more learning focus to be brought to bear on existing programmes and on measuring the outcomes.

It is likely that the need for new training and development programmes will have been identified, e.g. problem solving, management of innovation and special events that involve managers reviewing major projects and changes as a way of learning from past experience. It is also likely that use can be made of special project events that can be used to demonstrate the power of a learning focus. For example, where a new product or service is to be introduced then the core team can help design an approach covering team building, planning through to implementation and evaluation that emphasised all the elements of the learning approach. This use of demonstration projects is a key vehicle for organisational learning.

## *Creating the climate for the learning organisation*

In this development stage the move should be to create the climate or conditions that will allow the learning organisation to grow. It is important that the temptation to import a culture is resisted. The approach should be to set the conditions in which the existing culture can begin to migrate or move towards a more learning focus. In Chapter 5 the review of the dominant culture and sub-cultures in the enterprise will have provided a clear view of the status quo. Major culture change programmes may also be in various stages of implementation and changes in top management or external events may also be influencing the climate.

It is assumed that by now the vision and mission for the learning organisation,will have been communicated within the enterprise and a reasonable level of commitment or at least support to the notion and the underlying beliefs has been achieved.

The underlying principles for determining the actions needed to create the

**Implementation** 199

learning climate are:

- that actions must be in tune with the key interests of the enterprise
- they must build on the existing culture and provide obvious improvements
- they must use a change model that appeals to the perspectives on change held by the power groups and the wider management
- they must not threaten the outcomes of any previous change programmes.

The climate that will encourage the growth of a learning culture is one where:

- experimentation and risk taking are valued
- informal groups and professional practice groups form and operate in an open way
- information and knowledge on best practice are valued, collected and communicated within the enterprise. Moving knowledge from the tacit to the explicit is encouraged and rewarded
- the control and rewards systems encourage managers to declare their perspectives and confront their concerns when tackling work problems
- change is welcomed and seen as a demonstration of learning and progress.

The most obvious way to promote this climate is through the behaviour of the senior managers and leaders of the various functions and groups.

Two programmes will need to be set up to start this change. These should cover leadership development based on the principles outlined in Chapter 4 and the Management of Innovation. The latter programme should cover an appreciation of the personality and creativity concepts covered in Chapter 3 and the conditions that will enable idea generation and transfer through to implementation to take place. The target should be to expose all managers and teams to these programmes.

Four other activities that will promote the creation of this climate are:

- setting up and operating professional practice networks where individuals are helped to share their expertise and learning both internal and external to the enterprise
- forming specialised and multi-disciplinary task teams that set out to investigate and challenge perceived boundaries to enterprise performance, e.g. where cross-functional working is not proving effective, where lack of know-how or technology are restricting growth, where new ways of approaching clients or providing a service need to be explored
- establishing learning networks both internal and external to the enterprise using support from information technology solutions where appropriate
- setting up joint study teams with key customers and suppliers to tackle cost reduction and service development problems.

These activities will all place a high demand on learning and once again it is essential to measure and therefore demonstrate their worth to the purposes of the enterprise. Where an activity cannot be justified prior to implementation then it should only proceed if the longer term and intangible benefits can be argued convincingly.

A final event in creating the climate is to introduce the use of learning contracts. This is a method whereby a formal written agreement is made between a manager and a trainer or senior about what the manager will learn, how the learning will be carried out, what resources will be needed and how the learning will be assessed. The definitions of competences required are laid down and the workplace itself is used as the learning environment with the support of structured learning materials where appropriate. This approach has similarities to that of Management by Objectives and can be linked into a conventional Appraisal System.

## Linking rewards to learning

It is important that learning and the subsequent performance outcomes are linked to a reward or incentive system. The introduction of learning contracts and making links to the appraisal scheme is one way of starting this process. Another is to begin to integrate functional and management competences into a coherent system. This will involve aligning the existing enterprise systems for training and development more closely with the needs of the enterprise. Management jobs will need to be graded in terms of levels that have degrees of associated generic competences.

These generic management competences could include, for example:

- self-awareness and self-management
- effective management of subordinates and teams
- ability to interpret the needs and manage the local stakeholders and interfaces to outside agencies
- managing a major change programme
- setting and implementing strategic direction for the unit or enterprise
- initiating and contributing to the corporate vision building process and creation of mission, objectives and key strategies.

Managers need to acquire a particular degree of competence in all of these generic areas. A development programme should be set up so that as a manager moves up the corporate ladder the appropriate level of competence can be acquired and demonstrated. Most of the learning can be based on project and work-based activity.

## Implementation 201

## *Summary for the development stage*

The importance of continuing to identify and implement projects that contribute directly to the purpose of the enterprise cannot be over-emphasised. The project activities need to be much more closely directed towards the learning associated with problem definition, idea generation and decision evaluation. A range of possible techniques for doing this have been highlighted in this section to illustrate the increasing need to focus on creativity and to encourage managers to challenge their own and colleagues' mental models; acquiring this skill will create the core of the learning organisation.

In the early stages a skilled facilitator will be needed to help run these problem-focused project sessions but increasingly this skill must be developed within the senior and middle management ranks. The motive behind running these technique-based sessions is so that managers can become much more relaxed when using both the structured and unstructured techniques. In this way learning becomes the focus and the techniques merely the vehicle for achieving this end. Tangible and intangible outcomes from all these activities need to be constantly identified, measured and valued. The drive must be to ensure that the learning leads to a recognised outcome. Hence there must be a determination to capture and proceduralise these techniques, measures and applications.

During this stage the elements of the learning organisation will need to be perfected. Strategies for each of the areas of markets, services, delivery systems, funding and image building are suggested in this section and will help to embed the activities of learning into the enterprise activities while maintaining only a small core team.

Various events have been described in this section that will help to further develop the learning process. First, a review of existing training and development activities that will lead to identifying and closing the gaps between training and the purposes of the enterprise. A more learning focus to these programmes can then be introduced along with any new programmes. Programmes covering problem solving, management of innovation and projects reviewing past experiences can be likely contenders for filling these gaps.

Second there is the need to create the climate for the learning organisation. This is a key activity in this development stage. The aim is not to impart a culture but to generate initiatives and set up programmes and events that will move the existing culture to a more learning focus. These events will range from leadership programmes to setting up professional practice networks using specialised task teams and introducing learning contracts linked to appraisals. The other major activity in this stage will be to link the existing reward and incentive systems to the learning-focused structure that will begin to emerge.

## STAGE 3 – CONSOLIDATION (12 MONTHS)

Some broad guides can be given for this stage where the vision for the learning organisation of full integration with the enterprise is to be realised. The main activities will include:

- setting up all the processes that will enable the learning approach to be used and where appropriate developed
- establishing effective learning links and processes within the scope of the wider enterprise, e.g. customers, suppliers, etc.
- establishing ways of creating new knowledge and ensuring that it is captured and used to support the enterprise
- ensuring that the pay-off from individual, group and enterprise learning is recognised and linked to rewards and incentives for the managers
- ensuring that the culture emphasises values associated with learning.

This chapter has presented a very full and prescriptive coverage as to how to approach the implementation. It will help you to construct your own plans to suit your particular situation and is based on experience of what can realistically be expected to work in most settings.

The problem facing all potential implementors is to decide how big a step they are prepared to take. If the pressure for action and the personal commitment are of a high order then the way forward is often clearer. Whereas if you are trying to fight your way out of a corner or your commitment looks more like compliance, then the first step is often much harder. If the latter is the case it may be better to take very small steps and allow your learning to evolve. The decision is, as always, yours.

In Chapter 8 a series of examples of how others have tackled the challenge are presented. These are offered with the sole purpose of providing opportunities for what is known as creative swiping and perhaps to provide inspiration. The views given in these examples are based on interpretations made by the writer of this book and needless to say do not represent the policy or views of the corporations and organisations.

## *References:*

Boak, G. *Developing Managerial Competences*, (Pitman Publishing, Longmans Group, 1991).

Kepner, C.H. & Tregoe, B.B. *The New Rational Manager* (Kepner Tregoe Inc. New Jersey, 1981).

# 8

# LESSONS FROM PRACTICE

## INTRODUCTION

In this chapter the experiences of a wide spread of companies who have tackled the notion of the learning organisation are presented. They make no claim to being examples of best practice but they are real and expose some of the difficulties and successes surrounding implementation. All these examples illustrate learning at the levels of the enterprise itself (viewed as an entity), groupings of individuals (teams and functions) and that of the individual.

The notion of an enterprise having the ability to learn does require a leap of the mind. But there are perhaps a number of ideas surrounding this notion of enterprise learning that most managers would feel reasonably comfortable about. The question to ask is what sort of things does an enterprise need to be able to do well? Firstly to be able to interface to the outside world or environment in such a way that the stakeholders and customers achieve satisfaction (perhaps even delight). Secondly, it needs to be efficient and effective in conducting its internal affairs, in particular having a structure that supports key processes and delivers outputs to meet performance requirements. Thirdly, it needs to create an environment in which people can be effective in pursuing the purpose of the enterprise. It is not unreasonable to assume that managers at all levels are concerned with helping the enterprise learn how to achieve these three capabilities.

The next level of learning that is pursued within the enterprise is that of group and team learning. Once again it requires a small leap of the mind to be able to attribute learning to a group. Most managers would recognise an effective group but we need once again to ask the question: 'What sort of things does a group have to do well?' There are three requirements. Firstly, to be able to manage their interface to other internal groups while discharging their responsibility to the enterprise. Secondly, to contribute to the satisfaction of customers and stakeholders. Thirdly, to turn the tacit knowledge and understanding that the group acquires into explicit knowledge and make this available to other groups. Once again these would appear to be ideas on group learning that most managers would recognise and already be supporting to a large extent.

The final level of learning is at the individual level. Here everyone is quite happy with this notion. Not perhaps easy to agree on a definition about what it is but descriptions are plentiful. There are three areas of individual learning about which most would agree. Firstly, that of learning to understand oneself and set about mastering the local environment (e.g. interpersonal skills, acquiring information, becoming skilled at local politics, making decisions, integrating into work groups, communicating, etc.). Secondly, being able to contribute to the group or team through either a knowledge or personal style approach. Finally, being able to recognise and create opportunities for personal development and growth. These levels of learning needs are illustrated in Fig. 8.1.

How best to tackle enterprise, group and individual learning needs begins

---

**The Enterprise needs to learn how to:**

1. Interface to the outside world and provide stakeholder satisfaction.
2. Be efficient and effective in conducting its internal affairs.
3. Create an internal environment in which people can be effective.

**Groups need to learn how to:**

1. Manage interfaces to other internal groups.
2. Satisfy customers and stakeholders.
3. Turn tacit to explicit knowledge.
4. Work together effectively and efficiently.

**Individuals need to learn how to:**

1. Master the local environment.
2. Contribute to the team.
3. Pursue personal development and growth.

---

*Fig. 8.1 Learning needs*

to fall into place once the perspectives that people hold are surfaced and rigorously challenged. The perspectives may appear vague and suspect at times but it is this thinking that drives people to action and the adoption of their particular approaches to managing work and learning. This takes us much closer to understanding how the learning organisation can be made a shared reality.

The drivers for learning at these three levels stem from the requirements and demands of the enterprise itself. This will include directives from corporate and senior management, the managers perceptions of where the pressure for performance is coming from and what they consider is expected in terms of their behaviour. The other source of drive will be that which stems from tackling or conducting the work itself. These drivers create or encourage learning that is in the majority of cases tacit (where people and teams behave in intuitive or unspoken ways – the expertise of know-how) and in some cases the learning will become explicit (contained in procedures and best practice guides). In some organisations there is a view that tacit knowledge means power but a more reasonable interpretation would be that most managers do not find it easy to turn tacit into explicit knowledge. An area of learning that is rarely addressed.

This mixture of corporate drives, perceptions of pressure for performance, the work itself, tacit and explicit knowledge, control systems, change programmes and training and development actions, all contribute to the climate of the enterprise. This climate is recognisable by the competences and the norms of behaviour that are displayed. We have in effect created an ever changing culture or set of sub-cultures. Fig. 8.2 illustrates this notion in model form. This model provides a framework to help focus your thinking on implementation and also to help interpret the examples of practice given in the next section. Be critical about the model presented as it is intended for this purpose.

## Practice

These descriptions of practice are based on discussions with key individuals within the particular organisation, reviews of published articles and subsequent interpretations by the author. They do not therefore represent the policy or viewpoint of the organisations or the individuals named, although their publication has been approved. Their sole purpose is to provide a stimulus for thinking around implementation of the notions of the learning organisation contained in this book. They do provide a rich source of material and are offered as a vehicle for your learning.

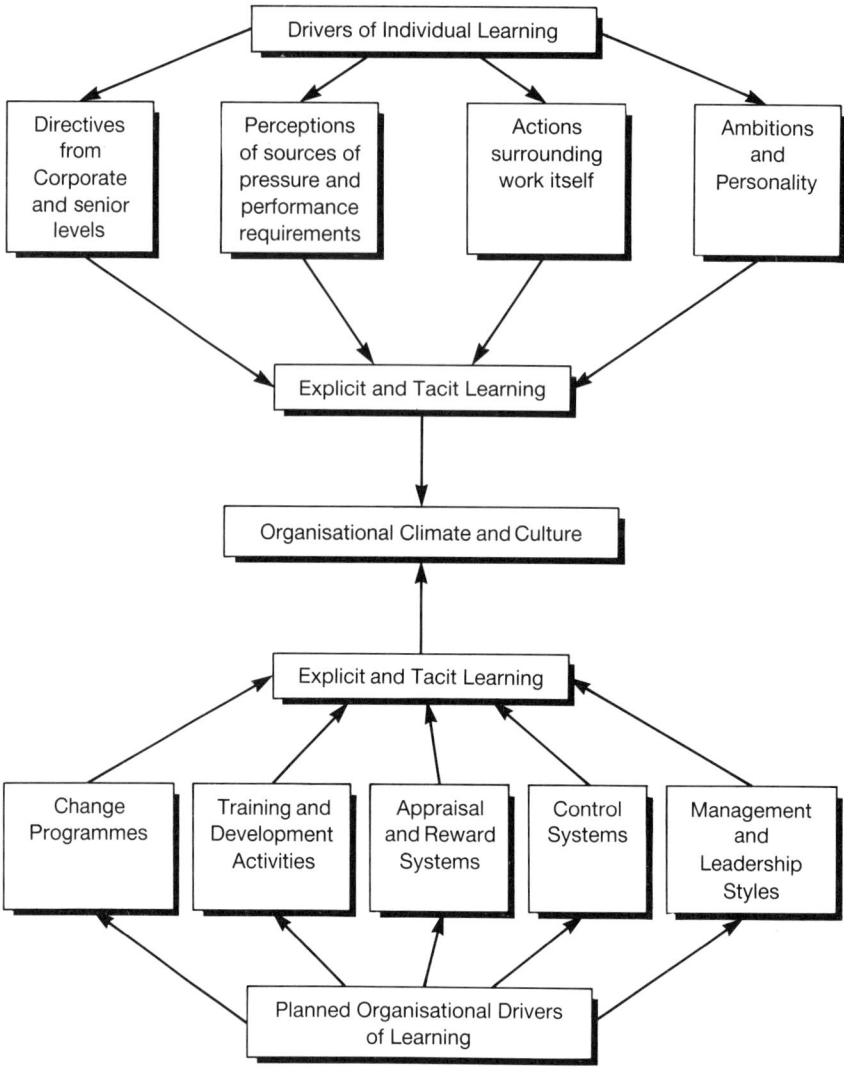

*Fig. 8.2 A model for interpreting lessons from practice*

## INTERNATIONAL COMPUTERS LIMITED

### Background

One of Europe's largest and most successful information technology companies formed from a merger in 1968 of two UK computer suppliers. The company design and manufacture a range of hardware, from mainframes and departmental systems to specialist workstations and personal computers. Over half of the business turnover is derived from software and services, offering international clients total solutions to business and financial problems. ICL is part of the Fujitsu family (since 1990), the second largest IT company in the world. ICL have businesses in 70 countries with Europe as the base, employing 25,000 people and generated revenues of almost £2.5 billion in 1992.

The company is fully committed to the Total Quality concept and in 1986 the Chief Executive, Peter Bonfield, and the Board instituted a programme of continuous quality improvement. An estimated £1 million each year is spent to ensure the success of this improvement programme. More than 100,000 man days have been invested to date in the training associated with this programme. The approach to training was top down, over 22,000 employees have attended the basic quality courses. This dedication to training and development of staff runs through all the company's activities.

## Practice

Elizabeth Lank, Managing Consultant of ICL Management Development at ICL Beaumont, UK, emphasised that the company prefer to adopt a very practical approach to the notion of the learning organisation and have in place a number of mechanisms to build what they see as – 'sustainable competitive advantage'.

The belief is that the ability to cope with the continuing pace of change in the industry can be attributed to its overall 'organisational capability'. This organisational capability is integral to understanding its environment and delivering on its business objectives and strategies. The elements of this capability are:

- leadership
- succession
- knowledge, skills and attitudes of all staff
- systems, processes and infrastructure
- organisation structure
- culture

All these elements are seen to require the involvement of people in the business. The model of organisation change that is seen as effective is one that is based on the critical dimension of the competence of staff to respond to change.

The company has a wide range of core and specialist training programmes in place and a number of programmes that focus primarily on development and learning. These learning events include:

(a) A number of self-development programmes including one for high potential managers. On this programme entry is by invitation for those managers who have been identified as key to the organisation via the 'organisation and Management Review' process, the HR side of the business planning process.

This focus on self development is seen as addressing the needs of the empowered 'knowledge worker', who needs to be well equipped to meet the challenges of continuing and escalating change. This programme is seen as contrasting with the traditional prescriptive and systematic training. The programme runs over 18 months and includes three distinct phases. A taster module where the principles of self-managed learning and the programme itself is explored. This is followed by a Diagnostic Module in which various tools are used to help the participants develop their strategic learning plan in line with ICL's business direction and form Development Network Groups comprising no more than six people. The final phase is where the Group help each other to manage and evaluate their learning. The overall aim is to help develop the knowledge skills and experience to tackle the challenges of general management.

(b) A company-wide appraisal system that includes a training and development plan for each individual, which they and their managers have responsibility for implementing.

(c) Training managers to act as coaches in support of the company's 'Investing in People' performance management processes.

(d) A willingness to 'learn from failure' such as when the senior managers involved in a less than successful acquisition shared their experience with the top 30 management teams across ICL; the objective being to dissect what went wrong and why and the lessons to be learned for the future.

(e) Learning across boundaries where cross-company networks are used to help transfer learning:

- Graduate level hires from across Europe meet regularly and form strong bonds. Graduates are recruited in their home country and after two to three months move to the UK for a ten-month training and development programme and exposure to the business environment.
- The general managers from the company's 25 software businesses meet regularly to share experiences and work together to develop strategies for the software and services business.

(f) Professional practice networks. Two networks of the company's most influential technical experts have been set up to help develop a technical vision of the future. These networks ensure that distributed teams of engineers who are working in the various autonomous business units can communicate and hence help maintain the company's technical edge in th global market place. The company has identified what are known as – 'Distinguished Engineers'. This approach supports the ICL Fellows programme where ten of the company's top engineers have been designated ICL Fellows who meet twice a year with the Chief Executive to discuss engineering and business strategy in ICL.

The distinguished engineers are invited to act as role models, organising strategic activities for engineers within the company. The scheme will eventually involve around 1000 engineers on an extended network linking in to 100 or so Distinguished Engineers.

The programme will focus on areas such as: technical capability through training in line with market trends, technical implementation through transferring successful engineering practice, technical management and technical acquisition including links to Universities and acquiring new technologies and involvement in broad-based research programmes.

The appraisal scheme identifies those who have potential to become a 'Distinguished Engineer' and the list is reviewed by ICL's Fellows who rank candidates on the basis of: technical ability, corporate mindedness and peer recognition (how they are regarded by colleagues). ICL's senior technical council make the final decision. This is seen as encouraging engineers to play a key role in the strategic development of the company and at the heart of the corporate culture.

(g) Two major functional networks involving Finance and Personnel managers from across Europe working together to ensure overall company business priorities and values are shared across ICL's autonomous business divisions.

These programmes and events provide a flavour of the way in which a learning focus is being applied to help ICL meet its business goals.

## MOTOROLA INC

### Background

Motorola is one of the world's leading providers of wireless communications and electronic equipment, systems, components and services for worldwide markets. Motorola was a winner of the first Malcolm Baldbridge National Quality Award in recognition of its company-wide management of quality process.

In 1992 net sales were over $13,000 million with some $100 million spent on training worldwide.

The elements of the strategy that produces the financial results are described as:

- Quality improvement to achieve total customer satisfaction and market leadership through empowerment of people.
- Cycle time reduction, both in customer service and product development, to reduce costs and lead new markets, as well as serving customers with products that help them manage time and become more productive.
- Technology leadership, leveraging strength in software, manufacturing, micro-electronics and radio communications.
- Investment in the future, training, research and development, production tools and facilities and in technology.
- Partnership with other companies, customers and within Motorola, to leverage available resources and enter growth markets while making efficient use of their financial resources.

Quality is the priority operational initiative relying on the empowerment of people to make it happen.

The major businesses are: Semiconductor Products, Land Mobile Products, General Systems, Paging & Wireless Data Group, Government Electronics Group, Automotive and Industrial Electronics Group.

Worldwide, Motorola employ around 103,000 people with some 10,500 in Europe of which 800 are in the Automotive & Industrial Electronics Group.

The company approach to the notion of the learning organisation is heavily influenced by three factors:

- a focus on Quality over the past 12 years
- a determination to empower every individual
- a fundamental desire to provide: 'Total Customer Satisfaction'

This desire to provide 'Total Customer Satisfaction' is encapsulated as follows:

Key Beliefs – How we will always act

- Constant Respect for People
- Uncompromising Integrity

Key Goals – What we must accomplish

- Best in Class: People, Marketing, Technology, Product: Software, Hardware & Systems, Manufacturing, Service. Increased Global Market
- Superior Financial Results

Key Initiatives – How we will do it

- Six Sigma Quality (no more than 3.4 defects per million opportunities)
- Total Cycle Time Reduction

- Product, Manufacturing and Environmental Leadership
- Profit Improvement
- Empowerment for all in a Participative, Co-operative and Creative Workplace.

## Practice

Nick Azelborn (Vice President & Director European Region, Automotive & Industrial Electronics Group) and Norman Finnis (European Quality Manager – AIEG) highlighted three elements that create the company focus on the learning process: The workforce itself (through the Total Customer Satisfaction Team competition); senior managers and executives (through their involvement in Functional Councils and strategic task teams) and the Motorola University in Shaumburg, Illinois (through the provision of central and regional training and consultancy).

### Total customer satisfaction teams

The company made extensive use in 1992 of over 4000 worldwide work-based Total Customer Satisfaction teams. These teams take part in a worldwide annual competition which has the following objectives:

- renew emphasis on the participative process at all levels of the organisation worldwide
- recognise and reward outstanding performance at the team level
- re-affirm the environment for continuous improvement
- demonstrate the power of focused team effort
- communicate the best team achievements throughout Motorola.

The teams can be of any size but are usually made up of six to eight members from all functions and levels in the organisation. They identify a work problem that they wish to use as a vehicle for their own learning and to demonstrate achievement in the five key initiative areas outlined above (e.g. six sigma quality, total cycle time reduction, etc.). The projects must demonstrate a high level of achievements and be linked to corporate initiatives. The emphasis is on the team process and results. The competition moves through various stages at local, European and eventually to the Corporate Competition in Chicago. Projects are assessed in terms of:

### 1. Teamwork:
participation, structure, meetings and attendance, communications and resolution of conflict, mutual respect, grasp of the process as a learning experience.

## 2. Analysis:
(a) use of statistical tools, problem diagnosis, solution and decision-making techniques
(b) mapping the process
(c) understanding the tools and moving to more sophisticated methods as learning increases.

## 3. Remedies:
(a) linking to the analysis
(b) implementation plan
(c) innovation in the remedies or implementation.

## 4. Results:
(a) links to the original goals
(b) documentation and verification

## 5. Institutionalisation:
(a) permanence of the solution
(b) applications to other projects
(c) grasp of the process of continuous improvement as a continuous process

## 6. Presentations
process and content.

The competition is judged by a panel made up of senior managers, customers and suppliers. Big operational cost savings are obtained through the efforts of all these teams and the problem-solving process is institutionalised.

A recent development, for the European Region, has been to hold an annual total customer satisfaction workshop during the fourth quarter with representation from each of that year's participating teams to share knowledge and further enhance cross site communications and hence learning.

### *Functional councils and strategic task teams.*

The company management processes include the operation of Functional Councils. These cover: Engineering, Manufacturing, Quality, Environmental and Safety, Financial, Materials and Software. These are expected to generate and support key strategic initiatives, produce the drive and direction for the company and to encourage sharing of information and learning.

An example of the Strategic Task Teams in operation is where the Chief Executive set 25 Vice Presidents worldwide the task of making the company a world leader in software by the year 2000. The task team then evolved a worldwide programme to change the culture to ensure this capability would be achieved. The Motorola University would be involved in this initiative and design suites of training programmes for all managers and appoint Regional Champions and Trainers to ensure implementation. The company culture is one where cross-functional teams working on problems are seen as the norm as is the use of benchmarking both internal and external to check performance.

## Motorola University

The University relies on the Functional Councils, Regional Advisory Boards and Client Groups to provide the strategic direction and information needed to develop services that meet the needs of the organisation. Key Motorola managers thus set the training priorities and determine which services the University will develop.

The University provides five types of services:

1. Applications Consulting Teams – these work on a contract consulting basis where financial and operational outcomes are described before the work is allowed to begin.

2. Regional Training Consultants – this is where a complete training plan is required for a large department or information for a local training programme.

3. Planning, Training and Conducting Quality Systems Reviews.

4. Information, literature and publications of Motorola authored books.

5. Instructional Design and development of educational products and services for Motorola businesses.

The University offer courses delivered in the following areas:

- Advanced Technology
- Centre for Distribution Channels
- College of Software Engineering Technology
- Executive Education and Development Centre
- Information System Centre
- Learning Methods Development Centre
- Quality Design Centre
- Six Sigma Research Institute
- Transcultural Development Centre

Programmes offered under the Executive Education label are seen to have a major impact on the organisational culture. Examples of these programmes are:

*Management Institute for Engineering, Manufacturing and Operations Excellence.*

- A two-week programme in world class operations, engineering and manufacturing. Including the strategic planning use in developing leadership, vision and decision-making skills.
- Conferences where past delegates share experiences and address selected topics.

*Manager of Managers Institute*

- A leadership programme using the Chief Executive's office as role models and teachers. The programme includes: creativity, championing change, leveraging with diverse teams, risk, trust, personal and professional development. The key leadership expectations are quoted as: envision, energise and enable.
- Senior Executive Programme. This involves small teams of executives working on business issues to enhance their leadership practices. Leadership teams of about 25 are chartered by the Chief Executive to develop and implement solutions to specific issues. Over a period of one to two years the teams define the issues, experiment with solutions, manage the change processes to execute the solutions, and transfer solutions to other parts of the company.

*Vice Presidential Institute*
A one-week forum on role expectations. How the company is performing against the six key initiatives, technology platforms, key governmental issues and interfaces and behavioural skills that executives should model.

*Institute for General Managers.*
This programme emphasises the leadership provided by the general manager. Balancing cutting edge business practices with the management of human capital. Practices are transferred back to the workplace through assignments.

*Executive Technique.*
Helping managers and senior executives strengthen their personal and presentational skills and interfacing to the press and media.

The University also presents many other associated programmes and services.

These three elements, Total Customer Satisfaction Teams, Functional Councils and the University activities illustrate both a bottom-up and top-down approach to creating opportunities for learning. The focus on Quality and hence Total Customer Satisfaction provides the foundation on which the learning can then take place and demonstrate contribution.

# ROVER GROUP LIMITED

## Background

Rover began making motor cars in 1904, becoming nationalised as part of British Leyland in 1975 and the Rover Group was formed in 1986 under Sir Graham Day. In 1988 Rover was purchased from the British Government by British Aerospace and established as Rover Group Holdings plc. of which Rover Group Limited is a part. Honda had been associated with Rover since 1979 and in 1990 a cross-share deal brought into play a much more constructive relationship. In 1992 car sales accounted for a revenue of some £3700 million (with 43 per cent coming from sales outside the UK) with a workforce of some 33,000.

Up to 1986 the company was profit driven and product led, processes were adhered to rigidly and people were somewhere about fourth. Sir Graham Day turned this on its head and put 'people first' as the only way to move forward; 1987 saw the introduction of a massive investment in Total Quality Management with a Board of Directors who were totally committed to TQM. The Total Quality programme is now owned by line management. As part of the Total Quality Process the company have identified nine key processes which provide the focus for all business development activities. These are:

- New Product introduction
- Manufacture
- Logistics
- Maintenance
- Sales and Service
- Product Improvement
- Management of People
- Corporate Learning

In May 1990, Sir Graham Day and the senior Directors decided that learning was key to the future of the business and set up the Rover Learning Business with Fred Coultas as Managing Director.

## Practice

Rover Learning Business (RLB) is an individual unit within the Rover Group with a staff of 60 specialists dedicated to providing a continuous learning and development environment for Rover Group associates (all employees), suppliers and franchised dealers. The annual company budget is in excess of £30 million. RLB focuses on the company policy of 'Success through People' as a way of supporting the company mission. RLB incorporates both training and learning activities with 30 trainers, 12 change agents and a small team dedicated to producing videos and training materials.

The unit operates as a profit centre and relies on gaining the support from the business line managers. The unit has an overwhelming determination to relate all learning activities to improvement in both the current performance of the business, future capability and maximise contribution from all employees. This is illustrated by the scope of the activities being undertaken:

**(a)** Ensuring that all employees have a total awareness of the learning opportunities available to them.

**(b)** Introducing the Performance and Development Review Process where managers and subordinates engage in a process focused on self-development and business related performance targets.

**(c)** Accrediting line managers as agents of change. This is achieved through coaching, mentoring and the provision of a range of skills training.

**(d)** Providing Corporate Learning in the form of workshops and conferences. Also providing a Corporate Learning Database to ensure that Best Practice learning principles will be available to line managers plus access to a network of experts.

**(e)** Supporting major business projects within the business through the use of change agents.

**(f)** Developing the Total Quality Leader programmme.

**(g)** Supporting the development of learning programmes with suppliers and franchised dealerships.

Some typical RLB driven projects include:

- acting as learning facilitators for the Environmental Strategy Committee to raise awareness across the company in environmental issues
- introducing a distance learning approach to increase financial and business awareness for staff in the Commercial Function
- designing and running workshops to help improve Distribution efficiency
- running 'Learning from Honda' conferences to capture the lessons from the business relationship
- producing videos for internal training of sales staff and a distance learning programme on 'right first time'
- running courses for all staff in the Franchised Dealer Network.

Fred Coultas, RLB Managing Director, believes that there are two fundamental reasons why an organisation should focus on learning. First, to support specific business performance objectives and measure the results. Second, to empower the individual on the basis that everyone has a right to learn and that individuals that value learning will make a greater contribution to the longer-term success of the total enterprise. Fred Coultas stresses that one of the keys to the success of the notion of the learning organisation in the Rover Group was the support and enthusiasm from the Board of Directors. Even with this top level support Fred believes that full transformation to a learning organisation needs to be viewed on a five to fifteen year timescale.

In the early days RLB underestimated the amount of time and energy required to get 'buy-in' from the middle management. This was linked to the belief that you could impose a culture of learning on to the company. Fred recognises that RLB learned by this mistake and then began the slower process of changing the culture by demonstrating to line managers that a learning focus could provide major benefits in areas that they saw as key to the work and performance. Fred believes that there is still a long way to go and that complacency and starting to believe that you have 'got it right' is something to be guarded against.

## ROYAL MAIL

### Background

Royal Mail is the 'Letters Business' of the Post Office. Royal Mail is one of the largest employers in the United Kingdom, with some 160,000 employees of which 13,000 are managers. Training and development have obviously played a major part in creating what is considered as one of the leading service industries in the world. But concern that training was not integrated into the business, the lack of individual and line management ownership and inconsistencies in measuring outcomes were seen as weaknesses in the existing training system. In December of 1992 the Executive Committee of the Royal Mail introduced a learning strategy that will provide learning for all its employees throughout their working lives.

The success of the business is seen as depending upon individuals being motivated, committed and capable of contributing to the achievement of business objectives. Royal Mail sees the future success of the business depending on the ability of staff at all levels and hence has introduced their learning strategy. The aim is to create an environment in which people can grow, one which ties in with its Employee Relations Strategy and the

European Foundation for Quality Management model which emphasises the importance of releasing the potential of employees.

Three strands or activities to support this learning strategy have been identified. Training which is seen as a structured process linking performance and business needs; Development around individual learning styles emphasising business needs and individual aspirations and education which is seen as formal learning which at the time has no direct impact on the achievement of business objectives.

## Practice

The emphasis is on individuals having ownership of their own development. The line managers will have a key part to play in developing the strategy which includes training, development and education. The approach is to link learning plans to business strategies. Individual development plans will be established with standards and performance levels agreed, set and then outcomes evaluated.

Royal Mail is committed to investing a minimum of 1 per cent of wage and salary costs each year in learning activities (with the employment costs of learners not included in the expenditure formula), but the emphasis is on promoting value for money and enhancing the role of the manager as a workplace coach.

Line managers from across the business are involved in the definition of competences and standards of performance expected, which form a framework for personal development plans. Learning initiatives in support of this might be locally or nationally based, but a key enabler will be the development of the coaching skills of line managers.

Jerry Cope, Personnel Director, and Jonathan Cawthra, Head of Resourcing and Development at Royal Mail see the learning strategy as having the following objectives:

- make a direct contribution to achievement of mission and values
- establish business objectives as the key drivers
- shift ownership to individuals
- provide a process for planning and prioritisation
- provide a framework for local action
- maximise value for money
- enhance the Royal Mail's reputation.

The programme is demonstrating a top-down business objectives-driven learning programme with a bottom-up empowerment programme for individuals. The programme is driven from the local Business Personnel function and implemented by a combination of managers, internal and external training programmes.

# CLUB 24

## Background

Club 24 specialises in customer management and is a subsidiary of NEXT plc, a leading UK clothing retail company. Club 24 offers a dedicated bureau service to other organisations, making full use of its expertise in high volume data processing and telephone based arrears collection operations. The arrears collection department has 56 full time and 49 part time staff and provides a full range of arrears management services.

Various initiatives aimed at gaining commitment from the staff to the idea of owning a mission statement and subscribing to a set of values had failed. The decision was made to bring a learning focus to bear and in this way develop a culture that was conducive to change and development of the services and hence the business.

## Practice

The start point was to adopt a learning focus that would develop commitment, competence and a capacity for change. Commitment was developed through a team building and personal development programme which emphasised learning to learn, problem solving and self-awareness. The outcome was a shared vision by the supervisors of how to improve departmental performance. This was followed by a series of team workshops using brainstorming techniques and focusing on quality. The business performance objectives for the department were now defined in both financial and non-financial terms along with a set of performance indicators.

Various learning modules were identified through this process in the areas of teamwork, communications and quality. The learning process that was used in these modules emphasised the now open culture and the focus on individual empowerment. Group advisors were trained to act as facilitators for these learning processes.

The outcomes to date have been a 5 per cent increase in individual productivity, absenteeism is reduced along with labour turnover. This example illustrates the notion of the learning organisation where the application is directly applied to the supervision and the workforce. Other departments within Club 24 are now taking the lead from the collections unit and seeking to adopt a similar learning process and hence learning culture.

## DIGITAL EQUIPMENT CO. LTD.

### Background

Digital, as a Corporation, has over 90,000 people working in 100 countries connected to one of the largest private computer networks known as Easynet. This network is increasingly being connected to customer systems, joint solutions partners, suppliers and public networks. Digital is one of the world's largest computer and computer service companies with worldwide revenues of almost $14 billion. The company aims to be the best provider of quality, integrated information systems, networks and services in the world.

Digital is a high-tech company that is business driven and relies for its success on being able to respond to the needs of its customers. The company aim is therefore to be a flat, flexible and continuously learning organisation capable of rapidly transforming itself.

The people development focus is on creating systems and facilities that will support learning at all levels. The drive is to facilitate individual, team and organisational learning. Three of the critical elements in this are seen to be:

- the ability of teams to learn together
- the change in the manager's role to one of coach and mentor
- the change in work practices such as flexible hours, working at home, mobile working, etc.

The general view is that the technology to support this is relatively simple compared to the changes required in how people work together.

### Practice

Some of the facilities being developed by Digital Learning Services at Reading are outlined below. Learning for the individual is supported by providing the following types of facilities:

- A networked computer-based training (CBT) package that allows people to diagnose their own individual learning styles and hence learn how to make use of additional learning opportunities. (This package is based on the Honey & Mumford learning styles questionnaire)
- A facility that provides Just-in-time learning opportunities at the workplace. An example of this is the Electronic Performance Support System. With this and other learning media the individual is able to call up the competences required for their job position, test their abilities, access learning materials and assess their progress. The move is towards a competence-based reward system.

For teams the following tools are available on the network to assist in learning and sharing knowledge:

1. An electronic mail system with distribution lists available for every user in the worldwide network, with connections to FAX and Telex systems.

2. Electronic Conferencing with Digital Notes. This is an interactive conferencing system that facilitates on-line, open discussion. At any one time there are thousands of conferences in progress covering all aspects of the business, products and services. The network is used for both informal and more formal types of information exchange and discussion. Teams and individuals are encouraged to initiate a conference on virtually any topic.

3. Videotext is used to provide an easily accessible method of distributing up-to-date information. The material may be required for reference, on-line retrieval or for inclusion in other documents.

4. Business Television is available at 120 Digital sites throughout the world. The sites are equipped with satellite TV receiving equipment and is used for Europe wide broadcasts to all the sales force for new product launches and CEO communications. The system is interactive, with questions telephoned or faxed into the originating site.

5. Video Conferencing is used for small team communications. Many of the Digital sites are equipped for video conferencing, and the UK/Geneva and UK/US team discussions are the most heavily used. The latest workstation technology is now making terminal to terminal video conferencing a reality.

The overall drive is to use these facilities and tools to develop a non-hierarchical approach to the generation, sharing and use of knowledge. One of the major learning tools being developed allows individuals to model their own skill profiles, identify development areas and map them on to available learning solutions. In this way the individuals and the network will develop a symbiotic relationship.

## SHELL INTERNATIONAL PETROLEUM CO. LTD.

The following material presents a commentary on an article printed in the magazine 'Marketing Intelligence and Planning – 1992', MCB University Press. The original article was written by Graham Galer (Group Planning – Shell International, London, UK and Kees van der Heijden, Strathclyde University, Glasgow, UK). The notion of 'planning as learning' and its implementation in Shell is explored.

Shell companies now form one of the largest business enterprises in the world. Shell's principal businesses are in oil, gas, chemicals, coal and metals. They represent the largest total investment in chemicals by any of the major oil companies. In 1991 net proceeds of Shell companies were around £58,000 million and net income £2,403 million. Some 130,000 people are employed worldwide and Shell has operations in some 100 countries. These worldwide operating companies are responsible for the performance and long-term viability of their own operations, but draw upon the experience of the service companies and through them other operating companies. In this way the full range of expertise built up within Group companies are available to them.

The more commercially orientated functions, including Group Planning, are located in London. New developments in, say, marketing techniques and various aspects of management stem from the London staff. For example, the Operating companies are provided with information to assist them in planning for the future. Global scenarios and their implications for energy supply and demand are supplied to operating companies to help them develop local scenarios as a basis for business planning. The operating companies in Shell are responsible for their own staffing, while the Group Human Resources and Organisation function plans for long-term management succession. This function also sets overall policy in the areas of reward and staff relations. A key role of this central group is to provide consultancy support to the Operating companies in terms of improvement to the effectiveness of the organisations and to the management processes which make them work.

Within Shell many of those working in decision support roles, such as planners, management trainers and organisational effectiveness specialists are trying both systematically (i.e. through formal programmes) and opportunistically to make managers aware of blockages to learning and to help overcome them. Among the formal programmes and processes are:

- quality management, which is widely employed throughout Shell
- programmes in organisation effectiveness and organisational capability
- management training programmes
- the processes of strategic planning, business planning and appraisal.

The Group's planning cycle provides a framework for periodic review of the strategies, plans and resource requirements of the operating companies and the business sectors. Strategic planning is driven by strategy development at the level of operating companies as is Business planning.

The appraisal of performance against plan takes place each spring and involves both operating company management teams and those from the Service Companies. It is this planning process that is seen as providing an enormous opportunity for accelerating corporate learning in Shell.

Galer and Heijden argue that, in business, learning is a process through which management teams change their mental models of their company, their stakeholders and the wider environment. The existence of this formal planning cycle brings together a wide range and level of managers and is aimed at reaching a high level of consensus on key business decisions.

Within Shell a Committee of Managing Directors (CMD), which is made up of the Managing Directors of the Service Companies, considers, develops and decides upon the overall objectives and long-term plans to be recommended to the operating companies. A small group, Group Planning, a service company division, reports into this CMD and has the following responsibilities:

- improving management understanding of the changing business environment in which the Group is operating
- the identification and study of strategic issues and options
- development of methods and techniques which assist in strategic thinking and which enhance capability in planning.

These three responsibilities all provide opportunities for accelerating individual, team and corporate learning. The authors emphasise the use of the learning cycle whereby managers experience feedback from action, review experiences, create mental models and plan next steps. Within Shell a series of formal and structured processes have been set up to make this learning activity explicit. There are three key opportunities for learning within this planning process that the authors describe:

- Scenario Planning
- Strategic Planning Workshops
- Business Appraisal

Scenario Planning (a technique often seen as synonymous with Shell) where various accounts of how the business environment might develop over time are prepared. This involves extensive use of creative techniques and 'what if' questioning. The whole approach is to try to grapple with a complex set of factors that are related to future uncertainty. This scenario building process is used to help surface the mental maps, held by teams, that link information about the environment to decisions. The authors argue that one of the main benefits of this scenario building approach is to ensure that what might be a simple natural learning process for an individual may not be so for a senior management team. Hedging against what they describe as the corporate 'one-track mind' (this has been described elsewhere as a form of 'group think'). This is tackled within Shell by helping managers develop commonality in both concepts and language in order for them to become skilful at observing and taking action in the fast changing business environment. Managers are encouraged to develop scenarios that are plausible to a critical mass of managers in the Group.

In order for this process to be effective in other organisations it will, of course, be essential to make use of skilled process facilitators and to have available techniques whereby ideas, information and conclusions can be readily captured. This is obviously a powerful learning approach for both Corporate and Senior Managers.

The authors describe how, historically, the outcomes of the thinking surrounding scenario building were rarely seen to be translated into the business strategy itself. This gave rise to the second area for learning around planning. The company instituted what are known as 'Strategic Planning Workshops'. In these workshops focused scenarios are linked with existing strategic vision, competitive positioning and the management of options. Existing strategies, visions and focused scenarios are brought together to determine the implications for the particular operating company. These implications are then related, in specific areas, to the competition and the internal capability of the company. This then follows a conventional strategic planning process. Once again the success of the approach must depend to a very large extent on the skills of the facilitator, the techniques available and the culture in which the process is being conducted.

In the period October 1992 to April 1993 some 50 workshops were run by Group Planning staff for Shell operating companies and business sector management teams throughout the world.

The authors argue that the characteristic 'learning' features of these workshops, are that they enable teams of managers to:

- review jointly their experience of what has been going on in the environment in which their business operates
- internalise this experience against the background of new information (e.g. new scenarios) and also to internalise the scenarios themselves
- infer conclusions for their business, at least of a preliminary nature.

Strategic planning workshops provide an environment and a structure in which the individual can learn and also a process for embedding that learning effectively in the management team.

The third area described by the authors is that of business appraisal. They describe appraisal as being about the formation of judgement as to how the Operating Company contributes to the Group company businesses. The appraisal adopts the usual criteria for judgement such as recent performance, performance in relation to competitors and how well the assets have been managed. New business issues and actions often arise from these appraisals. The process within Shell involves advice and consultation from a wide range of levels and interests.

This is a key business process for Shell and the management learning involved is seen as vital. Managers are encouraged to see the process more as one that leads to better business performance through coaching and learning than through control.

The success of this will obviously depend on how effectively Shell can create and sustain a culture of openness and trust. In times of expansion the learning may be greater than when the economy is on a down turn. In many ways it is exactly the reverse that is needed.

An overriding point made by the authors is the need to encourage what they describe as 'The Art of Organisational Conversation'. They argue that the process of debate must be managed and balanced with the need for profitable action. An example is given where the need for a review of the business appraisal process was seen as necessary. This review was tackled by:

- one to one interviews with key managers
- presentations of system solutions and possible changes
- workshops where the systems and suggested changes were exposed and challenged
- some principles posed and tested for acceptability.

This is seen by the authors as being more than a consensus-seeking exercise. The process involved many managers in a process of learning that required the surfacing and critique of firmly held mental models and the use of systems thinking. Once again the process relied heavily on the use of skilled facilitators and a careful design in order that it fitted the culture and was in tune with the perceived business needs.

The authors argue that these facilitator skills can be acquired by anyone. They see learning of these skills and their effective use as being key to the creation of a learning organisation.

A very important point made by the authors is that those within an organisation that have specialist roles to play, e.g. those engaged in quality management, training, organisational effectiveness, etc. need to have a high level of awareness of what learning entails. Those engaged in designing and supporting planning processes would no doubt qualify in the authors' eyes as being in the front line for learning these skills and transferring them to others.

Many organisations may feel that Shell are so large that their learning is hardly translatable to the smaller enterprise. This is not necessarily true. Many companies engage in Corporate, Strategic and Business Planning and the stories about how 'the plans' bear no resemblance to what actually happens are legion. It could be that one of the keys to the learning organisation, and also a good entry point, is that the process should focus on learning not on attempting to either forecast an imprecise future or establish unrealistic targets with associated punitive controls. To achieve this capability will no doubt require those responsible for the design and conduct of the planning process to take time out to understand how to encourage learning.

## CABINET OFFICE

The following material and five examples of practice, present a commentary on a report produced by the Development Division (Developing People for Results Through the Line – December 1991), Cabinet Office, Office of Public Service and Science. The review carried out by the Development Division set out to examine the extent to which line managers were involved in training and developing their staff in both public and private sector organisations in the UK. The overall concern was to determine good practice and how this might be more widely transferred. The survey covered some 100 companies in the private sector, government agencies and other public sector organisations.

For those considering implementation of a learning organisation the report is of major interest in that it demonstrates:

- how line management involvement was secured
- how the policies and initiatives were communicated to managers and staff
- what mechanisms existed to ensure action
- what systems were set up to support the policy
- how the systems were monitored and what criteria were used to evaluate success.

The report focuses on the role of the managers in training and developing their staff.

In companies where a policy statement about the role of the line manager as trainer and developer exists then the following obstacles to effective implementation of this policy were reported to be:

- mismatch between the policy and existing systems
- line managers not given the support and authority to deliver the training and development
- the significance of the policy is not highlighted
- lack of real commitment from the top
- lack of line manager accountability
- no effective means of monitoring performance.

All of these obstacles would be directly applicable to anyone setting out to implement a learning organisation. This is particularly relevant to organisations that have a large workforce where the line manager's role has been seen historically as that of supervision. The report provides some guidance as to how these obstacles can be addressed and overcome:

- top management must lead by example and show commitment
- line managers need to be convinced that development and training will directly contribute to the task in hand
- personnel management systems need to be in line with the line management activity
- line managers need training in the required skills
- line managers need resources and support from experts in how to improve the performance of their people.

Evidence from the organisations studied highlighted three areas that needed to be addressed if line managers were to take responsibility for development of their staff. These were:

- making the line managers accountable
- clarifying their role as trainers and developers
- giving them support.

The report presented some examples of what various organisations were doing to tackle these areas. Five extracts are presented here in order to provide some fresh ideas when considering implementing the learning organisation. They include Brooke Bond Foods, Nissan Motor Manufacturing (UK), Mobil, the Employment Service and the Department of Trade and Industry.

## BROOKE BOND FOODS

### Background

Brooke Bond Oxo was acquired by Unilever in 1984 and in 1987 merged with Batchelor Foods to form Brooke Bond Foods. There are some 3500 staff of whom 350 are managers.

### Practice

The approach reported highlights the involvement of the line managers in the design and implementation of a learning system. The start point was a determination to move away from an approach to training and development that was course-based and not clearly linked to the business needs. A top-down approach was adopted. The business direction and strategic intent being used to identify potential skill gaps. Seeking to focus on things that needed to be learned to help the business achieve its objectives.

This at first sight appears very conventional but two aspects make the approach special. Firstly, the involvement of line managers at Divisional level linking business targets to defined competences and secondly, the development by the managers themselves of a new appraisal system. The appraisal system emphasised the use of competences and job performance targets.

Here, as with other learning organisations, the appraisal scheme is linked to individual development plans that rely heavily on self-development approaches. Use being made of a wide variety of learning opportunities including: informal on-job learning, focused projects, job rotation, secondments and providing access to a resource bank of learning materials. The internal courses are reported to have been revised on the basis of the identified competences and a range of external qualification type courses.

The report emphasises the need to integrate all these activities through what is known as the Personnel Development Directory which ties together competences, appraisal and development opportunities including courses and open learning materials. This document acted as a guide for all managers on implementation of the new systems.

## NISSAN MOTOR MANUFACTURING (UK)

### Background

Nissan started production in the UK in 1985 and at the end of 1990 were producing over 75,000 cars per year. The achievement of excellence underpins the company philosophy throughout. All employees are issued with documentation that highlights the company's philosophy and emphasises the development of people, the involvement of staff in decision making, teamworking, good communications, target setting and seeking continuous improvement. The theme is quality throughout all activities.

### Practice

The report emphasises once again the importance of leading by example. Managers have the same terms and conditions as staff, eat in the same canteen, wear the same uniform in the plant. The company has a very flat organisation structure. The culture is reported as being very open and informal. The vast majority of training is seen as being within work teams, with supervisors trained to deliver training packages and take responsibility for recruitment and discipline.

Teams are used as the primary focus for the pursuit of quality. Teams concentrate on good housekeeping, close examination of targets, identifying critical areas in their work, setting up review processes and generating ideas for continuous improvement.

Team briefings on business development, setting targets, introducing changes and monitoring performance are a key feature of the Nissan approach. Here again the identification and use of competences is reported as being a major learning strategy. Competences are seen as providing a common language and allow training to be delivered and the individual's performance to be measured by agreed standards. Individuals then compile what is known as a Continuous Development Profile with their line managers. This is then used in the individual learning process alongside definitions of clear goals and target dates for achievement.

It is clear that the line manager can by use of the competence framework, the Continuous Development Profile and on-job training maintain a very close control of staff development. Competition between teams is encouraged in what is reported as taking place in a spirit of friendly competitiveness between teams.

This approach to staff development and training is obviously very closely matching job performance requirements and staff development and is supported by strong signals from management to demonstrate commitment to the overall aims.

# MOBIL

## Background

Mobil is a leading multinational company in the oil market. This international aspect means that the management systems and employees need to be able to operate across national boundaries. The company thus set out to create a flexible company culture in which responsibility is delegated to business units with line managers and employees fully involved in forming and giving feedback on company plans.

## Practice

The report describes the leadership of the company as both reinforcing the informal management style and demonstrating the importance that is attached to the setting of performance objectives. The line management are described as being highly involved in leading the training and development. Responsibility for objective setting, training, development and key areas of personnel work rest with line managers. The appraisal process is used for accountability in which managers are assessed on their ability to perform in these training and development areas.

Mobil use a Performance Management and Development System (PMDS) to increase emphasis on management practices by holding managers accountable for their ability to manage and develop staff. The PMDS is also clearly linked to business issues and quality. Through the PMDS managers set performance and development objectives, competences, management practices, review performance and conduct appraisals.

This approach to setting individual objectives in line with the business plans is a familiar approach. But with Mobil the link through to identify competences and management practices for the performance period does appear to go further than similar schemes. Measurable targets and the associated development plans then lead to coaching, formal training and secondments where appropriate. The individual development plans are backed up with a wide range of programmes, devised in conjunction with line management and delivered by the training function.

## THE EMPLOYMENT SERVICE

### Background

The Employment Service (ES) is an executive agency in the Employment Department Group. It became a government agency in 1990 and employs around 40,000 people spread throughout 2000 offices in Great Britain. Its purpose is to promote a competitive and efficient labour market by giving positive help to unemployed people through its job placement service and other programmes and payment of benefits and allowances to those who are entitled to them. The agency recognised that people were the most important resource and crucial to its success. A strategy focused on Human Resource Development (HRD) was thus launched.

### Practice

The emphasis in this programme was again on the line manager's involvement and commitment, breaking the reliance on centrally organised training events. The decision was taken to focus on line management accountability for the HRD strategy and to demonstrate that top management were fully committed to making it work. The approach was to commission a study of what senior managers could do to develop their staff and make HRD an integral part of the business. There was an obvious determination here to link development of the staff to the development of the business.

A top-down strategy was then evolved with a statement being made to all staff as to mission and values along with a clarification of business objectives. The role of every manager in ensuring that staff were highly motivated was spelt out. This is reported to have helped create a strong culture in which staff are involved in taking decisions to affect the future of the business and thus become highly committed to the achievement of targets.

A competency framework plays a big part in the new HRD scheme. There are plans to link this to the appraisal system. The competency framework helps line managers and staff identify the training and development that is required. The competences being based on the Management Charter Initiatives framework and adapted to suit the needs of the Employment Service.

## DEPARTMENT OF TRADE AND INDUSTRY (DTI)

### Background

The DTI employs around 11,500 staff. Its activities include contact with business, the UK's international trade, the promotion of a single market within the European community, consumer interests, regulatory functions, innovation, research and technology issues. The structure includes some nine executive agencies that account for over 50 per cent of the staff. They are widely spread geographically. The widespread diversity of activity and size has presented some interesting problems in devising suitable management systems within the department. The challenge was to move from a centrally run system to one that was owned and driven by line management.

### Practice

The approach focused heavily on consultation and involvement of staff in reviews of existing processes.

Competence frameworks incorporating Personal Development Plans have been introduced along with a revised appraisal system. The competence frameworks were devised with line managers and are used to help them assess performance gaps and training and development needs against performance targets and outputs.

The training and development activity now focuses on benefits to the line in terms of work outputs. The longer-term development of staff is recognised but the primary focus is on meeting customer and business needs. To ensure that the line managers are given adequate support for their new training and development role the DTI appointed Training Liaison Officers (TLOs) in each business area. All requirements for training are routed through them. They in turn consult with the Central Training provider and others in order to evolve strategies for training and put these into place.

This has resulted in several local, business based, learning and training strategies being established. The training is reported to be much more customer focused than before. The training now is only undertaken where there are clear objectives which the training is to meet. The focus is on improving performance and outputs in the job itself.

An open learning unit has been established to introduce Learning Resource Centres and produce in-house learning materials. Many of the courses are now run in collaboration with outside consultancies and educational establishments.

# THE HEALTH EDUCATION AUTHORITY

## Background

The Health Education Authority is a special health authority and is part of the NHS. Its mission is: 'to help the people of England to become more knowledgeable, better motivated and more able to acquire and maintain good health'. The Authority employs 200 staff and has a budget of over £30 million. It achieves its mission through mass media campaigns, working in partnership with other organisations and through the provision of resources to people involved in local health education throughout the country.

## Practice

In 1989, the Authority committed itself to becoming a learning organisation. This it defined as an organisation that would grow through the development of its staff, that would learn from its mistakes and that looked constantly to the external world in order to make sure it was focusing on the needs of its customers.

This philosophy was introduced at the same time as a new organisation structure based on matrix management. Development and training at first concentrated on the Executive team and on the senior managers who were the key people responsible for delivering the organisation's objectives. A ten-day programme was designed, with the help of a management consultant, for senior managers and in consultation with the managers. Its objective was to develop managerial skills as well as to create a team across the organisation that would facilitate matrix management.

Following the success of this programme the development programmes were introduced for project officers and support staff, to which the senior managers contributed, both in the design and delivery, thus helping make the development an initiative owned by all the organisation and not just the training department.

In conjunction with the programmes, a competency-based approach to development has been introduced. With the help of external consultants, competences for senior managers were identified using behavioural event interviewing and for project officers using a questionnaire and a focus group. These groups were then offered the opportunity to attend a Development Workshop following this they then had to produce development plans for a year. In constructing these plans, officers were encouraged to think more broadly than just attending courses but to set up mentoring, coaching and shadowing arrangements. The process of identifying the competences that created a successful organisation meant that organisational development and individual development were brought together.

During this time, the training department has issued annual training plans which are circulated to all staff, which detail the philosophy of training and development, interventions which will take place over the year such as development courses based on competences, language training and also policies such as the secondment policy and study leave.

## W. S. ATKINS – CONSULTANT ENGINEERS

### Background

W. S. Atkins is one of the largest and most diversified multi-discipline consultancy practices in Europe. The company is based in Epsom, Surrey, in the UK and employs over 2,500 staff in 17 European offices and five in the Middle East and Asia. Turnover in 1992 was around £120 million. Founded in 1938 by Sir William Atkins the practice now includes all branches of planning, management, engineering, architecture, and environmental consultancy. Projects range from those such as the prestigious Channel Tunnel and Docklands Light Railway programme to more modest single discipline activities.

The major sectors in which the company works are transportation, urban and rural development, water and waste treatment, public services, commercial development, industry, energy and power, oil and gas and defence. The focus is on engineering expertise and project management with some 300 specialists in transportation related projects and 200 involved in mechanical engineering. The company recruits over 50 honours graduates each year, most of whom then undertake professional development programmes in order to achieve their Chartered status.

## Practice

Roger Emberson (Group Personnel Director) sees the focus on learning as the key to the success that the company has achieved. Atkins is in effect a professional services company whose base is centred on:

- continuing educational development through professional updating programmes, presenting conference papers and participating in the activities of professional bodies
- demonstrating on-job professional training as a reqirement to achieve Chartered status
- providing demonstrable expertise in helping to identify and then meet the requirements of the client.

Atkins is an organisation that takes mentoring and coaching as a norm. The history of professional practice encourages learning and personal growth in all aspects of the work. Within this setting business requirements have raised a number of issues that have been addressed in terms of learning. Examples of these are given below:

1. The company had identified the need to review its capability of working, as a business, on projects that required multi-disciplinary working. A team was set to explore the potential for a business offering a new but more focused professional service. The team were given six months to review the success and failure of previous projects, identify the business opportunity and design the processes and organisational structure that would need to be implemented. External consultants were used as facilitators of this process and the outcome was presented to the Board as a business proposition. This approach to learning not only established a deeper understanding around business issues it also provided an essential review of how the strategic thrust of the company relied on the inter-working on these highly specialised groups.

2. Two major divisions of the company undertook a structured programme that involved looking at the present position of their business performance and operations and formulating stratetgies and plans for the next three years. These programmes involved the Managing Director of these busi-

nesses plus their senior managers. The learning covered all aspects of business and involved main Board members as part of the fact finding and evaluation process. The learning was then cascaded down through each of the Divisions through a series of workshops and involving middle management in the implementation of the plans that had been developed. This required 'buy in' from the middle managers and an opportunity for them to challenge the strategies and their implications. In this way the Divisions evolved new ways of working and a business focused ethos.

3. The consultants are obviously the main interface to the client and the need to share the learning in the area of consultancy skills (particularly selling skills) was identified. The approach taken was to engage a consultant with a brief to study what selling really meant in a consultancy environment and to relate this to the Atkins culture and then propose a development programme.

A three-year programme was then set up which involved: providing techniques, case studies and practical exercises. Some eight weeks after the programme support groups met to share experiences and learning. In this way the ability of staff to provide the client with a clear view of options to solving problems has been achieved. Some 200 senior consultants have so far completed this programme.

4. A 'Heads of Technology' concept is being used to help accelerate learning across the practices. In this the nominated leader of an area of technology (e.g. energy, off-shore, environmental etc.) sets up an informal network of senior people in the discipline who exchange information and experiences. These network members (say 16–20 people) meet quarterly to ensure that the company maintains its leading-edge capability. The current view is that this information is too dynamic to lend itself to capture on a database.

5. A leadership development programme was set up as a pilot to explore the ways in which individual leadership styles can impact on the work itself and the business performance.

6. A major learning need was how to get professional engineers to 'buy in' to the business plans and strategies that were cascading down through the organisation. The company has all the usual mission statement and business planning approaches built into the business process but there was concern that the plans produced were not always driving the business activity. An approach is now being used that involves getting managers to switch from a total concentration on the short-term problems of the business to thinking about the future. The approach centres on using a strict discipline for managing discussions and arriving at decisions. Using this more structured,

disciplined and focused approach to business planning and decision making is producing a high level of 'buy in' from the managers.

In summary, W. S. Atkins is unique in that the core population are all highly educated professionals, who are well versed in the techniques and approaches to creativity, innovation and problem diagnosis. The work itself provides ample opportunity for both intellectual and professional development. The triggers for organisational learning and group learning have primarily arisen from the business environment and the response has been to focus on learning that emphasises a business orientation and how to keep abreast of technological developments.

## RANK XEROX – THE DOCUMENT COMPANY

### Background

Formed in 1956 as a joint venture between Xerox Corporation and the Rank Organisation, Rank Xerox manufactures and markets Xerox document processing products and services throughout Europe, Asia and Africa. Some 27,000 people are employed across 80 countries with a turnover around £2.6 billion in 1992.

Rank Xerox (UK) Limited was established in 1972 as the UK sales, marketing and support subsidiary of the international company Rank Xerox Limited and employs some 4700 people in 50 locations with sales around £500 million in 1992.

The Xerox Corporation is located in the USA with a worldwide turnover of some $18 billion employing over 100,000 people in over 100 countries.

In 1990 Xerox Corporation and its subsidiaries repositioned themselves as the Document Company and have the stated strategic intent of being the leader in the global document market, by providing document services that enhance business productivity. They also state that they will lead in customer satisfaction, productivity, quality and technical excellence and in the use of innovative management techniques.

In 1980 Rank Xerox realised that it needed a minimum 18 per cent year on year increase in productivity for at least five years, to reach competitive parity with its fastest growing competition. To achieve that goal, the company transformed the way it did business. Rank Xerox became a quality company, with quality as its basic principle.

### Practice

Rank Xerox have taken a number of decisive steps since 1980 in order to become a quality company. The Rank Xerox quality programme, known as Leading Through Quality, has presented major opportunities for organisational, team and individual learning. The steps taken included benchmarking against competitors and recognised leaders in particular fields, employee involvement through empowerment, on-going assessment of managers against leadership role model criteria, obtaining National Certification for quality and introducing internal reviews in what is known as Business Excellence Certification (BEC). This involves senior management evaluating performance of the various business areas.

An example of this BEC process in operation is in the area of Management Development. Here the BEC requirement is that Management Development is conducted and measured against 16 key 'attributes'. Each attribute constitutes a best practice standard against which improvement action plans are determined and measured.

Some examples of these attributes are:

- evidence of links between Management Development Plans and the Business Planning process
- having a portfolio of skills and knowledge programmes for managers in place. This must include Empowerment and HRM topics to support employee motivation and satisfaction
- standards in place for internal management trainers
- evidence of benchmarking activities to understand 'best practices' at national level plus actions or plans to match these.

These examples show how the management development activities are closely tied into the other company processes particularly that of business planning.

The Company Education and Training Strategy is seen as being a key enabler in becoming a 'Learning Organisation'. This is stated as being an organisation which achieves business excellence through continuous improvement where employees:

- are aligned to a common vision and common values
- acquire the necessary competence (knowledge skills and values) that enable them to fulfil the requirements of their job roles
- optimise their potential and experience personal growth
- achieve their objectives and directly contribute to the goals and objectives of Rank Xerox (UK)
- are motivated
- are able to lead change, make productivity gains and improve on business performance.

There are four key ways in which the training strategy provides support to the above.

1. The Learning Process. A management training process has been instituted that involves:

(a) Translation of the business needs into learning requirements. This is a market driven focus for determining requirements based on the Rank Xerox 'strategic intent' and Corporate Priorities. The learning curriculum is linked to the business planning process and is benchmarked to other institutions. The focus is therefore both internal and external.

(b) Design and development of a core curriculum that is responsive to the defined learning need.

(c) Delivery of the modules using state-of-the-art learning technologies and methods.

(d) Evaluation of the delivery of content and effectiveness as a measure of expected versus actual results of training.

2. Establishing a Management Institute that will deliver the core management development programmes. These programmes deliver the Corporate vision, values and business direction plus key management skills. There are four levels of these courses: Development and Managing People (for first level managers), Business Leadership (for managers of managers), Advanced Management School (for Managers of Organisations) and New Executive Training (for new Executives and Directors).

3. All managers in 1993 are required to complete a minimum of 40 hours training and development from a combination of three curriculum areas.

4. The core curriculum covers three areas: Human Resource Management, Quality and Business Processes, Business and Systems Skills.

Managers support this training strategy through counselling sessions, coaching and conducting briefing sessions before and after and training events to set objectives and review outcomes.

The company emphasises that employee development goes beyond classroom-based training courses. It is seen as a continuous process of learning, training, experience and personal growth, enabling individuals to fulfil their potential while contributing fully to the company's business goals.

Underpinning this broad learning is the Performance Planning and Appraisal (PP&A) process, which helps everyone to focus on improving their current performance and to plan for future development needs. These are then incorporated into a personal Development Action Plan (DAP). Along with these two processes the company has produced the Xerox Employee Development Suggestions (XEDS) manual, which gives practical ideas for individual development and self-study where appropriate. XEDS also references numerous development tips, books and articles, distance learning materials plus in-house courses.

The DAP is the process that drives an employee's personal development. Once an action plan has been agreed, it is the responsibility of the individual to implement it using the resources and support provided by the Company. The DAP is reviewed twice yearly.

Currently Rank Xerox is introducing a major drive towards establishing seven re-engineered business processes. These will include processes covering: time to market (product development), market to collection (customer order, installation and payment), product maintenance (service). Top managers will drive these new processes across the existing functional organisation and be staffed by key managers who will be expected to own the processes. The move to re-engineer existing processes has arisen from an identified gap between current and required return on assets if Rank Xerox are to achieve their goal of being the most productive company in the industry. The company is also implementing a range of behaviour and culture change initiatives including a new style leadership programme and workshops for self-managed teams.

Empowerment as a way to energise people has been a cornerstone around which the company have developed the notion of the learning organisation and achieved impressive results in improving quality and productivity, making sure that decisions are made by the people who are closest to the action. Empowerment is seen as applying to teams as well as individuals. An empowered team being one that is focused on outputs, has a flat informal structure, responsible for daily actions and has a reward system that recognises both skill improvement and contribution to company profitability. The company see empowerment as helping to improve: productivity, quality, employee satisfaction and customer satisfaction. The benefits will include greater flexibility in jobs, faster response to technological change, ability to attract and retain the best people and helps all employees achieve a high level of satisfaction.

## LUCAS INDUSTRIES PLC

### Background

Lucas Industries is an international supplier of automotive and aerospace systems with sales of around £2.3 billion in 1992. It employs some 50,000 worldwide with approximately 50 per cent of these in the UK. There are currently 60 major manufacturing and assembly plants based in the UK.

## Practice

The Lucas Continuing Education and Training Scheme (Lucas CET), introduced in 1989, actively encourages individuals to take the responsibility for their own development, and provides support for employees to do so.

The scheme is funded by the Lucas Employees Benefits Trust Fund, which is currently supporting two initiatives for the benefit of Lucas employees; health care programme and Lucas CET. Launched in September 1989, two working parties had overall responsibility for establishing the scheme and determining the framework under which it would operate. The second of these, which looked at how to 'operationalise' the principle of CET, was a 'joint' Working Party which included members of the Trade Unions from all parts of the Lucas Group in the UK.

In 1991/92, the total expenditure on Lucas CET was £2.5 million and over 8000 employees (out of 24,000 UK based employees) took advantage of the scheme. Subjects covered include modern languages, information technology, electronics and supervisory training, and ranged from basic skills training through to degree level. Lucas CET has three main objectives:

- providing the opportunity for all employees to obtain the education and training which they consider will help them achieve their full potential in their working lives
- establishing within Lucas an approach to continuous learning which will increase the capability and confidence of all employees to strive for personal growth
- ensuring that the Lucas organisation comprises people who have the capability, flexibility and confidence to build a profitable and competitive business enterprise.

All employees are eligible for participation in the scheme, but one of the primary objectives is to assist those employees who have not had the level of education or development necessary for them to fulfil their potential.

The scheme operates in parallel with job-related training and is not intended as a substitute for the normal training arrangements which the businesses need to make. Business managers continue to have full responsibility for business-related training.

A key feature of the scheme is the Personnel Development Plan (PDP) which encourages an individual to think about long-term development rather than consider training courses on an ad hoc basis. The PDP is seen to be one of the foundation stones on which the learning organisation can be developed. Resources to provide vocational guidance and careers counselling have been put in place in order to help employees plan their development, and the process includes discussion with an individual's manager or supervisor.

Lucas operates some 20 Open Learning Centres on sites in the UK and makes full use of the latest technology. Lucas CET may be accessed through these centres, through on-site classes, at a local college or via distance learning courses. Typical programmes being studied cover basic numeracy through to degree courses. There is a strong emphasis on basic skills acquisition and wherever possible site-based classes are used.

The Lucas CET is part of the overall Lucas approach to employee development which has recently seen the introduction of an improved Management Development system. In this context Nick Everest, Director, Group Management Development and Training emphasises the importance of balancing the needs of 'running the business' with the need for individual career development. Where business needs become the sole driver for development then the individual may see options for personal development being narrowed. Equally, an over-emphasis on career development may lead to Management Development being marginalised. Nick sees the need to set up learning processes where individual and organisation needs are perceived to feed off and reinforce each other.

In order for Management Development to be seen as credible, particularly in the eyes of hard pressed managers, Nick believes that learning must be achieved wherever possible through 'real work'. In this way projects become major developmental opportunities with the addition of some prospective and retrospective learning discussions and minimise the problem of personal development and running the business being seen as competing priorities. The success of such an approach is seen to be very much linked to the boss having coaching skills and having people development as a personal performance criterion and, hopefully, a strong personal value.

At Lucas the flatter organisation, technological developments and the need for flexibility and continuous improvement create an environment in which no-one can be allowed to stand still. Through personal development planning, the Lucas CET Scheme, Management Development and other job-related training programmes Lucas is attempting to link short and longer-term bottom line business performance to 50,000 personal development agendas. There is a strong drive to link the development agenda to a future business scenario. This is achieved by integrating the rolling business plan known as CAP (Competitiveness Achievement Plan – a three year strategy for the business plus operational and performance plans for 12 months) with the individual Personal Development Plans. Lucas is not attempting to resolve this matching problem by identifying Group-wide generic competences. Each business is learning how to make the match and move towards solving the envisaged capability gap. This learning is then shared across the Group.

Business teams consider the strategic challenge facing the business and translate them into 'people' terms (skills, knowledge and attributes) which in turn provides the agenda for personal development planning. The general philosophy to meeting the resultant plans is to see 70 per cent of the development being derived from things people do (learning on the job), 20 per cent from learning from others and 10 per cent from off-line training programmes.

Nick Everest has some strong views about where the notion of the learning organisation fits in. Creating a climate in which senior management (who have a multiplier effect on organisational performance) as well as the shop floor craftsman engage in conscious learning is not easy. One of the obvious problems is that the timescale over which the effect of decisions and actions can be evaluated varies enormously with the level in the organisation, e.g. learning around strategic decisions as opposed to learning through turning a piece of metal and checking the results. The mistake here would be to focus on 98 per cent of the employees and exclude the executive team. Some of the factors that are significant in developing a climate for learning within Lucas are:

- valuing 'constructive disagreement' and 'feedback' as important elements of a genuine dialogue
- encouraging the development of inter-personal skills
- encouraging people to develop ideas and licensing employees to act on their own initiative
- recognising the power of learning at all levels in the organisation and regarding it as an investment
- learning from other organisations who are further ahead in developing people and learning strategies
- establishing a formal management development network to share the differing experiences of the businesses across the Group. This includes the international partners
- identifying and improving business processes and thus highlighting the connections between systems, tasks, people and information.

The focus at Lucas is very much on achieving the balance between developing individuals and developing the organisation; on improving the business bottom line whilst retaining good people and facilitating their personal growth against a background of organisational streamlining.

## BRITISH AEROSPACE PLC

### Background

The principal businesses of the Group are the Defence Business, Commercial Aircraft Business, The Rover Group, Arlington Securities (property assets) and Ballast Nedam (construction activity). The combined Group activities represent one of the UK's largest manufacturing organisations, and is the UK's largest exporter of manufactured goods with over 60 per cent of its sales overseas. Turnover in 1991 was £10,562 million with British Aerospace Defence Ltd contributing some 40 per cent, the Rover Group some 35 per cent and Commercial Aircraft around 16 per cent. The Group employs around 120,000 people.

### Practice

The subsidiary companies have in place extensive and sophisticated employee development and training programmes linked to the business itself; for example, the Rover Group which figures in this book as a leading exponent in the fields of Total Quality Management and being a learning organisation (Rover Learning Business). What this write-up provides is some examples of activities at Group level that support the notion of organisational learning that is linked to improving business performance.

The three activities highlighted by Rosemary Harper (Employee Development Director) are:

- an overall 'people strategy'
- Corporate Learning Days
- Priorities for Learning

#### 1. People Strategy

The strategy stems from the Business Plan. The two stated objectives of the strategy are to:

(a) maximise our people's contribution to the business

(b) gain a competitive advantage for the business through the utilisation of our people.

The strategy itself focuses on establishing organisation structures, obtaining the right people and skills, developing open communications and developing leaders; all of which are aimed at helping the Company achieve its goals and business plans. An additional two elements of this strategy are aimed at encouraging the creation of learning and development opportunities for all employees and creating an environment which provides individuals with confidence, purpose and recognition irrespective of level in the organisation.

Various actions to support the strategy have been identified. These include working with the subsidiary businesses to ensure:

- flat organisation structures with fewest possible levels
- appointment of key executives/leaders. This would include establishing succession plans for key posts and Development Centres for high potential people in critical functions
- optimum handling of manpower reduction/rationalisation programmes
- supply of qualified young people to meet future resourcing needs
- development of training and development programmes to improve the stock of potential leaders
- compensation planning to attract and reward the people needed in the business
- establishment of an open environment encouraging maximum contribution from all employees. To achieve this by developing a learning environment, involving employees in Customer Satisfaction programmes. Also to encourage employee contribution to process improvement and problem solving through the use of discussion groups, quality circles as appropriate to the individual business culture
- provision of 'Best in Class' personnel support within each of the businesses against established benchmarks

### 2. Corporate Learning Days.

At the most senior level (i.e. subsidiary company 'Management Committees') Corporate Learning Days have been introduced where themes identified by the Board and MDs as critical to the business are covered. The focus here is to share experiences, understand what the company is good at and not good at and learn from that. These events are supported by three day highly interactive workshops where the emphasis is on sharing knowledge, identifying gaps, risks and opportunities. These events also make use of inputs from academics who act as facilitators.

### 3. Priorities for Learning.

Each subsidiary has its own Business Plan from which critical success factors and key performance indicators have been developed. Combining these with the outcome of an in-depth analysis of training needs and an evaluation of current training programmes it has been possible to develop a core list of priorities for learning. These five priorities are:

(a) Critical Success Factors and Key Performance Indicators: How can training assist managers to play an effective role in the project plan process? All development programmes emphasise these as a core element in management processes.

(b) Business Awareness: Gaining greater understanding by all employees of Military Aircraft Division market structure and priorities, e.g. new modules for highlighting position in global markets and the tasks faced to win business.

(c) Business Process Redesign: Educating the team of facilitators who are helping in process improvements so that they have a better understanding of the principles, tools and techniques of business process design. For example one Division has three projects looking at the Spares Process, the Procurement Process and Project Control.

(d) Communication: Developing managers' communication skills to ensure effective internal communications is driven and achieved through the management structure.

(e) A continuous learning environment: It has been important to move to the creation of a culture where all employees are aware of the need to continually change and update skills – to continually learn. Examples include the provision of targets of open learning facilities at all sites. Personal Development plans are being created for all employees. In some of the subsidiary companies a cash allowance is given to employees who wish to take up a learning opportunity. The learning need not be work related and is seen as a strong reinforcer of culture change.

# INDEX

Allaire Paul 15
Adaptor 39
   Adaptor – Innovator Inventory 40
   Change agent as 64
Atkins W. S. – Consultant
   Engineers 233

Behaviour, individual and group
   levels 125
Benefits 138
   Cost Benefit Models 149
   Personal 135, 140
   Stakeholders 139
Boydell T. 1, 9
British Aerospace plc 243
British Telecom 17
Brooke Bond Foods 227
Burgoyne J. 9, 10

Cabinet Office Development
   Division 226
Change 125
   Culture influence on 104, 125
   Evaluating 148, 150
   Leaders role in 91, 128
   Management of complex 128, 132
   Power groups and leaders for 91
   Pressure for 57, 58
   Programmes for 116
   Rational logical approach to 128
Club 24 219
Competences 200
Consultants; approaches used by 12
Creativity
   Evaluation of personal style
     towards 39
   Use of 64, 72, 163
Culture 104
   Development of group and sub
     group 118, 124
   Evaluation of 11
   Impact of critical incidents on 121

Decision making in conditions of
   uncertainty 71, 129

Deming Edwards 27
Department of Trade and Industry 231
Digital Equipment Co. Ltd. 220

Entrepreneurs and organisational
   learning 123
Employment Service 230

Funding the Learning Organisation 183

Growth and the Learning
   Organisation 59, 60

Haley and Stumpf 64
Health Education Authority 232
Human Resource Development 19
   Learning Organisation links to 25
   Strategic Planning and 98

ICL plc 206
Innovation in developing
   organisations 72
Image for the Learning
   Organisation 183
Implementation of the Learning
   Organisation 156
   Exploratory Stage 171
   Development Stage 192
   Consolidation Stage 202
   Incremental approach towards 174
Influencing management and power
   groups 184, 188

Jones, Sir John Harvey 2
Juran J. 27

Kirton M. J. 39
Knowledge Management 14

Leadership
   Dynamic 70
   New roles in 96
   Personal style and 78, 161
   Visionary 69, 189

# Index 247

Learning
  Blockages to 104, 107
  Boundaries to 113
  Creating a climate for 198
  Complex 52, 74
  Contracts for 200
  Culture formation and 120
  Drivers of 205
  Explicit and tacit 54, 74
  Exploratory Stage applications of 176, 179
  Formal and informal structures for 74
  Levels of 175, 203, 204
  Model used in the study programme for 33
  Needs and 204
  Opportunities for 59, 61, 114, 115, 168, 176, 177, 178, 179, 182, 190
  Rewards for 200
  Tensions created by 73, 103
Learning Organisation 6
  Consolidation Stage for the 202
  Core values for the 184
  Definitions of 2, 7, 9, 10, 158
  Delivering services and staffing the 172, 181, 201
  Development Stage for the 192
  Elements of the 178, 196
  Evaluation of the 135, 148, 170, 172, 174, 183, 190
  Exploratory Stage for the 171, 174, 187
  Funding the 183
  Image for the 183
  Markets for and services provided for the 178
  Organisational Process identification and the 48
  Projects to help develop the 189, 193, 197
  Strategies for the 184, 196
  Triggers for the implementation of the 7
  Visions, missions and objectives for the 173
Lucas Industries plc 239

Management Development approaches to and limitations of 20, 90
McKinsey and Co.
Mobil 229
Models
  Demonstrating benefits by using 150
  Interpreting lessons from practice by using 206
  Mental 93
  Process 152
  Seven Step study programme 34
Motivation 24
Motorola Inc. 209
Munro Faure L. and M. 26

Networking as an aid to learning 51
Nissan Motor Manufacturing (UK) 228

Objectives
  Feasibility Study 42, 157
  Exploration Stage 175
  Development Stage 192
Organisations
  Analysing change programmes in 116
  Analysing functions in 47, 168
  External and internal environments of 44, 168
  Form and Development of 67
  Historical perspectives in 55, 166
  Informal processes and networks in 51
  Power groups in 91
  Rational approach to managing 69
  Stakeholders in the 166
  Using process models in analysing 48, 168
Organisational Development 21
Outcomes of the Feasibility Study 135, 139, 143

Paradox in managing organisations 73
Pedler M. 1, 9
Performance Measures
  Formal and informal 52
  Impact on learning of 53
  Stakeholders 139
Personality
  Bias created by 63, 120, 162
  Influence on the study of 36, 63, 161
  Self analysis of 36
Perspectives developed in the study programme 74, 100, 131, 152
Peters T. 2
Power Groups, identification and influence of 91
Practice in implementing learning in organisations 203
  British Aerospace plc 243
  Brooke Bond Foods 227

Club 24  219
Digital Equipment Co. Ltd.  220
Department of Trade and
    Industry  231
Employment Service  230
Health Education Authority  232
ICL plc  206
Lucas Industries plc  239
Mobil  229
Motorola Inc.  209
Nissan Motor Manufacturing
    (UK)  228
Rank Xerox (UK) Ltd.  236
Rover Group Ltd.  215
Royal Mail  217
Shell International Petroleum Co.
    Ltd.  221
W. S. Atkins Consultant
    Engineers  233
Pressures for change in organisations  57
Problem Solving
    Approaches to  182, 194, 196
    Personality and bias  65
Processes
    Analysis of organisational  48
    Informal learning  51

Quality see TQM

Rank Xerox (UK) Ltd.  236
Rewards and learning  123, 200
Risk taking and managing  71
Rover Group Ltd.  215
Rover Learning Business  215

Royal Mail  217

Senge P.  1, 11
Shell International Petroleum Co.
    Ltd.  221
Stakeholders
    Identification and analysis of  142
    Needs to satisfy  166, 186
    Outcomes and benefits sought
        by  143, 145
Strategic Development
    Direction and Planning Scenarios
        for  86
    Management and  72
    Enterprise and the Learning
        Organisation  90, 184
Training  19, 90
Total Quality Management in the
    Learning Organisation  25

Values in the organisation  126
    Core  184
    Influencing  146, 188
Visions
    Building  83, 93
    Learning Organisation Mission
        and  89, 173
    Learning Organisation and
        Enterprise  167
    Purposes and links to  85

Waterman R.  2

Xerox Corporation  15